FEDERAL ESTATE AND GIFT TAXATION

IN A NUTSHELL

By

JOHN K. McNULTY

Roger J. Traynor Professor of Law
University of California, Berkeley

FIFTH EDITION

ST. PAUL, MINN.
WEST PUBLISHING CO.
1994

 TEXT IS PRINTED ON 10% POST CONSUMER RECYCLED PAPER

 PRINTED WITH SOY INK™

For
Martha, Jennifer and John
McNulty

*

PREFACE

This book, now in its fifth edition, provides an introduction to the U.S. law of Federal Estate and Gift Taxation. It is thus a companion to my "Federal Income Taxation of Individuals in a Nutshell," now in its fourth edition (1988). It is intended to be used by lawyers, students and scholars from other legal systems, as well as by law students in this country as a supplement to usual law school courses and materials, and perhaps as a refresher or orientation for members of the bar. It attempts to summarize the law, frequently to mention the purposes of, and sometimes the alternatives to, existing legal rules. Only sometimes does it attempt a critical evaluation, or a history, or full justification, of the existing law. Chapters on some fundamentals of estate and gift and generation-skipping tax planning, and on reform of and fundamental alternatives to the federal transfer tax system, have been included.

The book is organized in a way that parallels many courses and teaching materials. It begins with an introduction to the gift tax, estate tax and reformulated generation-skipping tax as separate taxes. After the introductory chapters, however, the book is organized "transactionally" so as to take up both the estate and the gift tax (and generation-skipping tax) consequences of particular kinds of transfers, dispositions and situations.

PREFACE

Very little attention has been given to the matter of filling out required tax returns or forms and to other questions of compliance and administration of the laws. These matters simply have to be considered beyond the scope of a short volume of this kind.

The statutes themselves form the core of the subject matter and a copy of the Internal Revenue Code must be available to be read along with this book. Much the same can be said for the Regulations under the transfer taxes. Frequent references both to the Code and to the Regulations are given throughout the text. Citations to statutes are to sections of the Internal Revenue Code as amended through early 1994. These citations are usually given in the form "I.R.C. §§ __ " to distinguish them from cross references to other sections of this book itself, generally cited as "§§__, *infra*." Section numbers of the Internal Revenue Code, as cited, correspond to title 26 U.S.C. and title 26 U.S.C.A. (Subtitle B). Treasury Regulations under the Estate Tax are cited as, for example, "Regs. § 20.2035." Gift Tax Regulations are cited as, *e.g.*, "Regs. § 25.2512." Regulations issued under the Generation-Skipping Tax are cited as, *e.g.*, Regs. § 26.2601-1. Citations conform to sections of title 20 of the Code of Federal Regulations (Parts 20, 25 and 26). Rulings and other administrative pronouncements are cited to volume and page of the Cumulative Bulletin, abbreviated as "C.B."

Citations are given to a few leading cases, Revenue Rulings, Regulations, and collateral sources. These citations aim to offer access to some

PREFACE

central areas of authority but do not attempt to cover all relevant or helpful material.

In preparation of this fifth edition, I have relied heavily upon Douglas F. Carlson, a 1994 graduate of the University of California School of Law, Berkeley (Boalt Hall). He skillfully researched the statutory, judicial and administrative developments since the publication of the fourth edition in 1989, drafted textual additions to the book, screened the law for recent developments, selected the most important changes out of the great morass, prepared written descriptions, and reviewed the fourth edition for obsolescence, error or other flaws. His work proved excellent and reliable. It built on the fine and extensive contributions to prior editions by Seth M. Skootsky (Boalt, 1988), Charles Stepkin (Boalt, 1978) and Martina Marshall (Boalt, 1983). To all of them, my thanks.

I hope this short book will prove useful as an introduction, review or overview of the subject matter of U. S. Federal wealth transfer taxation. I must emphasize that it cannot substitute for, but at best can supplement, a thoroughgoing examination and analysis of the Code, Regulations, Rulings and cases, which are the principal sources of our Federal transfer tax law and which must be emphasized in the study of that law by law students in law school courses.

J.K.M.

Berkeley, California
April, 1994

*

OUTLINE

*

TABLE OF CASES

References are to Pages

XVII

TABLE OF CASES

*

TABLE OF INTERNAL REVENUE CODE SECTIONS

UNITED STATES

UNITED STATES CODE ANNOTATED
26 U.S.C.A.—Internal Revenue Code

XXVII

TABLE OF INTERNAL REVENUE CODE SECTIONS

TABLE OF INTERNAL REVENUE CODE SECTIONS

TABLE OF INTERNAL REVENUE CODE SECTIONS

TABLE OF INTERNAL REVENUE CODE SECTIONS

TABLE OF INTERNAL REVENUE CODE SECTIONS

TABLE OF INTERNAL REVENUE CODE SECTIONS

TABLE OF INTERNAL REVENUE CODE SECTIONS

TABLE OF INTERNAL REVENUE CODE SECTIONS

TABLE OF INTERNAL REVENUE CODE SECTIONS

TABLE OF INTERNAL REVENUE CODE SECTIONS

XLVIII

L

*

TABLE OF TREASURY REGULATIONS

TABLE OF TREASURY REGULATIONS

TABLE OF TREASURY REGULATIONS

TABLE OF TREASURY REGULATIONS

*

TABLE OF REVENUE RULINGS

REVENUE RULINGS

TABLE OF REVENUE RULINGS

FEDERAL ESTATE AND GIFT TAXATION

IN A NUTSHELL

*

CHAPTER I

INTRODUCTION

§ 1. Nature of the Federal Estate, Gift and Generation–Skipping Taxes

Taxation of property transferred by an individual to others at his or her death is one of the oldest and most common forms of taxation, at least in societies where property is privately owned. Death transfer taxes sometimes take the form of an *estate* tax, which is an excise tax levied on the privilege of transferring property at death and usually is measured by the size of the estate. Or, a death tax can be shaped as an *inheritance* tax, an excise tax levied on the privilege of receiving property from the decedent and usually measured by the amount of property received by each particular taker, rather than by the amount of the total estate, and by his or her relationship to the decedent. The Federal Estate Tax, as its name suggests, is an example of the former; many *state* death taxes are cast in the form of an inheritance tax. Both forms of tax usually, but not necessarily, employ a graduated rate scale; the larger the estate or the larger an inheritance received, the higher the *marginal* tax rates (the rates charged on the last $1 of taxable property) applied, and consequently the higher the *effective* or *average* rate of tax paid. The effective

1

tax rate consists of the total tax paid divided by the total taxable estate and is, necessarily, lower than the top marginal rate.

Since a transfer tax imposed at death can so easily be avoided by a lifetime gift (a gift *inter vivos*, by a living person), a federal transfer tax is imposed on the making of gifts during life. Many states also impose a gift tax to back-up their death transfer taxes. Gift taxes also can be progressive; the rate of tax varies with the amount of taxable transfers previously made during the donor's lifetime. Gift taxes and death taxes in the form of estate or inheritance taxes are known as "transfer taxes." Transfer taxes can be combined or integrated so that, for example, the rate of tax on transfers made at death is affected by the aggregate amount of gift transfers made during life.

The United States Constitution requires that all "direct taxes" be apportioned among the several states according to their respective populations. (After the income tax was held to be a direct tax, the 16th Amendment was passed to exempt the income tax from this apportionment rule.) The federal estate and gift taxes are not viewed as direct taxes. They are excise taxes, imposed on an event or a transaction (a gift or transfer of property at death), as distinguished from direct taxes, which are imposed on a person (a "poll tax") or on property itself (whether or not it has been transferred or otherwise made the subject of a transaction or an event). Consequently, the federal death and gift taxes fall outside the apportionment requirement.

§ 2. History and Evolution of the Federal Estate, Gift, and Generation–Skipping Taxes

A federal tax on transfers at death was first employed, in the form of an inheritance tax, in 1862. At first, it applied only to personal property, but later it was extended to real property as well. Rates were quite low. This tax was repealed in 1870, inasmuch as its revenue proved superfluous after the Civil War ended.

Later, and briefly, personal property received by gift or inheritance was treated as income subject to the income tax (enacted in 1894), before that tax was held unconstitutional the next year. In 1898 a mixed estate and inheritance tax passed Congress—it was progressive with the size of the estate and also graduated with respect to the relationship between the recipient and the decedent. The tax was construed, however, as a pure inheritance tax, and was upheld in Knowlton v. Moore, 178 U.S. 41 (1900), but was repealed by Congress in 1902.

In 1916 a Federal Estate Tax was enacted, in part out of pressure to raise revenue, and in part to attack undue concentrations of wealth through inheritance. The constitutionality of this tax was upheld in New York Trust Co. v. Eisner, 256 U.S. 345 (1921); it was viewed as an *indirect tax*, an excise, not requiring apportionment among the states. Meanwhile, many states had adopted estate or inheritance taxes. Some had not however, and rates varied widely from state to state. These disparities created an inducement for wealthy people to change domicile for tax purposes. To create uniformity, Congress (in 1924) enacted a credit against the federal tax for state death transfer taxes paid. As a result, states were induced to enact death transfer taxes and to bring their rates up to the maximum for which a full credit against federal tax would be allowed. Many states enacted such "pick-up" or "piggyback" taxes, taxes geared to the amount of the full credit against federal tax.

To avoid the federal and state taxes on transmission or receipt of property at death, some property owners made large transfers *inter vivos*. To counteract this technique and partly for political reasons, the Federal Gift Tax was enacted in 1924. (It was repealed in 1926 but reinstated in 1932.) This gift tax was imposed at a rate equal to three-quarters of the estate tax rate on equivalent transfers. The gift tax was, and is, progressive and cumulative over a donor's lifetime—the tax on a taxable gift of a given amount is higher if the donor has made many or large taxable gifts previously, even in prior years. Today's Federal Estate and Gift Taxes retain many of the essential features of their 1916 and 1932 forbearers. In the intervening years, however, the Federal government has modified the taxes in several significant ways.

Community-property laws in effect in some states created disparities in tax treatment that called for a cure. Under community-property law, the estate of a decedent husband, for example, if he were the first to die, would include only one-half of the couple's community property, whereas in a separate-property or common-law property state, the husband's estate would probably include all the couple's wealth. In order to take away most of the tax advantages of community property, the federal estate tax law was amended in 1942 to provide that the husband's taxable estate would include almost all of the couple's community property.

In 1948, a different rough equalization of community-property and separate-property decedents was accomplished by the opposite method: treatment of common-law decedents was made to resemble treatment of community-property decedents. As before, the surviving spouse's one-half share of the couple's community property was not taxed in the decedent spouse's estate. As a result of the 1948 changes, property that was *not* community property could be given by the decedent to his or her surviving spouse without estate tax on one half of its value, by virtue of the so-called *marital deduction*. Thus, in many instances (but not all), the Federal Estate tax treatment in separate-property situations equaled that given to community property.

Parallel treatment was afforded under the Federal Gift Tax—one half of the spouses' community property is owned by each and no gift tax is imposed regardless of whose services generated the property. And a gift tax *marital deduction* made one half of any gift of noncommunity property by one spouse to the other exempt from gift tax.

Between 1948 and 1976 Congress did not make any fundamental change in the transfer tax laws—

it merely dealt with the presumptions about gifts in contemplation of death, estate taxation of life insurance and other matters to be explained in greater detail later.

During this period, the separate lower rates on lifetime gifts, and the new start up the progressive rate scale provided by the separate taxation of the estate at death, offered great tax benefits for those families wealthy enough to be able to afford to make large *inter vivos* gifts. In an effort to eliminate most of previous advantages of *inter vivos* giving resulting from the separate gift and estate tax structures, the Tax Reform Act of 1976 restructured the estate and gift taxes.

Instead of two separate taxes, with two different rate tables and a new start up the progressive rate ladder for the taxable estate at death, there now is one unified tax structure, using one rate table. Moreover, the estate tax base now includes taxable gifts made during life, in much the same way that pre-1977 gift tax rates were based on cumulative lifetime gifts. Of course previous gift taxes paid are taken into account when calculating the estate tax payable, thus avoiding double taxation.

The 1976 Act also replaced the previously separate deduction/exemption ($30,000 cumulative lifetime deduction for gifts, $60,000 deduction for the taxable estate) with one unified *credit*, or "exemption equivalent". This unified credit was gradually phased in, beginning at $30,000 in 1977. Although originally slated to remain at its 1981 level of $47,-

000, the credit has since been increased still further by the Economic Tax Recovery Act of 1981 ("E.R.T.A."). It reached its ultimate level of $192,-800 in 1987. This credit corresponds, given the applicable rate table, to a deduction of $600,000 so that, for example, there will be no tax due on taxable estates of $600,000 or less for decedents dying in 1987 and thereafter. (See I.R.C. §§ 2010, 2505, and 6018 for the phase-in amounts of the credit prior to 1987.) Because the credit form has been used, however, the dollar savings to all taxpayers will be the same, whereas the old deduction/exemptions were worth correspondingly more to taxpayers in higher marginal brackets.

The 1976 Act also increased the available marital deduction, for both gift and estate tax purposes, by providing for a deduction of the larger of a fixed dollar amount of $250,000 *or* 50% of the decedent's net separate-property estate. This reform appears to have been a compromise with the Treasury Department's 1969 proposal to make all gratuitous transfers to spouses tax-free entirely. An unlimited marital deduction would have the effect of treating the married couple as a single unit for transfer tax purposes, on the theory that passage of accumulated wealth to the *next* generation is the appropriate event for triggering tax liability. (This Treasury position was in fact adopted by the E.R.T.A. in 1981, as more fully described below.)

Another major 1976 innovation was the creation of an entirely new tax on "generation-skipping transfers in trust." Under the old law it was possible for donors to split the beneficial enjoyment of donated property temporally. They could do so by creating generation-skipping trusts to avoid the federal transfer taxes. Thus, for example, a gift of income for life to Son, remainder to Grandson, gave the son the use and enjoyment of the property, but occasioned no additional estate tax on the corpus when the property passed to the grandson. Consequently the property, although of course taxed in the estate of the original grantor, could be passed through one (or more) succeeding generations with no transfer tax liability. The only limit was any applicable rule against perpetuities, with the result that over 100 years could pass without the property being again subject to a transfer tax. A new Chapter 13 generation-skipping tax effectively closed this avenue of tax avoidance by taxing the entire property *as though* it has passed through the estate of the skipped generation (S, in the example above). However, this new transfer tax was flawed, by administrative complexity and its inability to plug other significant gaps in the federal transfer tax scheme. Consequently, a completely overhauled Chapter 13 generation-skipping tax was enacted in the Tax Reform Act of 1986. The revised Chapter 13 tax is described in § 6 below.

The 1976 Act also amended some *income* tax statutes which have great importance for estate planning and distribution. The most important of these was an attempt at general equalization of the treatment of accrued but unrealized appreciation (or decrease) in property gratuitously transferred.

The old law was that the donee of an *inter vivos* gift took his donor's basis in the property ("carry-over" basis), while the donee of a testamentary gift took a new basis equal to fair market value at the date of death ("stepped-up"—or down—or "fresh-start" basis). Under the 1976 law, for all post-1976 transfers, both *inter vivos* and testamentary, the transferee was to take the transferor's basis ("carryover-basis"), subject to several adjustments which were to insure, among other things, that the new rule would not be retroactive and that there would be no double taxation. However, in 1978 this change was delayed until 1980, and "carryover basis" was ultimately repealed in 1980, without ever having gone into general effect. See former I.R.C. § 1023. The "old law" rules of "fresh-start basis" for testamentary transfers and "carryover basis" for *inter vivos* transfers remain in effect today. See I.R.C. §§ 1014, 1015.

Several other changes in the transfer tax and related income tax laws were made in 1976, relating to less pervasive features of the system. All these changes will be discussed in greater detail later.

The Economic Recovery Tax Act of 1981 (Pub.L. 97–34, 95 Stat. 172), hereafter "E.R.T.A.", drastically changed several provisions of estate and gift tax law that have an important bearing on estate planning. The most important of these changes is the adoption of an *unlimited* marital deduction in both the estate and gift tax contexts, which has the effect of treating the married couple as a single unit for transfer-tax purposes, thus relieving most inter-

spousal transfers from transfer tax liability. See
I.R.C. § 2056. E.R.T.A. also greatly increased the
amount of the unified credit, as mentioned above,
compressed the rate schedules applicable to high-
bracket estates and donors, and made many other
changes in the transfer tax area.

Following E.R.T.A., no major change in the transfer taxes was made until passage of the Tax Reform
Act of 1986. This act included a complete revision
of the Chapter 13 Tax on Generation-Skipping
Transfers. [Included also was an increase in estate
tax for individuals dying with an "excess accumulation" in a retirement plan (I.R.C. § 4981A(d)).
This small change is not given extensive treatment
in this text.]

Like the 1981 E.R.T.A., the Tax Reform Act of
1986 (P.L. 99–514, 100 Stat. 2085), hereafter
"T.R.A. '86," also amended some *income* tax statutes that have important connections with the
transfer taxes. For example, the tax income-rates
for estate and trust income were lowered and the
number of brackets was reduced. See I.R.C. § 1(e);
§ 1(g); § 1(h). In 1993, further changes were
made in the marginal rate structure of the income
tax, as a result of which the new 36 percent marginal tax rate applies to taxable income of an estate or
trust in excess of a rather low threshold, namely
$5,500. Compared with the thresholds for this rate
for individuals (married, joint returns: $140,000;
unmarried: $115,000), this low threshold, and the
rate schedule in general, make income of an estate
or trust taxable at relatively high rates, even at

fairly low levels of income. *See* I.R.C. § 1(e), compared with § 1(a), (b), (c) and (d).

Also, the so-called "kiddie tax" of I.R.C. § 1(g) makes the "unearned income" (including trust income or custodial income) of a child under the age of 14 taxable at the "applicable parental" rate, which often counteracts or reduces the income tax savings that could otherwise result from gifts, outright or in trust, for minor children. See also I.R.C. § 644, taxing gain on the sale or exchange of property by a trust within two years of the initial transfer of the property in trust at rates as if the gain had been included in the gross income of the transferor of the property. Section 644 is coordinated with the "kiddie tax" by I.R.C. § 1(g)(3)(C). The grantor trust rules of I.R.C. §§ 673–75 have been tightened to eliminate the so-called "10–year" or "*Clifford* trust rule." See I.R.C. § 673; § 674; § 676; § 677.

In particular, for transfers in trust after March 1, 1986, the former ten-year rule of I.R.C. § 673 has given way to a regime that taxes the trust's income to the grantor of a trust if the grantor has a reversionary interest in the corpus or income therefrom so long as, at the inception of the trust, such interest exceeds 5 percent of the value of the portion of the trust in which the grantor has the interest. See I.R.C. § 673(a). This rule does *not* apply if the reversionary interest will take effect upon the death, before the age of 21, of a beneficiary who is a lineal descendant of the grantor. As indicated above, children under 14 are now taxed at their parents' top marginal rate on unearned (investment) income over $1,000, the so-called "kiddie tax." See I.R.C. § 1(i); § 63(c)(5). [These and other significant income tax changes are discussed fully in the companion text, McNulty, Federal Income Taxation of Individuals in a Nutshell, fourth edition (1988).]

Just one year after the landmark T.R.A. 1986, Congress made a few small additional changes in the transfer tax scheme with the passage of the Revenue Act of 1987 (P.L. 100–203, 101 Stat. 1330).

The Technical and Miscellaneous Revenue Act of 1988 (TAMRA) (P.L. 100–647, 102 Stat. 3342) contained numerous, mostly technical amendments. The 1988 legislation also restricted the availability of the marital deduction in the estate and gift taxes for *noncitizen* spouses. A new 5% surcharge bracket was created so that large transferors will lose the benefit of both the lower, graduated rates and the unified credit. See I.R.C. § 2001(b); § 2001(c)(2); § 2052(a). A new section 2036(c) was added in an effort to place limitations on so-called "estate freezes," but it was repealed retroactively in 1990 by P.L. 101–508, § 11601(c).

In 1990, the Omnibus Budget Reconciliation Act of 1990 (P.L. 101–508, 104 Stat. 1388) added new I.R.C. Chapter 14 (§§ 2701–2704) to provide valuation rules for transfers of interests in corporations, partnerships, and trusts between family members. These sections replaced the former, short-lived § 2036(c).

Finally, in 1993, Congress fixed the maximum estate and gift tax rate at 55% for amounts over $3,000,000. See § 2001(c).

The more important legislative changes will be discussed in some detail in the analytical sections of this book.

§ 3. Revenue and Other Roles of the Transfer Taxes

The federal estate and gift taxes do not raise very large revenues now and they never have. As of 1992, they accounted for about $11.5 billion annually, or about one percent of federal budget receipts, a smaller percentage by far than each of those reflecting individual income (49.8%), corporate income (10.5%), excise (3.0%), and employment or payroll taxes (35.7%). See Table 4, *I.R.S. Annual Report* (1992). Rates are low and exemptions are high, and, as a result, most people are not subject to federal estate or gift taxes; among those who are taxable, many pay small amounts in tax. Declining tax rates and increases in the unified credit resulted in a real (adjusted for inflation) *decrease* in transfer tax revenues during the 1977–1987 period.

The transfer taxes were not enacted merely to raise revenue. In part they are designed to prevent people from accumulating large blocks of wealth and then transmitting those blocks from generation to generation. Also, these taxes make an important contribution to the progressivity of the entire tax system. Wealth and high income are closely associated, and estate and gift taxes mainly affect families with relatively high annual incomes.

For taxpayers whom the transfer taxes do affect, the impact can be great, so the prospect of these taxes looms large for such taxpayers and their lawyers. Enormous planning potential inheres in these taxes as presently structured. Structural features of the taxes have made for erratic results; the taxes often can legally and easily be avoided or drastically reduced by steps (such as regular annual gifts to children) that are perfectly acceptable on non-tax grounds. For society at large and for the finance of government, reform and revitalization of these taxes pose significant and difficult issues of redistribution of wealth, revenue potential, equity and economic effects.

§ 4. Introduction to the Estate Tax

As with all other taxes, the basic computation of the estate tax takes this form: *tax payable* equals tax *rate* times the tax *base*, minus *credits* (if any). The difficulty comes, for the most part, in determining the tax base.

Under the Estate Tax statute, the beginning point for determining the tax *base* is a concept labeled the *gross estate* (see I.R.C. § 2031 & § 2033.* From the gross estate are subtracted

---

* All references to the Internal Revenue Code are made by section number and the initials "I.R.C." The Federal Estate and Gift Taxes and the Tax on Generation-Skipping Transfers form part of the Internal Revenue Code (as does the Federal Income Tax). The Internal Revenue Code is embedded in the United

allowable *deductions* to determine the *taxable estate*, against which the tax *rates* must be applied. (See I.R.C. § 2051; § 2001).

The *gross estate* includes, at a minimum, the value of all property owned by the decedent at death which passes to someone else by will or intestacy. The gross estate includes more than this, however. It also includes some life insurance proceeds and some jointly-owned property. It may even include some property given away by the decedent before his death but treated by the law as if owned by him until death and passing then. So *gross estate* for tax purposes is not the same as "probate estate" for state law or as "wealth" and "estate" as commonly used.

Once the *gross estate* has been determined, allowable *deductions* may be taken to arrive at the *taxable estate*. (See I.R.C. §§ 2051–2057.) Such deductions include allowances for most transfers to a surviving spouse (*marital deduction*), [formerly some transfers to certain minor children (*orphans' deduction*)], contributions to charity (*charitable deduction*) and deductions for certain *debts* and *expenses*. (In addition, every decedent dying before 1977 was allowed a $60,000 deduction (*exemption*), now replaced by the *unified credit*, discussed in § 69 *infra*.) After subtracting these items from the *gross estate*, the *taxable estate* (if any) remains.

States Code (U.S.C.) and the United States Code Annotated (U.S.C.A.). Section numbers of the Internal Revenue Code (I.R.C.) cited in this book correspond to section numbers of Title 26, U.S.C. and Title 26, U.S.C.A.

Statutory, graduated *rates* apply against the sum of the *taxable estate* and all post-1976 taxable gifts not included in the gross estate, to determine initial tax due. The taxes already paid on those lifetime gifts are deducted, *credits* (including the immensely important *unified credit*) are subtracted and the residuum is the actual *tax payable*. See I.R.C. §§ 2010–2015.

(The rate of estate tax, prior to 1977, was not affected by the amount or number of transfers during lifetime, unless those transfers were formally includable in the estate tax base as equivalent to death transfers. See Chapters III and V, *infra*. That is, there were two separate trips up the graduated rate schedules, once for cumulative lifetime gifts, and once for the estate at death. Now, for decedents dying after 1976, the taxable estate is cumulated with post-1976 gifts, thus exposing it to higher rates as a function of the size of *total* post-1976 gratuitous transfers. Thus, in effect, the taxable estate is treated as one final gift at death. This is one aspect of the "unified" system.)

§ 5. Introduction to the Gift Tax

The gift tax is a companion tax to the estate duty. For pre-1977 gifts, its rates were lower, ¾ of the estate tax rates. Now its rates are the same as those of the estate tax, and this is a second aspect of the 1976 "unification" of the two taxes. See I.R.C. § 2502. It applies to any gratuitous transmission of property during life, since such a transfer serves to reduce the estate subject to the estate tax at death. (See I.R.C. § 2501; § 2511.) However, the two taxes do not fit together perfectly. As a result, some transfers made during life and taxable under the gift tax will nevertheless be included in the base of the estate tax, but for gifts made before 1977, a credit for gift taxes paid will attempt to eliminate any actual "double tax." For post-1976 gifts, this credit of § 2012 is inapplicable, since the credit is automatically taken into account by the new estate-tax calculation procedure of § 2001. (See § 2001(b)(2).) Other overlaps, gaps or conflicts may be found because the two federal transfer taxes are not *completely* "integrated."

The federal gift tax is now imposed and reported on a calendar-year basis and the appropriate tax rate is applied to the total of taxable gifts made during that year. (See I.R.C. § 2503.) (Note that from 1971 through 1981, the tax was, generally speaking, imposed and reported on a *quarterly* basis.) However, the rates are progressive not merely according to the current year's gifts but depend on the cumulative amount of taxable gifts made by the donor during his or her lifetime. The tax on a particular gift is determined by adding the amount of that gift to all taxable gifts of prior calendar years and imposing a graduated marginal rate on the current gift. Actually, the tax on the cumulated lifetime gifts is computed much as if they all had been made in the current year, and then prior gift taxes paid are subtracted, thus credited, the remainder being the tax due on the current gift. This system is explained more fully below.

Each year, a donor (any individual) is entitled to an *annual exclusion* for gifts in amounts up to $10,000 to *each* of any number of donees, to each donee. (See I.R.C. § 2503(b).)   Only when the donor gives more than the excludable amount to a donee in one year will the gift be taxable. Even then no tax may be payable because the donor may use up part (or all) of his remaining *unified credit* against any tax otherwise due. (See § 2505.) Once that unified credit and the available annual exclusions are exhausted, further giving becomes taxable. The tax liability is determined by cumulating all prior taxable gifts, adding the current year's taxable gifts, applying the graduated rates to this total and subtracting (from the total tax liability) the taxes that would be due on only the prior, non-current year's gifts. The remainder is the tax owing for current gifts. (See I.R.C. § 2052; § 2504.) Accordingly, except as statutory rates may change, and apart from annual exclusions, the amount of gift tax payable on a donor's lifetime transfers will be the same whether he or she gives everything in one year or spreads his or her gifts over many years. The timing of the tax may vary, however, and that makes for an important planning consideration.

For a given year, the gift tax *base* consists of gross transfers or *aggregate gifts* minus *annual exclusions* and minus some gift tax *deductions* (see I.R.C. §§ 2522–2524) to arrive at *net, taxable gifts*, against which tax *rates* are applied in the lifetime cumulative manner described. The result is gift tax liability, to be reduced only by any portion of the *unified credit* remaining to the donor, to determine the tax actually payable.

§ 6. Introduction to the Generation-Skipping Transfer Tax

The gift and estate taxes apply to gratuitous *transfers* of property. Holding a life estate, which expires upon the holder's death, therefore causes no additional tax burden on the decedent-holder's estate, since no property of the decedent "passes" to any third party by virtue of his death. The remainder interest (or successive life estate, etc.) which does then accrue to a third party is treated as "passing" from and through the estate of the original grantor, where it was of course taxed, and not through the estate of the decedent life-tenant. (See § 16, *infra.*) Thus a gift (whether *inter vivos* or testamentary), for example, by Grandmother of property in trust, with income for life to Son, remainder to Granddaughter, would be taxed as a gratuitous transfer by the grantor, Grandmother, but the passage of the use of the property to Granddaughter upon Son's death would occasion no further transfer tax under either the gift or estate tax alone.

This general rule, that interests terminating at death do not produce an estate tax, is the basis of much estate planning advice. The disposition illustrated in the example above accomplishes what is known as "generation skipping", and has been a source of some controversy in connection with proposals for reform of the estate tax.

By careful use of this slack in the gift and estate taxes, substantial tax savings could be accomplished. For this purpose, one might compare the taxes that would be paid if property were transferred outright through four generations with the tax saving that could be accomplished if the property were not transferred outright but rather similar interests were created. For example, a Patriarch in the family could give to his Son a life estate in property placed in trust, with the Son as trustee. In addition, the Son could be given a non-general testamentary power of appointment over the property. (See Chapter IX, *infra*.) To that could be added a non-general lifetime power of appointment. In addition, the Son could be given a power to invade the corpus of the trust to the extent necessary for his health, education, support or general maintenance. Moreover, the Son could be given the power to withdraw up to $5,000 or 5% of the corpus per year, whichever is greater, and that power would not cause the property to be treated as the Son's (if he did not exercise it) for the purposes of transfer taxes. If another trustee were appointed to act with the Son, the other trustee could be given a power to invade the trust still further for the benefit of the Son. The trustee could even be chosen by the family Patriarch.

As a result, the Son could have nearly the equivalent of outright ownership of the property, but nevertheless would not have to pay a transfer tax when the property passes on to someone else (at the death of the son). Still further, the Patriarch could have provided that at the Son's death the property would pass to a Grandson and then to a Great-Grandson with powers similar to those held by the Son. In each case, a transfer tax would not have to be paid when the property passed from one generation to another, so long as the interest held by each generation did not exceed those described and those permissible under the transfer taxes. Subject only to state law limitations on restrictions on alienation of property and rules against perpetuities, this kind of generation-skipping disposition could go on indefinitely. Even under those rules, the kind of outright transfer that would trigger a transfer tax usually could be postponed for a period ranging anywhere from 50 to 150 years. In a sense, then, the family could choose whether to pay the tax or not, because the dispositions of property that could be made without payment of the tax would so often suffice for family financial purposes.*

Dissatisfaction with allowing the use and enjoyment of large amounts of property to pass to successive generations and yet avoid any transfer taxes arose because of the need for uniformity in the operation of the taxing system. From a revenue-raising point of view, reasonably periodic collection of taxes is desirable. Also, horizontal equity (as between estates and gifts of the same size) demands

* See Cooper, G., *A Voluntary Tax? New Perspectives On Sophisticated Estate Tax Avoidance*, 77 Colum.L.Rev. 161, 205–210 (1977).

that such estates *all* be taxed with the same frequency, and therefore that the timing of the imposition of the tax not depend on the *form* of the
donor's gift (in trust versus outright), since then
the donor effectively has an election whether or not
to subject the property to further transfer taxes. In
addition, although all donors theoretically possess
the same option, actually only very large estates can
afford to use the generation-skipping device, since
the income alone of smaller estates is not sufficient
for the needs of the "skipped" generation. Vertical
equity, therefore, demands that the progressivity of
the transfer tax rates not be defeated by a device
available only to the very wealthy. Still another
undesirable effect of pre-1977 law was that many
dispositions of property were made in trust form
solely because of these tax consequences. Tax law,
however, should be "neutral," and ideally not influence primary activities in an unintended manner.
People should not be "forced" or induced to alter
their own dispositive desires because of a taxing
system which provides a premium for certain types
of transfers and not for other similar types (unless,
perhaps, there is a conscious Congressional policy to
encourage that favored type of transfer).

Efforts at reform of the transfer taxes in order to
prevent the kind of generation-skipping and tax
reduction that has been suggested in the foregoing
paragraphs from time to time reached the surface.
Those reforms included attempts to cut down on
the powers that could be given without taxation on
a constructive ownership or actual ownership basis.

Other reform proposals went further and suggested adoption of an inheritance or accessions tax scheme in lieu of the estate tax system presently enforced.*
Another possibility would be to treat inheritances or gifts as income under the income tax, particularly suitable if the income tax has a single rate or a flatter rate structure, as it does now, or if relatively generous averaging provisions softened some of the impact of taxing a once-in-a-life-time receipt of property as income under the income tax.†

Still another proposal was to impose an additional tax on the original disposition (by Grandfather, in the example) which has generation-skipping tax minimization as its object. This proposal was made by the American Law Institute "Federal Estate and Gift Tax Project", and also was advanced by the U.S. Treasury Department. (See Tax Reform Studies and Proposals, U.S. Treasury Department, 91st Cong. 1st Sess., Jt.Publ., Comm. on Finance of the U.S. Senate at pp. 116–7, 120.) Another possibility was to impose a tax at the time the skipped generation's representative dies, the "Son" in the above example. Imposing a tax at that time would more nearly resemble the tax treatment of a non-generation-skipping disposition, one in which the Grandfather made an outright gift of the property to his Son who used up the income but preserved the

* See McNulty, J.K., Fundamental Alternatives to Present Transfer Tax Systems, Ch. 6 in Halbach, E.C., Death, Taxes and Family Property, 185 A.B.A., West Pub. Co. (1977).

† See McNulty, J.K., A Transfer Tax Alternative: Inclusion Under the Income Tax, 26 Tax Notes 24 (1976).

property, and in turn made an outright transfer of the property at his death to the Grandson.

This last alternative is the one implemented by the entirely new Chapter 13 of the 1986 Tax Reform Act, entitled "Tax on Generation-Skipping Transfers", which entirely revised the more complex (and limited) "Tax on Certain Generation-Skipping Transfers", which had been enacted in 1976. This new tax is entirely separate from the gift and estate taxes, and is implemented via a multitude of new terms and concepts. (See §§ 2601–2663).

The Chapter 13 tax is imposed on "generation-skipping transfers" which, subject to important exceptions, are wealth transfers from a donor to a transferee who is two or more generations younger (a "skip person," § 2613) that escape the estate or gift tax at the intervening generation(s). See I.R.C. § 2601; § 2611; § 2612; § 2613; § 2651.

To be subject to tax, such a transfer must fit either the definition of a "direct skip" (an estate or gift taxable transfer to a skip person either outright or in trust), a "taxable distribution" (a transfer of trust corpus or income to a skip person), or a "taxable termination" (a shift to a skip person of the beneficial enjoyment of a trust), *e.g.,* if a trust pays income to a child for life, remainder to grandchild, the child's death results in a taxable termination. See I.R.C. § 2612.

The new tax is aimed at removing incentives to make gifts and bequests to persons more than one generation removed from a donor in an effort to avoid estate or gift taxation of the transferred property during the intervening generations.

In some ways, the new tax goes beyond its objective and actually creates incentives for transferors to ensure that property *will* be subject to estate or gift tax during intervening generations.

The generation-skipping transfer tax is a flat tax; its rate is fixed for *all* taxpayers at the highest marginal estate and gift tax rate (55% as of 1993). See I.R.C. § 2641. Unlike the estate and gift tax, there is no unified credit. Nor is there relief (comparable to the estate tax Section 2013 credit) for property that becomes exposed to the generation-skipping transfer tax twice within ten years.

There are, however, a number of very significant allowances in the generation-skipping transfer tax scheme. Every taxpayer has an exemption which can shelter from the tax either $1 million of direct-skip transfers or $1 million of trust assets (or a $1 million combination of direct skips and trust assets). See I.R.C. § 2631. Before 1990, transfers of up to $2 million per grandchild were exempt from the tax. [See P.L. 99–514 (Section 1433(b)(3)]. If a child has a parent who predeceased the child's grandparent, estate or gift taxable transfers from grandparent (or grandparent's spouse) to grandchild are exempt from the generation-skipping transfer tax. See § 2612(c)(2). Many section 2503(b), (c), (e) transfers excluded from gift tax are also exempt from any generation-skipping transfer tax. See § 2611(b); § 2612(c); § 2642(c). For example a grandparent can make medical or educational gifts to grandchildren without incurring any tax if the gift meets the requirements of gift tax § 2503(e). Finally, transfers to individuals *more than* two generations removed from the transferee are subject to only one application of the generation-skipping transfer tax. (This means that an individual pays the same tax on a direct skip to a great-grandchild as on a direct skip to a grandchild.)

This complex system will be described at greater length (and perhaps with greater comprehensibility) in later Chapters. See esp. § 15.

§ 7. Reporting and Payment of the Taxes

The most important requirement is that an *estate tax return* (Form 706) must be filed within nine months after the decedent's death, see I.R.C. § 6075, if any return is required. See I.R.C. § 6018. Also see Regs. § 20.6075–1. Payment of tax normally is due with the return. I.R.C. § 6151. An extension of time for filing can sometimes be obtained for a period up to six months, I.R.C. § 6081, and an extension of time for payment of up to twelve months, under I.R.C. § 6161, or sometimes up to fourteen years, under § 6166, if more than 35% of the value of the adjusted gross estate of a decedent dying after 1981 consists of an interest in a closely-held business. I.R.C. § 6018 requires that a return be filed in any instance when the gross estate of a citizen or resident exceeds the exemption equivalent of his remaining, unused unified credit. (See § 69, *infra*). If the decedent was a nonresident and non-citizen, a return (Form 706 or 706NA) must be filed if that part of the gross estate situated in the U.S. exceeds $60,000 reduced by the sum of decedent's adjusted taxable gifts (as defined in § 2001(b)) and any amount allowed as a specific exemption under old § 2521 after Sept. 8, 1976. See § 6018(a)(3). As a consequence of these rules and the exemptions they contain, a return need not be filed for every decedent. Furthermore, not every estate that is required to file a return will owe any tax; only a small percentage of deaths, under 2%, resulted in any federal estate tax liability even before the 1976 Amendments, which introduced still greater deductions and credits. See generally Galvin, C., To Bury The Estate Tax, Not To Praise It, 53 Tax Notes 1413 (Sept. 16, 1991).

A *gift tax return* must be filed by any citizen or resident who, within one calendar year, gives to any one donee property that exceeds or does not qualify for the annual exclusion of $10,000 under I.R.C. § 2503(b), the exclusion for certain transfers for educational or medical expenditures under I.R.C. § 2503(e), or the marital deduction under § 2523. See I.R.C. § 6019. (The return must be filed even if no tax is due because of other allowable exemptions or deductions, and must also be filed in order to elect gift-splitting under § 2513.) Gift tax returns must be filed before the 15th day of April following the close of the calendar year of the reportable gift, I.R.C. § 6075(b). An extension may be given under I.R.C. § 6081.

The tax, if any, is due with the return. See I.R.C. § 6151. Extensions sometimes can be obtained. See I.R.C. § 6161. (Further details about filing the returns and paying the taxes are set forth in the Statute and Regulations. See generally I.R.C. §§ 6001–7610 and the Regulations thereunder.)

With regard to the generation-skipping tax, I.R.C. § 2662 specifically authorizes the promulgation of Regulations specifying the person who must file the return and the time of filing, while providing guidelines to be followed by the Regulations "[t]o the extent practicable." (See Temp.Reg. § 26.2662–1, which provides that the return must be filed by the party primarily liable for the tax, under § 2603, *i.e.*, the distributee in the case of a taxable distribution, the trustee in the case of a taxable termination, and the transferor, in the case of a direct skip. In the instance of a direct skip other than from a trust, the guidelines require that the return be filed on or before the date on which an estate or gift tax return must be filed in connection with the transfer. Filings for other generation-skipping transfers are to be made within 4 months and 15 days after the close of the taxable year of the person required to file a return in connection with the transfer.

§ 8. Legislation and the Legislative Process

Although the Federal Estate, Gift and Generation-Skipping Tax laws are not altered as often as is the Income Tax, legislative changes must be expect-

ed from time to time. Congressional action usually
results from Presidential recommendations, filtered
through the Treasury Department.

In Congress, the legislative process begins with a
hearing before the Committee on Ways and Means
of the House of Representatives, because the Constitution requires all revenue legislation to originate
in the House of Representatives. (As a practical
matter, important legislation can begin in the Senate where it may be attached to a Revenue Bill as
an amendment, after which House action and Conference Committee action would have to follow.) At
the Ways and Means Committee hearing, the Treasury proposals will be presented by officials of the
Treasury Department. Representatives of various
private and public groups will also appear to present their views of the proposed legislation. Eventually, a Tax Bill and a Committee Report are reported to the House of Representatives. There the bill
is debated and possibly passed in some form by the
House. Next, similar hearings are begun in the
Committee on Finance of the U.S. Senate, which
considers the House bill. Eventually, the House
bill, as amended by the Senate Committee, and a
Senate Committee Report are brought to the floor
of the Senate. If passed by the Senate, the bill with
Senate amendments goes to a Conference Committee of the House and Senate which irons out the
differences between the two legislative chambers.
The action of the Conference Committee is reported
in a Conference Report, which then is usually approved by the House and the Senate. The legisla-

tion then goes to the President for his approval or veto. These various processes, and others that fill the gaps, provide rich legislative history for the tax lawyer or judge to use in understanding and interpreting the legislation.

§ 9. Administration and the Administrative Process

Revenue laws are administered under the Treasury Department by the Internal Revenue Service (I.R.S.) headed by the Commissioner of Internal Revenue. The principal office of the Internal Revenue Service is in Washington, D.C., but there is a field office in most cities of substantial size throughout the country. (The Treasury Department is mainly responsible for tax policy within the government; the Commissioner, appointed by the President, is delegated the task of assessing and collecting federal taxes.)

Each main field office is headed by a District Director. In addition, regional offices exist to coordinate the work of the field offices with the principal office in Washington. The taxpayer and his lawyer will usually be most concerned with the District Office. In the event a tax return is questioned or becomes the subject of a dispute, a conference will be held with an Internal Revenue Service agent or examiner in a field or office audit or other inquiry. Later, perhaps, the dispute will go to superior officers called group managers, and eventually (if necessary) to Appeals Office representatives. If the dispute has not been settled by then, it is necessary to "go to law." (See *Judicial Process and Procedure, § 10, infra.*)

Many disputes between the taxpayer and the Internal Revenue Service never reach litigation in court, as a result of the procedures by which Treasury representatives and the taxpayer may discuss and settle the controversy administratively. When a tax return is first filed, a Service Center office reviews the return for errors in arithmetic. Later, the Examination Division of the District Office inspects the return. If there is a problem, the return will be audited either in the office of the Internal Revenue Service or on the premises of the taxpayer (a "field audit"). During and after the audit, opportunities exist for the controversy to be settled or dropped as part of the administrative process. If the taxpayer so requests, the case will be referred to the Appeals Office, which will afford taxpayer an opportunity for a conference. The determination by the Appeals Office (formerly the Appellate Division) is final, so far as appeal rights within the I.R.S. are concerned. After that, the taxpayer may petition the Tax Court for review, or pay the tax. If the tax is paid, the taxpayer may still file a claim for refund and eventually go to court. (See § 10, below.)

Administrative interpretations of the tax laws are reported in general rules and policies announced by the Treasury Department and also are reflected by the administrative practices and litigation practices of the I.R.S. with respect to individual tax returns. The most important form of general administrative announcement is that made by the Treasury Department in the form of Treasury Regulations, specifically "Estate Tax Regulations," and "Gift Tax Regulations," authorized by Congress in I.R.C. § 7805. In addition, § 2663 specifically authorizes Regulations to be promulgated to implement the purposes of the Chapter 13 generation-skipping transfer tax. When a Regulation is amended, the amendment is issued as a "Treasury Decision" (abbreviated "T.D.").

Treasury Regulations are presumed to be valid; only rarely does a court invalidate a regulation as unreasonable, beyond the delegated power or inconsistent with law. These Regulations appear in the publication entitled "Cumulative Bulletin" (as well as in the Code of Federal Regulations (C.F.R.) and the Federal Register (Fed.Reg.)). Other authoritative pronouncements on tax law also appear in several forms in the Cumulative Bulletin (cited as "C.B.")—Revenue Rulings, Treasury Decisions and Revenue Procedures. The Cumulative Bulletin also publishes Senate and House committee reports on revenue bills.

Some, but not all, Revenue Rulings are published by the Internal Revenue Service. These rulings amount to decisions on given facts which usually involve a problem that is likely to recur frequently. Generally such rulings are issued pursuant to a request for a ruling by a particular (unnamed) taxpayer on an uncertain or difficult point of interpretation. The ruling procedure is outlined in Rev. Proc. 72–3, 1972–1 C.B. 698. Published rulings are referred to as Revenue Rulings (Rev.Rul.) and cited "72–1," the first number referring to the year of the ruling and the second number designating the ruling number for that year. Not all rulings are published; some private "letter rulings" or "determination letters," issued in response to taxpayers' requests, reach the light of day only in privately published tax books or newsletters, if at all, or only if disclosure is obtained by request or demand. See, *e.g.*, Tax Analysts and Advocates v. I.R.S., 505 F.2d 350 (D.C.Cir., 1974). I.R.C. § 6110 now provides for public inspection of I.R.S. "written determinations" (including private rulings), with a few exceptions.

Regulations and Revenue Rulings (but supposedly not Private Letter Rulings) are binding on the Internal Revenue Service and are followed by the Service in handling particular controversies and cases. Published rulings are applied retroactively unless they explicitly state to the contrary, and they can be revoked retroactively, unless doing so is held to be an abuse of discretion. See generally I.R.C. § 7805(b). A letter ruling ordinarily will not be revoked or modified retroactively as to the particular taxpayer to whom it was issued or as to someone else directly involved.

The Internal Revenue Service sometimes publishes a notice of "Acquiescence" or a "Non-acquiescence" when it loses a case in the Tax Court in order to indicate whether the Service will accept that case as authority in the future or not. Also, in some Rulings the Service lets it be known whether a decision or line of cases in a Federal Circuit Court of Appeals will be followed or not by the I.R.S. as to other taxpayers or other years.

§ 10. Judicial Process and Procedure

If proceedings are carried beyond the administrative stage, and into the courts, the taxpayer has a choice of tribunals. He or she may choose not to pay the tax deficiency (in which event interest will accrue at a statutorily determined rate, recently 10%) and to petition the United States Tax Court to contest the deficiency. Or, taxpayer may pay the tax and file a claim for refund, after adverse action on which he may then sue for a refund in the Federal District Court or in the Court of Claims. In the District Court, he may request a trial by jury. In the Tax Court or in a Court of Claims, the case will be heard by a judge without a jury. From the Tax Court or the District Court, taxpayer's case may be appealed to the appropriate Circuit Court of Appeals and from there to the Supreme Court of the United States. From the Court of Claims, the case can only go directly to the United States Supreme Court.

The Tax Court, which was formerly known as the Board of Tax Appeals, was once technically an agency in the executive branch of the government. As a result of 1969 legislation, it now has the standing of an "Article III Court," with all the limitations imposed by that provision of the U.S. Constitution. It handles appeals from deficiencies in tax which have been put forward by the Commissioner. It does not have jurisdiction over refund cases. (But, in a deficiency case the Court may order a refund as the proper remedy in the proceeding.) The Tax Court now follows Court of Appeals precedents in cases that would be appealed to that Court of Appeals. See Golsen v. Comm., 54 T.C. 742 (1970). The decisions of the Tax Court are reported in the Tax Court Reporter if they are "published decisions"; "Memorandum Decisions" of the Tax Court are not published in official reports but are made public by the tax services. 1969 legislation allows the Tax Court to use an informal procedure for cases involving small amounts.

§ 11. Supplementary Materials

The main sources of law and interpretation of the law are the Federal Estate, Gift and Generation-Skipping Tax statutes themselves and the Regulations and Rulings issued by the Internal Revenue Service thereunder as well as reports of decided cases by the Tax Court, Court of Claims and other federal courts. The regulations and rulings of the I.R.S. provide substantial explanation of the law. In addition, there are several useful books or texts about the Federal Estate and Gift Taxes.

These include Stephens, Maxfield, and Lind, Federal Estate and Gift Taxation, Warren, Gorham and Lamont, 6th edition, 1991 (1993 Supp.) and West-fall and Mair, Estate Planning Law and Taxation, Warren, Gorham and Lamont, 1989 (1993 Supp.). See also Lane & Zaritsky, Federal Income Taxation of Estates and Trusts, 1988 (1993 Supp.). The most up-to-date casebook is Campfield, Dickinson and Turnier, Taxation of Estates, Gifts and Trusts, 1991–1993, Commerce Clearing House. The most thorough discussion of the generation-skipping transfer tax (as of September, 1988) can be found in Kalik and Schneider, "Generation-Skipping Transfer Taxes Under the Tax Reform Act of 1986," 21 Univ. of Miami Institute on Estate Planning ¶ 900, Matthew Bender (1987) (also published at 39 Major Tax Planning ¶ 1600, Matthew Bender (1987).

An excellent article is Halbach, Living with the Generation Skipping Tax, 22 Univ. of Miami Institute on Estate Planning ¶ 800, Matthew Bender (1988). A fine set of essays (and American Assembly Report), on transmission of property and transfer taxes is Halbach (ed.), Death, Taxes and Family Property, A.B.A. (West Pub. Co., 1977).

On the transfer taxes in recent years, see Aaron and Munnell, Reassessing the Role for Wealth Transfer Taxes, 45 National Tax Journal 119 (1992); Donaldson, The Future of Transfer Taxation: Repeal, Restructuring and Refinement, or Replacement, 50 Wash. & Lee L.Rev. 539 (1993); Cooper, A Voluntary Tax? New Perspectives on Sophisticated Estate Tax Avoidance, 77 Colum.L.Rev. 161 (1977) and, revised, Brookings (1978); Graetz, To Praise the Estate Tax, Not to Bury It, 93 Yale L.J. 259 (1983); Gutman, Federal Wealth Transfer Taxes After E.R.T.A.: An Assessment, 69 Va.L.Rev. 1183 (1983); Gutierrez, Taxation of Wealth Transmission: Problems and Reforms, Ch. 5 in Halbach (ed.) Death, Taxes and Family Property (Essays and

American Assembly Report), ABA Tax Section, (West, 1977).

On the economics of transfer taxes, see Pechman, Federal Tax Policy, Ch. 8 "Estate and Gift Taxes" (Wash., D.C.: Brookings, 5th ed., 1987); Jantscher, The Aims of Death Taxation (Wash., D.C.: Brookings, 1978); Shoup, Federal Estate and Gift Taxes (Wash., D.C.: Brookings, 1966); Steuerle, Equity And The Taxation of Wealth Transfers (Treasury Dept., O.T.A. paper 39, 1980).

Longer, multi-volume tax services published by Commerce Clearing House and Research Institute of America provide elaborate material on the administrative and judicial interpretations and decisions under the estate and gift tax laws.

An important one-volume book on the federal transfer taxes is Shoup, Federal Estate and Gift Taxation, Brookings Institution, 1966 Edition. A fine but shorter treatment of this subject is to be found in Chapter 8 of Pechman, Federal Tax Policy, The Brookings Institution, 5th ed. 1987.

§ 12. Constitutionality of the Transfer Taxes

The constitutionality of the early federal "death duty" was tested in Knowlton v. Moore, 178 U.S. 41 (1900) and the (then inheritance) tax was upheld as an excise tax, not a direct tax, valid despite its progressive rates. The present federal estate tax was upheld in New York Trust Co. v. Eisner, 256 U.S. 345 (1921), again as an indirect tax free of the apportionment requirement for federal direct taxes.

The tax also was held to comply with the requirement of Art. I, § 8 of the Constitution that taxes be uniform throughout the U.S.

Because the estate tax is an excise tax on a transfer of property, not a direct tax on the property itself (however thin the line between these two categories, especially when the excise tax is geared to the value of the property transferred), the tax can apply to a transfer of property that itself might be exempt from federal tax. So, state and local municipal bonds, whose interest is free from income tax, can be included in the base of the estate tax. Similarly, property that is exempt by federal statute from direct tax and from claims of creditors may nevertheless give rise to estate (or gift) tax liability. One example is the proceeds of National Service Life Insurance policies. Foreign real estate may be included in the base of the transfer taxes without constitutional objection. See MacDonald v. U. S., 139 F.Supp. 598 (D.Mass.1956).

The Federal Gift Tax was held to be constitutional in Bromley v. McCaughn, 280 U.S. 124 (1929) over arguments based on the apportionment clause, the uniformity and the due process requirements.

There is no reported case challenging the constitutionality of the Generation–Skipping Transfer Tax. The Federal Estate and Gift Tax precedents cited above would appear to protect this more recent transfer tax from constitutional attack.

When the transfer taxes first appeared, questions of unconstitutional retroactivity often presented themselves if a tax were levied on a transfer made before the tax was enacted. Some courts upheld such taxpayer objections, based on the due process clause. See Nichols v. Coolidge, 274 U.S. 531 (1927) (estate tax); Untermyer v. Anderson, 276 U.S. 440 (1928) (gift tax). As a result, the taxes often have been construed to apply only to post-enactment transfers. See, *e.g.*, Shwab v. Doyle, 258 U.S. 529 (1922); Carlton v. U.S., 972 F.2d 1051 (9th Cir.1992), cert. granted 114 S.Ct. 55 (1993). Nonetheless, some degree of retroactivity, in the form of higher rates or in slightly different technical dimensions, can constitutionally be allowed. See, *e.g.*, Milliken v. U. S., 283 U.S. 15 (1931). Sometimes, difficult questions arise about which event is the key one for determining whether a new tax rule is retroactive, when some events preceded its enactment and others occurred later. See, *e.g.*, U. S. v. Jacobs, 306 U.S. 363 (1939); Fernandez v. Weiner, 326 U.S. 340 (1945); U. S. v. Manufacturers National Bank of Detroit, 363 U.S. 194 (1960).

The Gift Tax explicitly applies only to post-enactment gifts. See I.R.C. § 2502(c). In contrast, the Estate Tax contains a general rule looking in the direction of retroactivity. I.R.C. § 2045.

The revised Generation-Skipping Transfer Tax contains very specific effective date provisions. Generally, it will apply to transfers made after October 22, 1986, which come within its terms. There are, however, some rather significant exceptions to this general rule. See Tax Reform Act of 1986, § 1433(b).

The old "Tax on Certain Generation–Skipping Transfers" has been repealed retroactive to its date of enactment. No tax is due under the old law, and any tax actually paid will be credited, or refunded (with interest) as an overpayment. The statute of limitations has been waived as to refund claims filed before October 22, 1987. See Tax Reform Act of 1986, § 1433(c).

CHAPTER II

THE FEDERAL ESTATE, GIFT, AND GENERATION-SKIPPING TRANSFER TAX LAWS IN OUTLINE

§ 13. Outline of the Estate Tax

The Federal Estate Tax occupies a small number of sections of the United States Internal Revenue Code of 1986. The Estate Tax is the lineal descendant of the 1916 legislation which in turn became a portion of the 1939 Internal Revenue Code and later the Internal Revenue Code of 1954. The Estate Tax begins with I.R.C. § 2001, which sets forth the rates of tax. Perhaps better starting points, however, are §§ 2031 and 2033.

Section 2031 provides that the value of the gross estate of the decedent shall be determined by including "the value at the time of his death of all property, real or personal, tangible or intangible, wherever situated." Section 2033 makes it clear that the value of the gross estate shall include the value of "all property"—to the extent of any interest in that property held by the decedent at the time of his death.

Section 2032 provides for an alternate valuation date. Under this section, the executor may elect to

41

value the property included in the gross estate as of
a date *six months after* the decedent's death, or, in
the instance of property already sold or otherwise
disposed of by the estate, the value at the date of
disposition, instead of at the date of death. Special
valuation rules are granted by § 2032A for property
used in some farms and small businesses. (Valuation will be covered in greater detail below at
§§ 47–52.)

Under I.R.C. § 2034, the value of the gross estate
includes all of the property of the decedent *without*
any reduction for an interest in the nature of dower
or curtesy in favor of a surviving spouse.

These basic sections defining the *gross estate* of
the decedent are supplemented by additional sections which provide for the inclusion of some property interests held by the decedent at his or her
death and also for the inclusion of some property
interests transferred before death, transfers which
are treated by the law as substitutes for testamentary dispositions. As a result of these latter sections, the *gross estate* may exceed the actual wealth
of the decedent at the time of his death.

I.R.C. § 2040, for example, provides that in many
instances jointly-owned property will be taxed in
the estate of the first of the joint owners to die.
Under § 2035, the gross estate will include the
value of some property that was gratuitously transferred within three years of death. See Chapters V
& VI below for greater detail.

I.R.C. § 2036(a)(2) and I.R.C. § 2038 deal with interests gratuitously transferred by the decedent in trust or otherwise during his lifetime and over which he has retained powers to alter or amend or revoke the transfer. If the decedent retains the specified powers, the property will be included in his gross estate at his death. Under I.R.C. § 2036(a)(1) a similar rule is imposed for property transferred by the decedent during his lifetime if he has retained a life estate in the property or a right to the income in the property for his life or for any period which does not in fact end before his death, or which is not ascertainable without reference to his death. Again, such property will be included in his gross estate because of the retained interest.

Section 2036(b) triggers § 2036(a)(1) inclusion where the transferor retains "the right to vote (directly or indirectly) transferred shares of stock of a "controlled corporation." Newly enacted § 2701 governs the valuation of transfers between family members of distribution rights in an entity that the family controls. Section 2702 provides the rules for determining whether a transfer of an interest in trust to a member of the transferor's family is a gift and, if so, the value of that gift. Section 2703 governs options and restrictive sales agreements, and section 2704 provides rules for valuation of lapsing rights.

Under I.R.C. § 2037, gratuitous transfers made during life but taking effect at death will cause inclusion of the transferred property in the decedent's gross estate if the decedent retained a reversionary interest of more than a minimal value.

I.R.C. § 2042 provides that the gross estate will include the value of proceeds of insurance—but only if the proceeds are receivable by the executor *or* if the decedent at his death possessed any of the incidents of ownership of the life insurance. Under I.R.C. § 2041, property over which the decedent had a general power of appointment, as defined in the statute, will be included in his gross estate even if the power had not actually been exercised and thus disappeared at death.

I.R.C. § 2039 provides that the gross estate of the decedent shall include the value of an annuity or other payment receivable by a beneficiary who survives the decedent if, under the annuity arrangement, an annuity or other payment was payable to the decedent or if he possessed the right to receive some annuity or payment alone or with somebody else for his life or for a period defined by his death or for a period that does not in fact end before his death.

I.R.C. § 2043 deals with the problem of defining transfers made for insufficient consideration. In particular, subsection (b) provides that marital rights relinquished by a spouse shall not be considered to be consideration "in money or money's worth" for purposes of the estate tax, except in the case of property settlement agreements entered into within a few years of a divorce. See I.R.C. § 2043(b)(2); § 2516.

The tax rates of I.R.C. § 2001 are applied against the *taxable estate* of every citizen or resident of the United States. The *taxable estate* is defined by I.R.C. § 2051 to consist of the *gross estate*, as defined by §§ 2031 and 2033 and the other inclusion sections, minus allowable *deductions*. The *deductions* are set forth in I.R.C. §§ 2053 through 2056. Under I.R.C. § 2053, deductions are allowed for: funeral and administrative expenses, claims against the estate, unpaid mortgages and other indebtedness in respect of property included in the gross estate, and for certain state and foreign death taxes. Under I.R.C. § 2055, a deduction is allowed for transfers made for public charitable and religious uses. Section 2054 allows a deduction for uncompensated casualty or theft losses that arise during settlement of the estate. Section 2056 grants an unlimited deduction for qualified bequests to a surviving spouse.

After the *taxable estate* has been determined by subtracting deductions from the *gross estate*, the tax is determined by applying the rates and computation method of I.R.C. § 2001 to the base: the taxable estate. Prior to 1977, the rate of tax on the taxable estate was independent of the size and number of any *inter vivos* gifts the decedent had made. Under the unified rate schedules of new § 2001, however, those prior gifts push the taxable estate into higher and higher rate brackets, depending on their cumulative size.

There is no longer a separate trip up the rate scale for the taxable estate at death. This result is achieved in a manner very like the cumulative calculation of the gift tax under both prior and current law. To the taxable estate is added all *adjusted taxable gifts*, defined in § 2001(b) as all gifts not otherwise included in the gross estate, made after Dec. 31, 1976, taking into account (*i.e.*, not adding in) either any allowable $10,000 per–year per–donee exclusion, or the spouse's share of any split gifts. Only post '76, *i.e.* post effective-date, gifts are accumulated under § 2001, so the "unification" of the gift and estate taxes operates only prospectively. This grand cumulative total is then subjected to the rate schedule of § 2001(c), and the result is a "tentative tax", from which is subtracted a second tentative tax (using the same progressive rate table) on just the adjusted taxable gifts.

The result is the estate's tax liability, which amounts to a tax on the value of the taxable estate, at the progressive rates of not just the estate, but of the estate plus all post-'76 gifts. However, the amount thus ascertained is not the final tax liabili-ty, for certain *credits* are allowed against the tax otherwise payable. I.R.C. § 2010 provides for the *unified credit*, gradually phased in through 1987, which replaced the old deduction/exemption of § 2052. Credits are also allowed in I.R.C. §§ 2011 through 2015 for: death taxes paid to a state or states, for estate tax paid on prior transfers, for foreign death taxes paid, and for gift taxes paid earlier. These creditable amounts are subtracted from the tax liability determined by applying the rates and computational mechanics of § 2001 against the taxable estate. By subtraction of these credits the actual amount of tax that must be paid is determined.

Income tax basis. For income tax purposes, I.R.C. § 1014(a) contains the basic "fresh start" basis rule for property acquired from a decedent. This rule says that the person to whom such property passes shall take a basis equal to the fair market value of the property at the decedent's death. (Alternatively, it may have to be the fair market value at the optional valuation date (under § 2032) or the § 2032A special valuation if either of those alternative valuation rules is elected by the estate.) In other words, the heir or legatee gets a basis that has a "fresh start" rather than a basis determined by reference to the basis in the hands of the decedent, or "carryover basis." This rule applies for all property acquired by bequest, devise or inheritance, or by the decedent's estate from the decedent. See § 1014(b). It also applies to other property that is included in the decedent's gross estate, although transferred by him or her during life, because of retained strings—such as a life estate, power of revocation, etc. The fresh start basis, a *higher* basis if the ("appreciated") property's fair market value exceeds its basis in the hands of the decedent, seems to be a link of integration between the income and estate taxes and it gives income tax basis for value taxed under the estate tax. In light of this understanding of the rule of § 1014, the next step becomes somewhat surprising.

If decedent owned community property at his or her death, the surviving spouse takes a one-half interest in the property by virtue of community property law. If the decedent transfers the other half to the survivor, she or he gets ownership of the entire community property item. One half did not come from the decedent; the other half, which did, will qualify for the estate tax unlimited marital deduction. The question is whether all, one-half or none of the property will receive a fresh-start basis in the survivor's hands. The answer, provided by § 1014(b)(6), states that the surviving spouse's one-half share of the property receives a fresh start basis if at least one-half of the whole of the community interest was includable in determining the value of the decedent's gross estate. It was included, of course, because the marital deduction comes *after* determination of the gross estate, which includes the decedent's community property one-half interest in the asset. So the survivor will get a fresh start basis in the *entire* asset. No comparable effect is provided in § 1014 for joint and survivorship property, or other joint ownership, even though it may closely resemble the community property on which § 1014(b)(6) operates.

Section § 1014(c) specifies that the fresh start basis rule will *not* apply to property that constitutes a right to receive income in respect of a decedent under § 691.

Section 1014(e) blocks one device for improperly obtaining an advantageous fresh start basis. If an owner of appreciated property transfers it to a person nearing death, with assurance that the imminent decedent will bequeath the property back to the owner, § 1014(e) will fend off the § 1014(a) step-up if the first transfer occurs within one year of the decedent's death.   Unless and until that period elapses, the death will result in retention of the property's old basis.

International Aspects.   An individual who is a citizen or a resident alien of the United States is taxed by the Estate Tax on all property owned ("world-wide").   See I.R.C. § 2031(a).   If that property is located in another country, or if the person is a citizen of another country, or if another country— applying its own rules of residency—treats the person as a resident of that country, some (or all) of the decedent's property may be subjected to estate tax or "capital transfer tax" by the other jurisdiction, as well as by the U.S.   Such "international double taxation" of a transfer can occur under the gift tax as well.

International double taxation is eliminated or ameliorated by two main devices.   One is the statutory *credit* for foreign taxes, in § 2014.   The § 2053(d) *deduction* for foreign death transfer tax can, alternatively, provide some lesser relief.   Another is the use of bilateral tax treaties between the U.S. and other countries, under which—typically— the country of citizenship (or domicile or residency) agrees to allow a tax credit (with some limitations) for foreign death taxes paid to the country of situs or source.   The treaties define situs, and other key terms, in an effort to provide certainty and to fend off different or inconsistent applications of the treaty by the two countries. Some treaties provide a foreign tax credit of their own.

The U.S. has entered into transfer tax treaties with a number of countries, but with many more there is no treaty, and so the § 2014 foreign tax credit becomes the crucial source of relief from double taxation. That credit uses the "situs" rules of I.R.C. §§ 2104–2105 to determine the location of property in question. Sometimes both the § 2014 (statutory) credit and a treaty could apply. In that event, taxpayer may choose the most favorable relief. (Usually any tax credit leaves in place the higher of the two competing death taxes.)

The U.S. also sometimes taxes non-resident aliens, but it does so only on their property situated in the U.S. See I.R.C. § 2103; § 2105; § 2106. The estate of the non-resident decedent may be entitled to a credit or other relief in the country of citizenship or domicile/residence under a tax treaty or under internal, domestic law.

As to gift transfers by nonresident aliens, and some major exemptions, see §§ 2501(a), 2511(a) and 2511(b).

If an American citizen expatriates (gives up U.S. citizenship and residence) to avoid high U.S. estate tax, the trick won't work—at least for a while. I.R.C. § 2107 applies the U.S. estate tax even to a non-resident alien if he or she was a citizen within 10 years of death, unless it can be shown that avoidance of death tax (or income tax) was *not* a principal purpose of the sacrifice of citizenship. § 2501(a)(3) and § 877 contain parallel rules for the gift and income taxes.

§ 14. Outline of the Gift Tax

The Federal Gift Tax also is set forth in a very few sections of the Internal Revenue Code, beginning with I.R.C. § 2501. The brevity and occasional vagueness and incompleteness of these sections leaves much to be determined without the benefit of direct statutory command.

I.R.C. § 2501(a) decrees that a tax shall be imposed "on the transfer of property by gift" during the calendar year "by any individual, resident or nonresident." I.R.C. § 2511 goes further in providing that the tax imposed by § 2501 shall apply "whether the transfer is in trust or otherwise, whether the gift is direct or indirect, and whether the property is real or personal, tangible or intangible."

In general, the Gift Tax applies to any transfer made without consideration or an equivalent value received in return, without regard to intent. In other words, the common-law requirement of intent to make a gift is not necessary for a taxable gift for Federal Gift Tax purposes. Thus, a transfer made without consideration *equal in money or money's worth* will be taxable, except for business or arm's-length transfers, transactions required by or made under compulsion of law (such as alimony), and incomplete transfers—the incompleteness of which local law will govern.

Under I.R.C. § 2512, the *valuation* of any gift shall be made at the date of the gift. When property is transferred for less than an adequate and full consideration in money or money's worth, the amount of the gift is the amount by which the value of the property transferred exceeds the value of the consideration received.

The method of computing the Gift Tax is set forth in § 2502. The rates are the progressive Estate Tax rates of § 2001(c), and the tax is applied cumulatively, over the lifetime of the donor.

Every donor is allowed an *annual exclusion* of $10,000 per donee. See I.R.C. § 2503(b). An unlimited exclusion is also allowed for amounts paid on behalf of a donee directly to an educational institution for tuition payments, or to a health care provider for medical expenses, without regard to the relationship between donor and donee. See I.R.C. § 2503(e). An unlimited *charitable deduction* is granted by I.R.C. § 2522. In addition, an unlimited *marital deduction* is to be found in I.R.C. § 2523(a).

Under I.R.C. § 2513, a gift by husband or wife *to a third party* may be considered as made one-half by each spouse. This is the so-called *split-gift* provision, which attributes one half of the gift to the spouse of the donor, if the spouse consents to such treatment. This split-gift provision enables spouses to take advantage of two lifetime unified credits and two annual exclusions, as well as enabling them to use the lowest of two graduated tax brackets for gifts by either or both of them, whether they are giving separate or community (or other jointly-owned) property.

Further experience will reveal more fully what, if any, will be the continuing *need* (in planning or compliance) for the split-gift provision, given the new unlimited marital deduction.

Gifts may occur in disguised or subtle forms; special statutory rules apply to some of these special forms. I.R.C. § 2514 provides that the exercise of a *power of appointment* may constitute the making of a taxable gift. Under I.R.C. § 2516, some *property settlements* made in connection with divorce will *not* be treated as taxable gifts; in contrast, transfers not made in compliance with the conditions of I.R.C. § 2516 will be subjected to the more general rules in determining whether there has been a transfer for a full and adequate consideration in money or money's worth or a taxable gift. (Contrast § 1041 which, for income tax purposes, deems many property-settlement and other transfers between spouses, or to ex-spouses incident to a divorce, to be gifts.)

The Federal Gift Tax, then, has a structure that resembles that of the Federal Estate Tax, although the statutory language tends to cloak this resemblance. The gift tax begins with the notion of a net transfer—the value of the total gift under I.R.C. § 2512, minus the $10,000 annual per-donee exclusion—which is reduced to the concept of a *taxable gift* by the subtraction of deductions in §§ 2522 through 2524. There is only one *credit* available against the gift tax, the new post '76 *unified credit* of § 2505. This is a cumulative credit, and in any given year only the amount remaining unused may be taken. Moreover, the use (and consequent exhaustion) of this credit is not elective, since § 2505(a)(2) specifies that the amount allowed as a credit in any given year is to be $192,800 (for example, in 1993) reduced by any amounts "allowable" (as opposed to "allowed") in previous years.

The actual computation of the gift tax is not quite so simple, however, since it is *cumulative* over the lifetime of the taxpayer as well as *progressive*. To make the tax cumulative in this way, the tax for current gifts must be determined in the following fashion. First, total taxable gifts made since the enactment of the gift tax to the end of the taxable year of the gift in question must be aggregated and a tax on that amount computed at current rates. From the tax so determined must be subtracted a tax, again computed at present rates, on the total taxable gifts made up to the beginning of the current year. The difference is the amount of tax that must be paid on gifts made in the year in question. See I.R.C. § 2502. The progressive rates and this cumulative computation of the gift tax result in taxing larger gifts or gifts in succeeding years at higher and higher tax rates, up to the maximum rate, i.e., 65% in 1982, 60% in 1983, 55% in 1984, and 50% in 1993 and thereafter.

Income tax basis. As to gifts of property during life, § 1015 states the income tax basis rule to be that the basis of the gift property in the hands of

the donee shall be the same as its basis in the hands
of the donor (carryover basis), except that if such
basis is *greater* than fair market value at the time of
the gift, then the basis for purposes of determining
loss (only) shall be such fair market value.   [This
means that if the donee sells for a price between
carryover basis and lower fair market value at gift,
a "grey area" results—no gain or loss to the donee.
See Regs. § 1.1015–1(a)(2)(ex.).]

Section 1015(d) entitles the donee to step up the
§ 1014(a) basis by the amount of gift tax paid with
respect to the gift.

§ 15. Outline of the Tax on Generation-Skipping Transfers

The Generation-Skipping Transfer Tax, completely revised by the Tax Reform Act of 1986, occupies
only the 22 Code sections of Chapter 13, beginning
with § 2601.   These sections are very complicated
and contain a multitude of new terms with mutually dependent and interlocking definitions.   An overview of this new tax was given in § 6, *supra*.   Now
comes the more detailed and technical treatment of
the statute which implements the scheme.

This outline is organized in five parts: (1) *What
is a generation-skipping transfer?*   (2) *How is the
tax on generation-skipping transfers determined?*
(3) *Who pays the tax?*   (4) *What credits are available?*   (5) *What basis effects and other consequences
follow a generation-skipping transfer?*   The simplicity of this outline belies the morass of new terms
which implement the scheme.   It may be tempting

for students (and their instructors) to pay scant attention to the tax on generation-skipping transfers. After all, today only a tiny number of well-advised households pay estate or gift tax. Because of generous exemptions, it appears that far fewer will ever pay any generation-skipping transfer tax. With the population living longer and longer (and the elderly becoming increasingly wealthy), however, a well-drawn estate plan must consider its effects not only on the testator's children, but also on grand- and great-grandchildren and unborn generations. In addition, inflation could make today's "gaping" exemptions look downright stingy by the time the estate plan goes into effect. For these reasons, practitioners involved in planning all but the simplest and smallest estates are remiss if they do not take the time to wade through the complexities of I.R.C. Chapter 13.

(1) What is a generation-skipping transfer?

Section 2601 of the I.R.C. purports to impose a tax "on every generation-skipping transfer." Section 2611(a) states generally that a generation-skipping transfer is either a *taxable distribution*, a *taxable termination*, or a *direct skip*. There will not be any Chapter 13 tax applicable unless a transfer can be classified as one of these three generation-skipping transfers.

Direct Skips. The great innovation of the new generation-skipping transfer tax, enacted in T.R.A. 1986, was the taxation of "direct skips." The classic direct skip is the bequest or *inter vivos* gift from

a transferor to a grandchild. Had the property
been transferred first to the transferor's child, there
would be some additional estate or gift tax "consequence" when and if the property passed from the
transferor's child to the grandchild. At least, some
or all of the grandchild's parent's unified credit or
$10,000 annual exclusion might be extinguished,
and perhaps some estate or gift tax would have to
be paid.

By "skipping a generation" and transferring directly to a grandchild, the transferor (prior to the
1986 T.R.A.) could be sure that no estate or gift tax
consequence would be incurred that might diminish
the gift or reduce the estate and gift tax planning
options available to members of the "skipped" generation.

Example: Decedent D (Grandmother) leaves her
entire estate of $750,000 to her wealthy son. This
bequest will be reduced by federal estate tax of
$55,500 [$248,300 tax (I.R.C. § 2001(c))–$192,800
unified credit (§ 2010)]. Son will receive $694,500
(assuming no state inheritance tax). Ten years
later, son dies and leaves his entire estate to his
daughter. Since son's estate contained other assets
in addition to the $694,500 received from D, his
inheritance, assuming it enlarges his estate, directly
or indirectly, by $694,500, will completely use up
son's unified credit (amounting to a $600,000 ex-
emption), incur a federal estate tax of $34,965 and
"push" the remainder of son's estate into, and
probably beyond, the 37% bracket. Until the
T.R.A. of 1986, D and other members of wealthy

families could avoid such consequences by planning direct-skip gifts or bequests directly from grandparent to grandchild.

The new generation-skipping transfer tax (G.S.T.) imposed in the 1986 T.R.A. applies a direct skip generation-skipping transfer tax on transfers otherwise subject to estate or gift tax which transmit an interest in property to a "skip person" (generally a person two or more generations below the transferor). See I.R.C. § 2612(c). The precise definition of "skip person" will be discussed *infra*.

Example: Grandparent transfers $100,000 *inter vivos* to a grandchild. The transferor is *subject* to gift tax (though grandparent's unified credit may shield the transfer from actual taxation) and the transferee is two generations below the transferor. Therefore, this is a direct skip (though special rules and the G.S.T. exemption, see discussion *infra,* may allow this generation-skipping transfer to escape actual taxation).

Example: A makes an outright *inter vivos* gift of $10,000 to her great-grandchild, B. Is this a generation-skipping transfer? *No.* Surprised? This transfer meets all the requirements for a direct skip *except* for the § 2612(c)(1) requirement that the transfer be "subject to a tax imposed by chapter 11 or 12." This transfer is not subject to Chapter 12 gift taxation because of I.R.C. § 2503(b), which provides an annual exclusion for present-interest gifts of up to $10,000 to any number of individuals. Similarly, if A had made a § 2503(e) qualified transfer to pay medical or educational expenses, an even larger amount could have been transferred to B without either gift or generation-skipping transfer tax liability. See § 2611(b)(1).

Special Rule for Direct Skips From Grandparent to Grandchild With Predeceased Parent. I.R.C. § 2612(c) grants relief in the case of a direct skip transfer to a grandchild if, at the time the transfer is made, the grandchild's parent is no longer living and that parent was the child of the transferor (or of the transferor's spouse). Such a grandchild will be treated as a child of the grandparent (not a skip person). In other words, no Chapter 13 liability will attach to direct transfers between a grandparent (or a grandparent's spouse, or former spouse), and a grandchild who has lost the parent who stood between her and her grandparent in the line of descent.

This rule may be reapplied. For example, if a great-grandchild's parent and grandparent have predeceased a great-grandparent transferor so as to leave two "holes" in the line of descent from great-grandparent to great-grandchild, the great-grandchild will be treated as a child of the great-grandparent (not a skip person) for the purpose of analyzing Chapter 13 tax liability. This Rule does not apply to taxable terminations or distributions. It only applies to direct transfers that occur *after* the death of the transferee's parent (or other appropriate lineal ancestor).

Special $2 Million Per Grandchild Direct Skip Exclusion Until January 1, 1990.   Section 1433(b)(3) of the 1986 Tax Reform Act (P.L. 99–514) states that a direct skip "shall not include any transfer before January 1, 1990, from a transferor to a grandchild of the transferor to the extent that the aggregate transfers from such transferor to such grandchild do not exceed $2,000,000."   (This is familiarly known in lobbying circles as "the Gallo exception".)

Note that the two special rules only exclude from generation-skipping transfer taxation those transfers that would otherwise be direct skips.   Many transfers of wealth involving trusts will not be eligible for these special exclusions.   (See discussion of taxable distributions and terminations below; note, however, that a technical amendment to § 2612(c)(2) extended these exclusions to certain trusts that are fully "vested" in the eligible grandchild.

Taxable Terminations.   Unlike direct skips, taxable terminations were made subject to the original generation-skipping transfer tax when it was first enacted in 1976.   (The computation of the tax on terminations was, however, significantly changed in the 1986 revision.)

Prior to 1976, a wealthy person could save tax by setting up a trust that paid income to child for life, then income to grandchild for life, then income to great-grandchild for life, etc.   Even though a beneficial property right would be shifted at each death, there would be no estate (or gift) tax consequence upon the death of the child, grandchild, or great-grandchild. Such a trust could give a family a great deal of estate planning flexibility. (Recall discussion of the pre-1986 tax avoidance motivation for direct skips, *supra.*)

The generation-skipping tax closes this loophole by viewing such an arrangement as one involving a series of taxable terminations. Section 2612(a) defines "taxable termination" as "the termination (by death, lapse of time, release of power, or otherwise) of an *interest in property held in a trust*" (emphasis added) when immediately after such termination, only skip persons hold an *interest* in the property.

"Interest" is a term specially defined by I.R.C. § 2652(c) which states that "[a] person has an interest in property held in trust if (at the time the determination is made) such person has a *right* (other than a future right) to receive income or corpus from the trust" or "is a *permissible* current recipient of income or corpus." (Note that the defined term "interest"—meaning, in effect, a present interest—is also included in the definition of direct skips. I.R.C. § 2612(c). This appears to be an error since direct skips may involve property free of trust.)

Example: A creates a trust and makes son B the life beneficiary, with remainder in grandchild C. Upon B's death, B's interest terminates, and C has the right to take the trust corpus. This is a taxable termination. Notice that no estate or gift tax is incurred when B's life interest terminates. If, upon B's death, the trust income becomes payable to B's spouse, there would be no taxable termination since B's spouse is not a skip person. (See full discussion *infra.*) If, then upon the death of B's spouse, the remainder passed to C, there would be a taxable termination, because C is a skip person.

Estate planners might be tempted to create nominal or token interests in non-skip persons so as to avoid causing a taxable termination upon the conclusion of a life estate. See I.R.C. § 2612(a)(1)(A). With this possibility in mind, § 2652(c)(2) permits the I.R.S. to disregard "an interest which is used primarily to postpone or avoid the [generation-skipping transfer] tax." As of this writing, no regulation has been promulgated to explain how the I.R.S. is to identify such nominal interests.

Anticipating efforts to avoid the tax on terminations (or distributions) by creating non-trust arrangements that are "trust equivalents," Congress has defined "trust" broadly to include "any arrangement (other than an estate) which, although not a trust, has substantially the same effect as a trust." I.R.C. § 2652(b)(1). Congress specifically contemplated "arrangements involving life estates and remainders, estates for years, and insurance and annuity contracts." See I.R.C. § 2652(b)(3).

Taxable Distributions. If a distribution from a trust to a skip person is neither a direct skip nor a taxable termination, it is a taxable distribution.

Example: Grandparent A creates a trust to pay income (and principal, in the trustee's discretion), to son S, daughter D, and their children as long as one of these beneficiaries is alive. The remainder goes to A's favorite charity. Payments of trust income or principal to the grandchildren are taxable distributions subject to the generation-skipping transfer tax. Payments to S and D are *not* taxable distributions, of course, because S and D are not "skip persons."

Who Is a Skip Person? All three generation-skipping transfers involve transfers of property to "skip persons." Since a skip person is necessary to trigger a generation-skipping tax, it is important to have a precise definition of "skip person." In most cases, it suffices to say that a skip person is a person who is two or more generations younger than the transferor. Sections 2613 and 2651 fill in the details.

Section 2613 defines the skip person as a person "assigned to a generation which is 2 or more below the generation assignment of the transferor." A skip person may also be a trust if all the interests in the trust are held by skip persons or if only skip persons can receive distributions (including distributions on termination) from the trust.

Note that, in the case of trusts, the definition of skip person requires reference to the § 2652(c) definition of "interest", discussed *supra*.

The definition of skip person requires reference to section 2651 in order to determine a transferee's generation assignment relative to that of a transferor. Section 2651 divides transferees into two categories—those who have some family relationship with the transferor and those who do not.

Family Member Transferees. The most common generation-skipping transfers will be ones that are made within the family, either directly between family members or with a trust as an intermediary.

Section 2651(b) gives the generation-assignment rules for a transferee who is a lineal descendant of a *grandparent of the transferor* or a grandparent of the transferor's *spouse.* They require one to compare the number of generations between the grandparent and the transferee with the number of generations between the grandparent and the transferor. The difference is the number of generations between transferor and the individual. Adoptees and half-blood relatives are considered full family members. § 2651(b)(3).

Section 2651(c) gives the rules for those who are (or who have been) married at any time to the transferor or to a lineal descendant of the transferor or the transferor's spouse. Those married to the transferor are assigned to the transferor's generation. Those married to a § 2651(b) lineal descendant are assigned to that descendant's generation.

Transferees Outside the Family. Sometimes the transferee is an individual who has no family relationship to the transferor. Such a person is not a lineal descendant of the transferor or the transferor's spouse; nor has such a person been married to the transferor or to any lineal descendant of the transferor (or the transferor's spouse). Section 2651(d) gives the generation-assignment rules for such strangers to the transferor. The generation assignment is made on the basis of a comparison of the date of the individual's birth with the date of the transferor's birth. A simple formula results in a generation-assignment. "[A]n individual born not more than 12½ years after the date of birth of the transferor" is assigned to the transferor's generation. See § 2651(d)(1). "[A]n individual born more than 12½ but not more than 37½ years" after the transferor is assigned "to the first generation younger than the transferor." See § 2651(d)(2). Individuals born more than 37½ years but not more than 62½ years after the transferor are assigned to the second generation younger than the transferor. If necessary, additional generations may be created at 25 year intervals to determine proper generation assignments. See § 2651(d)(3).

It is conceivable that several different generation-assignment rules could apply to the same individual, placing him or her in more than one generation. Section 2651(e)(1) anticipates this possibility by assigning the individual "to the youngest such generation." (When will this choice-of-generation rule apply?) Note that the drafters of the subsection explicitly gave the Treasury the authority to modify this rule by Regulation.

Section 2651(e)(2) deals with the possibility that people will try to avoid tax by taking transfers through "an estate, trust, partnership, corporation, or other entity." In such a case, the veil of such purportedly separate entity will be pierced. "[E]ach individual having a beneficial interest in such an entity shall be treated as having an interest in such [transferred] property and shall be assigned to a generation" according to the generation-assignment rules described above.

Certain transfers to charitable organizations or trusts are effectively exempted from the generation-skipping transfer tax by assigning these entities to the transferor's generation. See I.R.C. § 2651(e)(3).

The generation-skipping tax is added to any estate or gift tax otherwise payable by the transferor, in his or her estate, on the transfer. However, if a gift or estate tax is paid by the skipped generation, no added generation-skipping tax is imposed. See § 2611(b)(1). To illustrate, suppose grandmother transfers property in trust with income to be accumulated during the life of her child (second generation) with the remainder and accumulated income at that child's death to be paid to the child's child, grantor's grandchild (third generation). This would ordinarily invoke a generation-skipping tax, since the transfer skips the second generation and is a taxable termination. But, if that second generation has a power to invade the trust for his or her own benefit such as to make the trust property included in that second generation's estate, e.g. under § 2041, the transfer to the third generation at the death of the second generation will *not* be taxable as a generation-skipping transfer—since, for tax purposes, the second generation was not skipped.

(2) Computing the tax.

I.R.C. § 2602 presents a (deceptively) simple formula for computing the generation-skipping transfer tax incident to a direct skip, taxable termination, or taxable distribution. In all events, the tax is equal to the *taxable amount* multiplied by the *applicable rate.*

Taxable Amount. For direct skips, the taxable amount is the value of the property *received* by the transferee. See I.R.C. § 2623. If $100,000 is transferred by direct skip and the applicable rate is 50%, the *transferor* must pay $50,000 of generation-skipping transfer tax. See § 2603(a)(3). The tax on direct skips is *tax exclusive.* The $50,000 tax is not considered to be part of the direct skip. Thus, there is *no tax on the tax.* (However, § 2515 makes payment of the G.S.T. tax itself a taxable gift, in addition to the gift of the property transferred.)

Compare with direct skips the treatment of taxable distributions and taxable terminations. Suppose a remainder of $150,000 is to be delivered to grandchild upon the termination of his father's life interest. At a 50% rate, the trustee will have to pay a *tax-inclusive* $75,000 generation-skipping tax out of the trust corpus. Thus, grandchild will receive property worth $75,000 following this $150,-000 taxable termination. To understand the difference between tax-inclusive and tax-exclusive taxes, note that for the grandchild to receive $75,000, grandparent must leave him $150,000; grandparent must begin with $150,000 so that grandchild ends up with $75,000. This tax is tax inclusive. In contrast, for grandchild to receive $75,000 by *direct skip*, grandparent can transfer $75,000 to grandchild and then pay 50% tax on $75,000, which totals only $37,500. Thus, grandparent needs to start with only $112,500 to ensure that grandchild ends up with $75,000. This tax is tax exclusive.

Like the tax on taxable terminations, the tax on taxable distributions is *tax inclusive*. There *is* a tax on the tax. Clients planning generation-skipping transfers may wish to favor direct skips over taxable terminations and distributions in order to gain the benefits of tax exclusivity. The disparate treatment given to direct skips, as opposed to the other two generation-skipping transfers, is not unique in the federal transfer tax system. The gift tax also is tax exclusive, while the estate tax is tax inclusive.

For taxable terminations and distributions, the taxable amount may be reduced by certain deductions. See I.R.C. § 2622; § 2621(a). If any of the generation-skipping transfer tax is paid out of the distributing trust, such amount paid is also treated as a taxable distribution to the transferee. § 2621(b).

In general, property is valued at the time of the generation-skipping transfer. See I.R.C. § 2624. For the purpose of computing the taxable amount, the value of the property will be reduced by the amount of any consideration provided by the transferee. § 2624(d).

Alternative valuation and special use valuation elections may apply to certain direct skips and taxable terminations. See I.R.C. § 2624(b)–(c); § 2032; § 2032A.

Section 6166(i) grants an option to defer payment of generation-skipping tax arising on a "direct skip" that occurs at the death of a transferor who owns an interest in a closely-held business.

Applicable Rate. The applicable rate is "the product of (1) the *maximum Federal estate tax rate,* and (2) the *inclusion ratio* with respect to the transfer." I.R.C. § 2641 (emphases added).

I.R.C. § 2641(b) states that the maximum Federal estate tax rate is the maximum rate imposed by Section 2001 on the estates of decedents dying at the time of the generation-skipping transfer. As of 1993, the maximum rate is 55%. See § 2001(c). In 1987, Congress established a special 5% surcharge on large estates in order to recover both the unified credit and the benefits of the graduated rates below the top rate. See § 2001(c)(3). This surcharge will not affect the applicable rate on a generation-skipping transfer.

Inclusion Ratio (I.R.). Section 2642(a)(1) defines the inclusion ratio (I.R.) for taxable terminations and distributions as "the excess (if any) of 1 over the *applicable fraction* determined for the trust from which such transfer is made." For direct skips, the I.R. is the excess (if any) of 1 over the applicable fraction determined for the skip. The applicable fraction depends on the amount of G.S.T. exemption allocated to a transfer and the value of the property transferred.

G.S.T. Exemption. Section 2631 grants every individual a G.S.T. exemption of $1 million, which may be allocated by the individual (or his executor) to any property for which the individual is the transferor. Once an allocation of any of the G.S.T. exemption is made, the allocation is irrevocable. § 2631(b). Section 2632 gives rules for allocation of the G.S.T. exemption in the event that the transferor (or the transferor's executor) does not make the allocation. A married couple may elect to treat a lifetime transfer by either as made one-half by each, and thus they can "double" the $1 million individual exemption as well as the annual $10,000 exclusion. See I.R.C. § 2652(a)(2).

Absent a contrary election by the transferor, the G.S.T. will be applied first to lifetime direct skips, then—after the transferor's death—to testamentary direct skips, and finally to trusts from which a taxable termination or distribution might occur. See § 2632(b)–(c). It will often be important for the transferor to elect out of this scheme. Reg. § 301–9100–7T prescribes the time and manner for making the allocation of the G.S.T. exemption.

Direct Skips: Computing the I.R. The I.R. (inclusion ratio) is simple to compute in the case of a direct skip. In general, the I.R. is 1 minus the applicable fraction—the numerator of which is the portion of the G.S.T. exemption allocated to the direct skip and the denominator of which is the value of the property involved in the direct skip.

Example: Grandparent wishes to transfer $100,000 in a direct skip to grandchild. Grandparent allocates $100,000 of the $1 million exemption to this gift. The I.R. $= 1 - \dfrac{\$100,000}{\$100,000} = 0$

With the I.R. equal to zero, no tax will be payable, but grandparent will be left with only $900,000 of G.S.T. exemption to shelter future lifetime or testamentary generation-skipping transfers.

Taxable Terminations and Distributions: Computing the I.R. Computing the I.R. for the other two generation-skipping transfers is more complicated. *A trust's I.R. is established when property is first transferred to the trust.* This I.R. continues for the duration of the trust, unless there are future additions to the trust. Subsequent taxable terminations or taxable distributions will result in tax liability only to the extent that the trust's I.R. permits. [This general rule does not apply to charitable-lead annuity trusts. See § 2642(e).]

When a trust is established, its I.R. equals 1 minus the applicable fraction—the numerator of which is the amount of the G.S.T. exemption allocated to the trust and the denominator of which is the value of the property transferred to the trust (possibly reduced by a charitable deduction or a deduction for state death or federal estate taxes attributable to the property and paid by the trust).

See § 2642(a). The I.R. for trusts can be expressed symbolically:

$$\text{I.R.} = 1 - \frac{\text{G.S.T. exemption allocated to property transferred}}{\begin{matrix} \text{Value of} \\ \text{property} \\ \text{transferred} \end{matrix} - \begin{matrix} \text{state death} \\ \text{and federal} \\ \text{estate taxes} \end{matrix} - \begin{matrix} \text{charitable} \\ \text{deduction} \end{matrix}}$$

Example: A transfers *inter vivos* $1 million cash to a trust. A elects to allocate her entire $1 million exemption to this property. 20 years after A's death, with the trust worth $3 million, the trustee makes a $100,000 distribution of trust income to A's great-grandchild, B. Does this taxable distribution incur tax liability? No. The inclusion ratio was determined *when the trust was created,* not when the distribution was made. In this case, the inclusion ratio is 0, and the applicable rate is (50% × 0) 0. A generation-skipping transfer has occurred, but no tax is payable.

Example: Suppose A had allocated only $400,000 of her G.S.T. exemption to her $1 million transfer; the I.R. then would equal 60%. The applicable rate (50% × 60%) is 30%. B will receive $70,000 following the taxable distribution.

Several insights spring from these simple examples:

(1) From a tax computation point of view, knowledge that the I.R. is equal to zero makes irrelevant any information about whether or not a skip person is a transferee. No matter who receives the income

or corpus of such "exempt trusts", there will be no generation-skipping transfer tax to pay. As a matter of trust management, however, it is desirable that corpus and income of such exempt trusts go only to skip persons, if other non-exempt funds are available for non-skip beneficiaries, since only transfers to skip persons can incur generation-skipping transfer tax liability. Estate planners can ensure that the benefit of the G.S.T. exemption will not be partially "wasted" on non-skip persons by creating non-exempt trusts (with I.R.s of 1) that have assets sufficient to provide for the needs of a decedent's spouse, children, and other non-skip person beneficiaries. As a general rule trusts should be either wholly exempt or wholly non-exempt, with no I.R. between 0 and 1.

(2) Since the applicable fraction is determined at the time of the transfer to the trust, much more than $1 million can ultimately be sheltered in an exempt trust. In the first example, A transferred $1 million and completely exempted this property from future generation-skipping taxes by allocating the entire $1 million G.S.T. exemption to this property. So long as no addition is made to this trust, any distribution of income or appreciation of the trust property (including distributions on termination) will also be exempt from generation-skipping transfer taxes. If A was 30 when she made the transfer and the property grew by 7.2% per year (as a result of after-tax income accumulations) until A's death at age 70, the trust would have grown to $16 million. This entire amount (as well as further

income and appreciation after A's death and before the trust terminates) would be available for tax-free generation-skipping transfers. In theory, the exempt trust can grow (and shelter generation-skipping transfers) for as long as it is permissible to hold property in trust under the perpetuities rules of the applicable state property law.

Transfers made to existing trusts may require recomputation of the applicable fraction. See I.R.C. § 2641(d).

Section 2642(c)(2) gives inclusion rules for *nontaxable* gifts. A nontaxable gift is defined as a § 2503(b) annual exclusion gift or a § 2503(e) educational or medical exclusion gift. See § 2642(c)(3). With one narrow exception, nontaxable gifts to a trust *are* taken into account for G.S.T. purposes; thus, to avoid taxation of these trusts, a portion of the G.S.T. exemption must be allocated to the trust. The exception applies—and, thus, the inclusion ratio is zero—only when (1) the transfer to a trust is a direct skip, and (2) the trust is exclusively for the benefit of a single individual and must be includable in that individual's gross estate should he or she die before the termination of the trust.

G.S.T. Exemptions or Exclusions. Overall the new G.S.T. has three exemptions or exclusions. The first is the $1 million exemption for each transferor, for the total of lifetime and testamentary transfers that are taxable by the G.S.T. See I.R.C. § 2631(a). The second is for transfers excluded from gift tax by the § 2503(b) annual, per donee exclusion. See I.R.C. § 2642(c). The third is for *inter vivos* medical and tuition expense transfers that are exempt from gift tax by § 2503(e). See § 2611(b)(2). And, as mentioned, a married couple may double the first and second exemptions by electing, under § 2513, to have a gift by either considered as made one-half by each spouse. See I.R.C. § 2652(a)(2).

(3) Who pays the tax?

Once the tax is computed, I.R.C. § 2603(a) gives the rules for who is personally liable for the tax. The tax in a taxable *distribution* is to be paid by the transferee. The tax in a taxable *termination* (or *direct skip* from a trust) is to be paid by the trustee. The tax on a *direct skip* (other than a direct skip from a trust) is to be paid by the transferor.

Unless provided otherwise by a specific reference in the governing instrument, the generation-skipping transfer tax is charged to the property constituting the transfer. See § 2603(b). (Recall the tax exclusivity of direct skips as compared with the tax inclusivity of taxable terminations and distributions, in the discussion of the taxable amount, *supra.*)

(4) State tax credit.

Section 2604 provides a limited credit to offset any state tax on generation-skipping transfers (other than direct skips) occurring "at the same time and as a result of the death of an individual." This credit is similar to the § 2011 limited estate tax credit for state death taxes. It can be expected that most states will enact limited generation-skipping taxes to take advantage of the revenue sharing opportunity afforded by § 2604.

(5) Post generation-skipping tax consequences.

Multiple Skips. It is important not to lose sight of the purpose of the generation-skipping transfer tax. It was designed to fill in gaps in the estate and gift tax by ensuring that family wealth would be taxed at least once per generation. In addition to the enormous shelters offered for pre-existing trusts, the $1 million G.S.T. exemption, incorporation of § 2503 exclusions, the § 2612 predeceased parent exclusion, and the $2 million grandchild's exclusion (which expired in 1990), the generation-skipping transfer tax is inherently "leaky" inasmuch as a direct skip is taxed only once—regardless how many generations are skipped.

Example: A transfers *inter vivos* $100,000 to B, A's great-grandchild. The tax on this gift will be identical to the tax on a gift to a grandchild. If A had instead transferred $100,000 to A's grandchild, the parent of B, there would have been an additional tax (an estate or gift tax) when B's parent transferred the property to B.

Except for direct skips, the generation-skipping transfer tax aims (with some success) at guaranteeing that there will be a transfer tax each time the benefits of trust property descend through a generation. Application of a generation-skipping transfer tax more than once to the same generation, however, would lead to harsh results (particularly since the tax is imposed at a flat rate of 55% and since Chapter 13 has no analog to the estate tax § 2013 credit for prior transfers).

Section 2653 helps ensure that property which has been subjected to the generation-skipping transfer tax at a particular generation level will not be subject again to Chapter 13 tax upon a subsequent transfer to a transferee at that level. In the case of a direct skip free of trust, there is no problem. Section 2652(a)(1) defines "transferor" as the decedent, in the case of a transfer subject to estate tax, or the donor, in the case of a transfer subject to gift tax. If a donor makes a direct skip, the donee's subsequent transfer of the property to members of the donee's generation (or to the one immediately below) will *not* be a generation-skipping transfer because: (1) application of estate or gift tax will convert the prior transfer's donee into the "transferor" for Chapter 13 purposes and (2) none of the transferees will be skip persons relative to the donee transferor.

As to trust property, however, trust distributions or terminations will not incur an estate or gift tax unless a trust beneficiary has an *inter vivos* or testamentary general power of appointment. See Ch. IX, below. Without Section 2653, distributions or terminations at the generation level of the skip person who triggered the initial tax will continue to trigger the generation-skipping tax, since these individuals will also be skip persons relative to the original transferor.

Section 2653 handles this situation by treating the trust "as if the transferor of such property were assigned to the 1st generation above the highest generation of any person who has an interest [see § 2652(c)] in such trust immediately after the transfer." § 2653(a)(2). An example illustrating the effect of § 2653 appears in Ch. 15 at § 78, below.

Effect on Basis. If property with an inclusion ratio of 1 is transferred by a taxable termination occurring at the same time as, and as a result of, an individual's death, the basis of the property is adjusted in accord with income tax Section 1014(a). If the inclusion ratio of such property is less than 1, any increase in basis called for by § 1014(a) is limited by multiplying the increase by the inclusion ratio. Thus, terminations (upon death) of an exempt trust (inclusion ratio = 0) result in no change of basis. See § 2654(a)(2).

The basis effects of other generation-skipping transfers are given by Section 2654(a)(1). Transferred property retains its prior basis, adjusted (but not in excess of its fair market value) by an amount equal to that portion of Chapter 13 tax (without regard to the § 2604 state tax credit) which is attributable to the excess value of such property over its adjusted basis immediately before the transfer. Section 2654 is to be applied after any basis adjustment under § 1015 (relating to property acquired by gifts and transfers in trusts).

The I.R.S. has issued proposed regulations for the generation-skipping tax. See 57 Fed.Reg. 61,353 (1992). These proposed regulations include special rules for taxation of transfers by nonresident aliens.

For a discussion of planning under the generation-skipping tax, see Philip J. Michaels, *Drafting With the GST Exemption in Mind,* 208 New York Law Journal 1 (Aug. 5, 1992), and Hamlin C. King, *Telling Gramps That One or Two Just Won't Do (Generation–Skipping Trusts),* 71 Taxes 339 (June 1993).

CHAPTER III

THE ESTATE AND GIFT TAXES APPLIED TO TRANSFERS AT DEATH AND DURING LIFE

§ 16. Application of the Estate Tax to Transfers of Property at Death

The *gross estate* is determined or defined under I.R.C. §§ 2031 and 2033. Section 2031(a) states that the value of the gross estate of the decedent shall be determined by including the value at the time of his death of "all property, real or personal, tangible or intangible, wherever situated." To make it clear that an interest in property will be included in the gross estate of the decedent even if he does not own title or all of the bundle of rights in the property, § 2033 goes on to state that the value of the gross estate shall include the value of all property "to the extent of the interest therein of the decedent at the time of his death." Not just property in the probate estate or subject to claims of creditors or distributed as part of the administration of the decedent's estate, but much more, can fall within the tax concept of gross estate.

However, not every item of wealth or every economic resource of the decedent becomes part of his or her gross estate under I.R.C. § 2033. (Some difficult questions of the scope of § 2033 have not arisen because the arrangements and transactions to which it might apply are covered by later sections, such as §§ 2039, 2041 and 2042. Other questions have arisen in contexts where the inclusion must occur under § 2033 if at all, or in cases that came up before the enactment of the later, more specific sections.)

Thus, the general question is raised: What will be included in the gross estate of a decedent under the terms of § 2033? The statute and the cases and the Regulations (see Regs. § 20.2033) shed some illumination. Obviously, property decedent owns in the form of real estate, bank accounts, stocks and bonds (including dividends whose record date precedes that of the date of death), causes of action that survive the decedent's death, claims against debtors (including accounts receivable), contractual rights entitling the decedent to royalties on an invention, interest in an unincorporated business and the decedent's interest in community property or a tenancy in common will be included in his gross estate. See Regs. § 20.2033–1(b). In contrast, property held by the decedent in the form of joint-tenancy or tenancy-by-the-entirety, which carries survivorship rights and where the interest of the decedent expires at his death, lies beyond § 2033 (but will be governed by I.R.C. § 2040). Similarly, special rules in § 2042 govern the proceeds of insurance on the decedent's life. But, if the decedent is the owner of an insurance policy on the life of *another* person, who survives the decedent, § 2033 will require the inclusion of the value of that interest in the life insurance policy on someone else in the decedent's gross estate.

Legal title to property or an interest in property is not necessary or determinative for inclusion in the gross estate. For example, property held by decedent as trustee or guardian or some other fiduciary will not be included in his gross estate under I.R.C. § 2033. The interest of the decedent must be a beneficial interest to result in inclusion. Any beneficial interest, however, will do. For example, if the decedent holds a vested remainder in a trust established by someone else, the value of that interest will be included in his or her gross estate. Even a contingent remainder held by the decedent will be included if that remainder is not destroyed by the death of the decedent and if it passes from him or her to someone else at or by reason of the decedent's death. Thus, § 2033 ranges broadly to embrace interests in the gross estate.

Can Congress limit the scope of Sections 2001 and 2033 by enacting a statute outside the estate tax code? Yes it can, but it must do so unambiguously. This is the import of a Supreme Court case, U.S. v. Wells Fargo Bank, 485 U.S. 351 (1988). The background is this: In 1937, Congress passed a housing act authorizing local authorities to issue tax-free obligations, termed "Project Notes." The Project Notes were exempted by statute, "from all taxation now or hereafter imposed by the United States." Appellants contended that the notes could be transferred without federal estate tax liability.

Following a review of the legislative history, the Court in *Wells Fargo Bank* held that "the presumption against implied tax exemptions [is] too powerful to be overcome" even by the express exemption from "all taxation." This holding is not entirely surprising for two reasons. First, *no* court had upheld a challenge to the estate taxation of Project Notes until 1984. See Haffner v. U.S., 585 F.Supp. 354 (N.D.Ill.1984). Second, a contrary holding would have created a gaping hole in the estate tax (the Supreme Court in *Wells Fargo* noted a " 'rush to market' for Project Notes" had been caused by the *Haffner* decision).

It is unlikely that the Supreme Court will be called upon to decide additional questions of Congressional intent in this area. Congress reacted to *Haffner* by stating that no "law exempting any property (or interest therein) from taxation shall exempt the transfer of such property (or interest therein) from Federal estate, gift, and generation-skipping transfer taxes" unless Congress does so by specific reference to an appropriate provision of the Internal Revenue Code. See Deficit Reduction Act of 1984, Pub.L. 98–369, § 641, 98 Stat. 494, 939 (1984).

Thus as a general rule, it might be said that the transfer taxes apply to state or municipal bonds even when the interest paid on such bonds is exempt from federal income taxation in the hands of the bondholder, by reason of I.R.C. § 103.

Even in the absence of such a demonstration by Congress, the compass of I.R.C. § 2033 is by no means unlimited. In particular, the "substantial ownership" rule which plays such an important role in the income tax, sometimes known as the *"Clifford* doctrine," has expressly been curtailed under the estate tax with respect to the reach of I.R.C. § 2033. See Helvering v. Safe Deposit & Trust Company of Baltimore, 316 U.S. 56 (1942). In that case, the Supreme Court held that I.R.C. § 2033 does not require inclusion in the gross estate of property subject to an unexercised general power of appointment. Since that case, § 2041 has been enacted and includes property subject to an unexercised general power; the remaining impact of the case mainly lies in its conclusion that Congress did not intend the general rule of § 2033 to grasp every form of economic power or resource available to the decedent before or at death. Other, specifically phrased sections, of course, will be applied according to their terms.

Nevertheless, some questions about the application of § 2033 to items of value and economic worth that may not seem clearly to constitute "property owned by decedent" or property "in which he had an interest at his death," continue to arise despite the enactment of Code sections subsequent to § 2033 and dealing with more specific problems of inclusion in the gross estate.

By way of illustration, the scope of § 2033 has been questioned in applying it to employee death benefits and rights to payment after death. I.R.C.

§ 2039 covers much of this area, but there is room for attempts by the Commissioner to assert the application of § 2033 as well. For example, § 2033 has been held to require inclusion in the gross estate of payments made by a partnership, pursuant to a partnership agreement, of profits attributable to work performed by the deceased partner before death. The estate was found to possess an enforceable chose-in-action which had passed from the decedent to the estate. See Estate of C. A. Riegelman v. Commissioner, 253 F.2d 315 (2d Cir. 1958); Rev.Rul. 66–20, 1966–1 C.B. 214.

The Tax Court has held that § 2033 does *not* require inclusion by reason of *discretionary* death benefits paid by the employer to a widow of the decedent—neither the employee nor his widow had any right to payment nor did either own any property in this form. See Estate of Salt v. Comm., 17 T.C. 92 (1951). See also Revenue Ruling 66–20, 1966–1 C.B. 214; Estate of William E. Barr, 40 T.C. 227 (1963) (so-called wage-dividend death benefit paid by Eastman Kodak Company to the widow of the decedent did not amount to a property interest in the decedent at the time of his death such as to require inclusion under I.R.C. § 2033).

Consistent with this reasoning, § 2033 does not bring a lump-sum payment received by the executors or administrators of an estate under the Social Security Act into the decedent's gross estate, because the decedent had no control over the designation of the beneficiary or the amount of payment, both of which are fixed by statute. See Revenue

Ruling 55–87, 55–1 C.B. 112. Similarly, damages payable to close relatives for wrongful death under the Federal Death on the High Seas Act are not includable. Rev.Rul. 69–8, 1969–1 C.B. 219.

It seems clear that where employee death benefits are payable only to those beneficiaries whom the employer designates, § 2033 does not apply. Where employee death benefits are payable to the decedent or to his estate, § 2033 is applicable. If the employee may appoint the benefits to anyone, including his own estate, § 2033 requires inclusion. If the employee may appoint the benefits to anyone except his estate, an argument could be made that he has an "interest in property" or the equivalent for purpose of § 2033, but the Helvering v. Safe Deposit & Trust Company case doctrine, *supra*, would argue against inclusion.

If the employer retains the right to terminate the plan prior to the employee's death, some court cases have held that no property need be included under § 2033. See Molter v. U.S., 146 F.Supp. 497 (E.D.N.Y.1956), where the court expressly found G.C.M. 27242 inapplicable and held that no contractual relationship, and thus no property, exists when an employer possesses an absolute right to revoke a death-benefit plan. If the possibility of forfeiture lies solely within the control of the employee, however, (for example, if death benefits are to be paid so long as the employee does not engage in a competing business after retirement), inclusion under § 2033 would appear inescapable. In general, an expectancy (not includable) must be distinguished from a contract or property right held at death (includable). For a case examining § 2033 and § 2039 as to employee death benefits, see Estate of Wadewitz v. Comm., 39 T.C. 925 (1963), affirmed on appeal, 339 F.2d 980 (7th Cir. 1964).

Recoveries for wrongful death under statutes that create a new cause of action for the benefit of the surviving spouse or children are not includable under § 2033. Conn. Bank and Trust Co. v. U. S., 465 F.2d 760 (2d Cir., 1972). Now it has also been held that a recovery or settlement for wrongful death under a survival statute is not includable either under § 2033 or § 2041, even if distributed under a will. Morgan v. U. S., 356 F.Supp. 546 (D.Iowa 1973). The Service has acquiesced in this line of cases (see Rev.Rul. 75–127, 1975–1 C.B. 297), while continuing to include any such proceeds representing damages to which the decedent had become entitled during his lifetime, *e.g.*, for medical expenses or pain and suffering.

In general, whether a decedent did have any interest or ownership right in property is to be determined under state law. However, whether the rights and interests held by the decedent amount to ownership of property or an interest in property sufficient to require inclusion under I.R.C. §§ 2031 and 2033 is a Federal question. Accordingly, the courts and administrators must look to state law to determine the interest of the decedent in property.

State court litigation on the rights of the particular decedent in question will be exceedingly pertinent, of course. The question then arises whether such a state court decision is binding upon the federal court for purposes of the Federal Estate Tax. The problem can be difficult because some state court litigation of questions such as this is not actively contested and is decided, perhaps, with some implicit consideration of the tax consequences that will follow. The Supreme Court of the United States has attempted to provide some guidance for federal courts in connection with this problem. In the *Bosch* case, Comm. v. Estate of Bosch, 387 U.S. 456 (1967), the Supreme Court said that lower court decisions of the states are not controlling for Federal tax purposes. "Proper regard," not absolute finality, should be given to such decisions of the lower state courts. The state's highest court, however, was regarded as the best authority on the state law. If no decision in the highest court of the state bears on the point the federal authority must apply what it finds to be the state law after giving "proper regard" to pertinent rulings by other courts of the state. As an example of this problem, see U. S. v. O. M. Neel, Executrix, 235 F.2d 395 (10th Cir. 1956) (only one-half of the property standing in the name of the decedent husband and one-half of the joint bank accounts standing in the names of the decedent husband and his wife should be included in the decedent's gross estate because there did in fact exist a general partnership between the decedent and his wife from the date of their marriage to the date of the decedent's death; a partnership in business as well as in romance having been made out, the court found the decedent to have owned only a one-half interest in the property held in his name or in the names of his wife and himself).

Income in Respect of a Decedent—§ 691. If a decedent has earned income that he or she had not received before death and was not *entitled* to receive before death, such income is known—for Federal Income Tax purposes—as "income in respect of a decedent", (I.R.D.). For example, if the decedent earned fees or salary or wages for work done before death but not payable until later, and if decedent was a cash method taxpayer (versus an accrual method taxpayer), that earned but unpaid income would not properly be shown on the final income tax return filed for the decedent, for that taxable period ends with the date of death. Rather it is I.R.D. that becomes taxable to the estate of the decedent. See I.R.C. § 691(a). (If the income had been earned and was payable before the date of death, but simply had not been collected by the decedent, it would be treated as constructively received by the decedent and includable on his or her final individual tax return. I.R.D. is income the decedent was not *entitled* to be *paid,* though earned, before death.)

Paralleling I.R.D. are expenditures that were incurred but not paid before death. They would not be deductible on the decedent's last individual tax return. If otherwise deductible, such expenses must be taken on the estate's income tax return on deductions in respect of a decedent (D.I.R.D.). See § 691(b).

I.R.D. is taxed to the actual recipient (the estate, a legatee or devisee or other person entitled to receive it) of the income, in the year of receipt. See § 691(a)(1). D.I.R.D. may be taken by whomever is obligated to pay the expense and who actually does so.

An item of I.R.D. is not "property" and hence is not entitled to a fresh start basis for income tax purposes at the death of the owner. In fact, I.R.D. has no basis for income tax purposes; its collection produces taxable income in the full amount received. Nevertheless, for estate tax purposes, I.R.D. is included in the decedent's gross estate, as something of value passing at death.

I.R.C. § 691 requires the income tax return of the estate of a decedent, or of a recipient, to include in gross income all items of income "in respect of a decedent" not includable in the taxable period covering the date of death, or a prior period. [Such items include deferred payments from sale of property, deferred compensation, accrued rent or interest, and other contingent or delayed receipts. See Regs. § 1.691(a)–1.] Some related costs and other expenditures are allowed as deductions. See § 691(b). I.R.D. retains the character it would have had if received by the decedent. § 691(a)(3).

Section 691(c) of the I.R.C. allows an *income* tax deduction, in the last tax return filed for a decedent, in an amount equal to the excess of the *estate* tax paid over the amount that would have had to have been paid if the value of the right to receive income in respect to a decedent had not been included in the estate tax calculation. Because of this § 691(c) deduction, an *estate* tax is payable on almost all, if not all, items of income in respect of a decedent; the § 691(c) deduction avoids "excess taxation" of I.R.D. included in the gross estate.

§ 17. Future Interests and Contingent Interests Under § 2033

Future interests in property often must be included in the gross estate under I.R.C. § 2033. Because such inclusion will increase the estate tax payable even though the interest is still suspended and the economic value it represents is not available to pay the tax, I.R.C. § 6163 permits the executor to elect to postpone payment of the portion of the estate tax generated by including in the gross estate "a reversionary or remainder interest" until six months after the termination of the preceding interest. The Commissioner has authority to extend the date for payment an additional three years upon a showing of reasonable cause. See § 6163(b).

To include some future interests in property in the gross estate seems logical enough with respect to remainder and reversionary interests that are *vested* at the time of the decedent's death. However, some question has arisen about including a future interest that is *contingent*. Such an interest is one that will not come into possession and enjoyment unless a certain contingency or condition is met or is an interest that may fail upon the occurrence or non-occurrence of an event sometime in the future, an event such as the death of a certain person without issue or without surviving to a certain date specified. Should such contingent interests be subject to estate taxation and thus included in the gross estate of the decedent? The problem seems to be particularly difficult when it ultimately appears that the interest did not come into possession or enjoyment of the decedent or of anyone to whom he passed the chance of enjoying the interest at all, because the right conditions did not fall into place.

At one time, it was thought that the pertinent question was whether the remainder or other future interest held by the decedent at death was a vested or a contingent remainder. If the interest was contingent, some courts held that the interest would not be included if it never took effect in possession or enjoyment. See, *e.g.*, Commissioner v. Rosser, 64 F.2d 631 (3d Cir. 1933). However, it is now apparent that the decisive question is not whether the interest of the decedent was vested or contingent. The appropriate question is whether the interest of the decedent expired upon his death, in which case it will not be included in his gross estate under I.R.C. § 2033, or whether it survived (despite the decedent's death) and passed to someone else at the death of the decedent, in which case inclusion under § 2033 will and should follow. See Estate of Hill v. Comm., 193 F.2d 724 (2d Cir. 1952); Williams v. U.S., 41 F.2d 895 (Ct.Cls.1930);

Martin v. U.S., 121 Ct.Cl. 829 (1952). For example, X gives Blackacre to Y for life, remainder to Z, but if Z should die before Y, then to A. If Z predeceases Y, then nothing is included in his estate because his death has terminated his interest. However, if A predeceases both Y and Z, his interest is not terminated because Z could still predecease Y and Blackacre would go to A's estate upon Y's death. Thus, if the death of the decedent is itself the contingency or if it prevents the required contingency from happening, so that the decedent's interest ceases to exist at and after his or her death, as in the case of Z predeceasing Y in the example, there will be no inclusion in the gross estate even though the possession or enjoyment of the property itself shifts to someone else following and as a result of the death of the decedent. In such case, the taker does not receive the interest of the decedent but rather takes and enjoys an interest created in him by someone else. In other words, a shifting of possession and enjoyment from one person to the other is not the same as the taxable passing of an interest *from the decedent* to someone else. On the other hand, if the decedent's death fails to terminate his interest (as in the case of A predeceasing Y and Z, above) the value of his reversionary interest is included in his gross estate.

As a more general rule, any property interest that expires upon the death of the decedent is not included in the gross estate under I.R.C. § 2033. For example, if grandfather at his death puts property in trust and provides that all income shall be paid

to his son for the life of the son, and at the death of
the son the trust will terminate and the trust
property be distributed to the grandson, there will
be no inclusion in the gross estate of the son at his
death even though his enjoyment of the income
from the property terminates and the grandson
begins to enjoy it. What has happened conceptually
is that the son's life estate has terminated at the
death of the son and the grandson's vested remainder has taken effect in possession or enjoyment at
the death of the son.

Such an arrangement may, however, be subject to
the generation-skipping tax upon the son's death,
when his interest in the property terminates.

In general then, under I.R.C. § 2033, there is
included in the gross estate not only all property
owned by the decedent but also all property in
which the decedent has an interest, to the extent of
that interest. The interest must be a beneficial
one, not mere title. Property interests that expire
on the death of the decedent, whether contingent or
not, are not included in his gross estate under
§ 2033. A remainder interest or other future interest in property, if it is not a contingent remainder
or other future interest that terminates upon the
death of the decedent, falls within I.R.C. § 2033.
(A separate question is a *valuation* of such interests, which may present difficult problems.)

Consequently, shares of stock, salary, rents and
interests accrued at death and dividends declared to
shareholders of record on or before the date of

decedent's death all are includable property interests. Some statutory death benefits are not includable in the decedent's estate because he did not at
his death have an interest in or control over the
disposition of the property. As to death benefits
arising out of employment, such benefits will not be
includable in the gross estate unless the employer is
obligated to make the payments and the decedent
had at least some control over those payments.
(Many employees' death benefits are governed by
I.R.C. § 2039(c), to be analyzed later, § 43 *infra*.)

An inter-vivos power of withdrawal, akin to an
inter-vivos power of appointment, will not produce
§ 2033 inclusion in the estate of the decedent holding the power so long as the power was not exercised before death and thus expired at death. See
Gertrude L. Royce, 46 B.T.A. 1090 (1942). For
inclusion under § 2033, the taxpayer must possess
a beneficial interest which survived him so that he
could alienate it or so that it would pass at his
death.

§ 18. Application of the Gift Tax to Inter-
vivos Transfers of Property

The gift tax statute provides in I.R.C. § 2501 that
a tax, as computed in a later section, is imposed "on
the transfer of property by gift ... by any individual, resident or nonresident." I.R.C. § 2511(a) goes
on to say that "the tax imposed by § 2501 shall
apply whether the transfer is in trust or otherwise,
whether the gift is direct or indirect, and whether
the property is real or personal, tangible or intangi-

ble; but in the case of a non-resident not a citizen of the United States, shall apply to a transfer only if the property is situated within the United States.'' Under I.R.C. § 2512, the value of a gift made in property is the value of the property at the date of the gift. By virtue of § 2512(b), if property is transferred for less than an adequate and full consideration in money or money's worth, the amount by which the value of the property exceeded the value of the consideration received shall be deemed to be a gift and included in computing the amount of gifts made.

Under I.R.C. § 2503, the term *"taxable gifts"* is defined as the total amount of gifts made during the calendar year, minus the *deductions* provided in I.R.C. § 2522 and following. An *exclusion* is granted by I.R.C. § 2503(b) in the amount of $10,000 per year per donee ($3,000 for pre-1982 gifts). This exclusion applies only in the case of a present interest in property; a gift of a *future interest* in property does *not* qualify for the per donee annual exclusion.

Under § 2513, a gift made by one spouse to a third person may be considered to have been made one half by him and one half by his spouse if both spouses consent to this gift splitting, which enables them to use both their § 2503(b) exclusions and unified credits.

These sections comprise the basic legislation on the gift tax. Some more specialized provisions, such as I.R.C. §§ 2514 through 2517 will be consid-

ered later, as will the provisions for deductions in
§§ 2522 through 2524, and most importantly, the
unified credit, given by I.R.C. § 2505.

These deceptively simple statutory rules give rise
to difficult questions about what is a "gift" for
federal gift tax purposes. In the absence of more
detailed statutory assistance, regulations, rulings
and cases are important aids in construing the
statutory rules. The regulations under I.R.C.
§ 2511 prove especially helpful in explaining the
appropriate treatment of a variety of commonly
encountered gift situations. See Regs. §§ 25.2511–
1, 25.2511–2. One of the first questions encountered in applying the basic statutory gift tax rules is
what will be regarded as "property" for purposes of
the gift tax. (A "gift" of services is not taxed as a
gift by the Federal Gift Tax—which raises serious
questions of equity, efficiency and transfer tax (and
income tax) policy.)

§ 19. What Is "Property" for Federal Gift Tax Purposes?

As implied by the valuation section, I.R.C.
§ 2512, the question of whether "property" was
transferred is to be viewed as of the time of the
transfer. Thus, even though later facts show that
the donor never enjoyed anything possessory and as
it turned out did not transfer anything that came
into possession and enjoyment in the donee, there
still may have been a taxable gift of "property."
This general rule is illustrated in the case of a
transfer of a contingent or defeasible remainder

interest which ultimately does not come into possession and enjoyment by either the donor or the
donee.

For example, suppose that Muriel establishes a
trust that provides a life estate to taxpayer Dorothy,
with remainder to Dorothy's children then living at
her death, but goes on to provide that if Dorothy
outlives her children then the property shall go to
Dorothy in fee simple. If one month before her
death Dorothy conveys all of her remainder interest
in the trust to Roger and then dies survived by two
children, Dorothy will be deemed to have made a
transfer subject to the Gift Tax. This will be true
even though at Dorothy's death her life interest in
the trust ended and the contingent interest she
conveyed to Roger never vested because she was at
that time survived by her two children. Still, at the
time of the transfer one month before her death,
she did transfer to Roger "property," her contingent remainder (or vested remainder subject to
divestment). In other words, she gave Roger the
chance of enjoying the property and taking a fee
simple interest if at Dorothy's death she were not
survived by any of her children. The *valuation* of
that interest is a separate question; all that is
asserted at this point is that there was a taxable
gift. See Goodwin v. McGowan, 47 F.Supp. 798
(W.D.N.Y.1942). For these purposes the interest of
the decedent or donor in the case of an inter-vivos
gift must be distinguished from the physical property itself or the economic value which that property
constitutes.

It has been said more generally that "property" as used in the gift tax law is to be given a broad meaning and should include every species of right or interest protected by law and having exchangeable value. Thus, the assignment of a judgment or an insurance policy or even the forgiveness of a debt will be treated as a gift for gift tax purposes. A promissory note is property for purposes of gift tax, (although if the note transferred is the donor's own note it will not constitute a gift until the note is either paid or negotiated by the donee). If the donor owns less than a complete interest in the property in question, the gift will be deemed to be a gift of that interest which he or she in fact owns and does in fact transfer. If the donor transfers less than his or her entire interest in the property, he or she is deemed to make a gift only of the portion actually transferred.

§ 20. What Is a "Transfer" For Federal Gift Tax Purposes?

Taxable Transfers. I.R.C. § 2511 broadly states that a gift will be deemed to exist whether the transfer is in trust or otherwise and whether the gift is direct or indirect. Therefore, a gift may consist not only of an outright transfer from one person to another of some property interest, but also by such other techniques as, for example, the gratuitous discharge of the donee's obligation by the creditor or by a third party.

As to non-taxable transfers, it has been held that substitution by a wife of her promissory note to a bank for notes of her husband's was *not* a taxable (gift) transfer. See Bradford v. Comm., 34 T.C. 1059 (1960). To be sure, a gift that is not complete for income tax purposes, such that the donor remains taxable on the income from the property as its constructive owner, may nevertheless be deemed to be a completed gift for transfer tax purposes. See, e.g., Lockard v. Comm., 166 F.2d 409 (1st Cir.1948). [The estate tax may then produce another uncorrelated decision; for example, a gift may be complete and taxable for gift tax purposes even though it is deemed incomplete for estate tax purposes, and hence taxable, again, by the estate tax when the decedent dies and "completes" the gift for purposes of the estate tax. See., e.g., Comm. v. Beck's Estate, 129 F.2d 243 (2d Cir.1942).

Rendering *services* for someone without compensation will not be taxed as a gift, even if those services produce definite, ascertainable financial gain for the recipient. See Comm. v. Hogle, 165 F.2d 352 (10th Cir.1947) (father's expert and profitable financial and investment management for children). But interest-free demand loans do constitute taxable gifts of the value of the money lent. See Dickman v. Comm., 465 U.S. 330 (1984) (interest-free demand loan has two components: an arm's length loan from lender to borrower, with "constructive" interest, and a "constructive" gift from the lender to the borrower in the amount of that interest).

Disclaimers. A renunciation or disclaimer of an interest in property can constitute a gift, as when a beneficiary renounces a testate or intestate share in an estate or a trust. For gifts made before 1977, the actual decision of whether a taxable gift was made will depend partly upon state law and on whether the interest vested in the renouncing beneficiary before renunciation was made. In that event the renunciation will be treated as a transfer, taxable as a gift, by the renouncing beneficiary. If the renunciation succeeded in preventing the interest from vesting as a matter of state property law, the act of renunciation will not be deemed to be a gift. See generally Hardenbergh v. Comm., 198 F.2d 63 (8th Cir. 1952), cert. den. 344 U.S. 836 (1952); Brown v. Routzahn, 63 F.2d 914 (6th Cir. 1933), cert. den. 290 U.S. 641 (1933). But in addition to the above requirement, a pre-'77 renunciation must also have been "made within a reasonable time after knowledge of the existence of the transfer." See Regs. § 25.2511–1(c). Therefore a renunciation, valid under state law, of an unvested contingent remainder, 33 years after its creation, was held to be a transfer subject to the gift tax. Jewett v. Comm., 455 U.S. 305 (1982).

In order to provide definitive and uniform rules concerning disclaimers, I.R.C. § 2518, providing a federal disclaimer rule for the first time, was passed as part of the 1976 Reform Act. All post-1976 putative transfers will be evaluated under the *federal* rule. If the disclaimer qualifies under the terms of § 2518, then it shall be deemed that no transfer took place at all, with respect, at least, to the disclaimant. The effects of such a qualified disclaimer extend also to the estate tax and the generation-skipping tax. See §§ 2046 and 2654(c) which incorporate § 2518 into those two tax structures, respectively. Section 2518(b) defines a qualified disclaimer as an "irrevocable and unqualified refusal by a person to accept an interest in property," made in writing. The refusal must be made within 9 months from the date of the "transfer" creating the interest, or from the day on which the disclaimant reaches the age of 21, whichever is later. See, in general, Regs. § 25.2518–2.

Two additional conditions must be met, and they introduce some uncertainty into the operation of the new law. First, the disclaimant must not have accepted the interest or "any of its benefits." This creates some confusion as to the allowability of partial disclaimers, permitted under the laws of some states. Compare also § 2518(c)(1) relating to disclaimers of an "undivided portion" of an interest. Even more importantly, § 2518(b)(4) decrees that, to qualify, the interest refused must pass to some person other than the disclaimant, without any direction on the part of the disclaimant. This means that the disclaimer must also be valid under state law. The result was then not a uniform federal disclaimer rule pure and simple, but rather a set of federal conditions having to be met, in addition to the disparate local rules already in existence.

In order finally to provide a purely federal rule, I.R.C. § 2518(c)(3) was enacted as part of E.R.T.A. (1981). It provides that any written transfer of the transferor's entire interest to the person who would have received it if a valid disclaimer had been made under applicable state law will be effective, if otherwise valid under federal disclaimer law.

Great complexity remains, however, because the new rule only applies to the disclaiming of interests created *after* 1981. Thus there are 3 sets of rules covering interests created before 1977, after 1976 but before 1982, and after 1981, respectively. Note also that new § 2518(c)(3) covers only disclaimers of "the transferor's entire interest in the property", so that partial disclaimers are still governed by § 2518(b) and (c)(1) and (2).

Indirect Transfers. A reimbursement of someone else's expenses will be a taxable gift, if the other requirements of the gift tax are met. A transfer to a corporation is sometimes regarded as a taxable transfer by the donor to the shareholders of the corporation. See Regs. § 25.2511–1(h)(1). A transfer of property by a corporation to a donee will be treated as a gift to the donee from the stockholders of the corporation. See Regs. § 25.2511–1(h)(1). If a person makes a gift to one transferee on condition that the transferee make a further payment over to a third person, the whole transaction will be regarded as a gift from the original transferor to the third party, to the extent of the property received by the third party from the intermediary. Such a determination will affect, among other things, the number of available annual per donee exclusions. See Estate of Bartman v. Comm., 10 T.C. 1073 (1948); Regs. § 25.2511–1(h)(2) and (3).

Net Gifts and Gifts on Condition the Donee Pay the Gift Tax. If a person makes a gratuitous transfer of money or other property and conditions the gift, or otherwise requires the donee to pay any gift tax levied on the transfer, several interpretations would seem possible. One is the "net gift" approach. This implies that the value of the property or cash equal to the gift-tax liability was not part of the gift itself, and that the donor made a "net gift" of the property less the gift tax liability. See, *e.g.*, Harrison v. Comm., 17 T.C. 1350 (1952). Another view is the part-gift, part-sale analysis; the donor sold the property for the amount of the gift tax paid, and has a gain or loss, for income tax purposes, equal to the difference between the amount realized and basis.

In Comm. v. Turner, 410 F.2d 752 (6th Cir. 1969), the Circuit Court held that when a donor made a gift of stock on condition that the donee reimburse the donor for his gift taxes, there was a net gift of the value of the stock minus the amount of the gift tax (not a part-sale, part-gift, or a full-gift and a gift-back). Other courts had adopted the part-sale, part-gift analysis, and the issue finally had to be decided by the U.S. Supreme Court.

In Diedrich v. Comm., 457 U.S. 191 (1982), an income tax case, the U.S. Supreme Court rejected the net gift theory and ruled that the donor realized income when the donee paid gift tax that exceeded the donor's basis in the "gifted" property. It was a part-sale, part-gift. For gift tax purposes, since the gift tax is primarily imposed on the donor, a donee's payment must be regarded as a benefit provided to this transferor. So, if that benefit is offset, the result is a net gift amounting to the difference in values. The net gift rule and a formula to determine the amount of gift tax due on the net gift are set out in Rev. Rul. 75–72, 1975–1 C.B. 310; and Rev. Rul. 71–232, 1971–1 C.B. 275. The *Diedrich* rule does not apply to gifts made before March 4, 1981. See § 1026 of the Tax Reform Act of 1984.

Interest-Free Loans. Until very recently it was possible to make interest-free loans without incurring gift tax liability. Interest-free loans were an effective and simple technique for the tax-free transfer of wealth. Suppose a borrower needed a loan of $200,000 to start a business. A bank would charge 15% simple annual interest on the loan, requiring an interest payment of $30,000 per year. If the borrower could obtain an interest-free loan from a wealthy parent, there would be an implicit transfer of $30,000 in wealth (assuming the parent could have loaned the money at a 15% rate), without gift tax. If, on the other hand, the wealthy parent transferred $30,000 to the borrower to pay the borrower's interest expense, the $30,000 would be subject to the gift tax, though $10,000 of this amount would be eligible for a Sec. 2503(b) exclusion.

As early as 1953, the Tax Court ruled that a loan in exchange for a below-market-interest note would expose the transaction to gift tax liability to the extent the value of the loan exceeded the value of the note. See G.H. Blackburn, 20 T.C. 204 (1953).

Subsequently, however, a distinction was made between interest-free (or below-market-interest) *term* notes and interest-free *demand* notes. In theory (though not often in practice), a demand note could be called by the lender for full repayment at any time.

In one 1966 case a federal district court, without citing *Blackburn,* found it significant that the lending parents had no duty to invest their money. Since the lenders (parents) could have kept their money in cash (perhaps in a mattress?), there was no reason to imply a gift of interest on a loan to the children. E.M. Johnson, 66–1 USTC ¶12,386.

It was not until 1973 that the I.R.S. announced its intention to ignore *Johnson* and to apply the logic of *Blackburn* to interest-free demand note cases. See Rev.Rul. 73–61, 1973–1 C.B. 408.

The I.R.S. position was challenged in the courts. By 1984, there was a conflict in the federal courts of appeal. One circuit followed the reasoning of *Johnson* (L. Crown, 585 F.2d 234 (7th Cir.1978)), while another affirmed the I.R.S. position (E.C. Dickman, 690 F.2d 812 (11th Cir.1982)).

The U.S. Supreme Court resolved the conflict by affirming *Dickman* and the I.R.S. position—interest-free demand loans constitute a gift of (uncharged) interest to the borrower, much as if the lender had charged and collected interest and then given the interest back to the borrower. See E.C. Dickman, 465 U.S. 330 (1984).

Dickman did not end the controversy surrounding the use of interest-free loans as tax avoidance devices. Such loans remained popular because the $10,000 annual exclusion sheltered some fairly large loans from the gift tax. Even at a 10% implied rate, for example, spouses electing the § 2513 gift-splitting provision could make a $200,000 loan to a child without incurring gift tax on the uncharged $20,000 interest. In addition, any *income* generated from the loan property (e.g., bank account interest) would be attributed to the child and taxed at the child's (probably lower) marginal income tax rate. This income tax avoidance technique is called *income shifting*.

After standing on the sidelines of the interest-free loan controversy for a decade, Congress resolved most of the interest-free loan questions when it enacted I.R.C. § 7872 in 1984.

In the event of any below-market rate (or interest-free) loan, the foregone interest is treated as a gift from lender to borrower. In order to eliminate income-shifting opportunities, the foregone interest is considered also to be *interest income to the lender*. See § 7872(a)(1). In other words, Section 7872 creates an imaginary world in which the recipient of an interest-free loan pays "interest" to the lender and the lender transfers this "interest" back to the loan recipient as a gift. Section 7872 applies to both term and demand loans. Interest is imputed at an "applicable Federal rate" in effect under Section 1274(d).   See § 7872(f)(2).

Section 7872 provides a general *de minimis* exception, from both its gift and income tax provisions, for loans between individuals not exceeding $10,000 outstanding at any one time.   § 7872(c)(2). However, this exception does not shelter an income-shifting gift loan.   And see § 7872(c)(2)(B) (disallowing the exception whenever loan assets are invested by the borrower in income-producing assets).

Time of Gift.   As to the *time* of a *transfer* by gift, there is some authority that a taxable transfer takes place upon the making of a contract or promise to transfer in the future, rather than at the later time when property is transferred in satisfaction of the contractual promise.   A gift after the wedding pursuant to an antenuptial contract exemplifies this problem.   See Comm. v. Estate of I. C. Copley, 194 F.2d 364 (7th Cir. 1952), acq. 1965-2 C.B. 4.

The Internal Revenue Service has issued a ruling to attempt to clarify its position with respect to the effective date of the gift of property pursuant to a legally enforceable antenuptial agreement.   See Rev.Rul. 69-347, 1969-1 C.B. 227 (holding that the effective date for gift tax purposes is the date on which the promise to make a future transfer became enforceable under state law, not the date on which an actual transfer of property is made, if the gift is susceptible to valuation at the time the agreement became enforceable; if not, the gift was considered not to have been made until a later time (there the death of the husband) at which time the amount of the gift was determinable).

In general, however, a transfer is deemed to be complete when the donor has fully relinquished dominion and control over the property that is the subject of the gift. Some special rules have been established to govern particular problems such as the gift of a note or check. For example, the gift of a donor's own check is not complete until the check is paid or negotiated for value to a third person and the gift of the donor's own promissory note is not complete until the note is paid or transferred for value. The gift of a check or note of a third party, however, is complete at the time of transfer of the note or check. With respect to gifts of checks and notes, see Rev.Rul. 67–396, 1967–2 C.B. 351; 84–25, 1984–1 C.B. 191.

Of course, a gift is not complete if it is revocable. Since the donor can get the gift property back at any time by exercising his power of revocation, the occasion for imposing a gift tax has not arisen. Even if the donor cannot exercise the power of revocation, but if he or she retains a right to change beneficial interests, even in a way that will not benefit the donor, the gift will be regarded as incomplete. So, if a donor establishes a trust and retains a power to alter the beneficial interests in the trust (though not in donor's favor), the creation of the trust does not constitute a completed gift at the time. As amounts are paid over to beneficiaries by the trust, the donor will be deemed to have made a completed gift since those amounts are then no longer under the donor's dominion and control.

So, the time of the transfer for tax purposes does not depend upon when the donor relinquishes all power to revoke or get the property back nor even upon the time when a donee becomes assured of his interest, but upon whether the donor has relinquished dominion and control over the property. See generally Regs. § 25.2511–2. If a gift *causa mortis* is revocable, it is not a completed gift for gift tax purposes. A gift made in connection with a separation or divorce is deemed to take place at the time when the transferee first has an enforceable right to the property. A transfer of property subject to a life interest in the transferor will be deemed to be a completed gift of the whole property minus the interest retained by him, in other words, a completed gift of the remainder interest—for gift tax purposes. If he or she later were to make a transfer of the retained life interest, there would be another taxable gift at that time.

If the donor does retain some interest in the property given away, that interest must be susceptible of valuation or else the gift will be deemed to be a gift of the entire property without any subtraction for the retained interest. If a gift is regarded as incomplete because the donor has retained dominion and control, a completed gift for gift tax purposes will occur when dominion and control terminates or when it is transferred by the donor or taken away from him by some other event. In general, the amount of control that the donor must retain in order to render a gift incomplete for gift tax purposes is somewhat greater than what must be retained to render a transfer incomplete until death for estate tax purposes.

In general, the rules about when a gift is complete for Gift Tax purposes do not coincide exactly with the rules about when a gift is complete for Estate Tax purposes. Therefore, a transfer that is complete and thus incurs a gift tax may nevertheless be regarded as incomplete for estate tax purposes, with the result that estate tax is payable on the same property or interest at the time of the donor's death (with a credit for the gift tax).

§ 21. Liability for Gift Tax

Primary liability for the gift tax rests with the donor, but the donee is secondarily liable for the tax, to the extent of the value of his gift. In fact, the donee will be liable even if it has not been proven impossible to collect from the donor. The donee may be assessed any time within one year after the expiration of the period of limitation for assessment against the transferor. Also, the gift tax forms a lien against the gift property for a period of ten years from the date of the gift. Moreover, the recipient of a tax-free gift can be held liable (only to the extent of the value of his gift) for tax unpaid on all other gifts made by the donor in the same year. See I.R.C. §§ 6324(b), 6901(a)(1)(A)(iii), § 6901(c)(1), and related sections.

§ 22.   Application of the Generation-Skipping Tax to "Transfers" at Death and During Life

Sight must not be lost of the fact that the new Chapter 13 tax on certain generation-skipping transfers constitutes a separate and special tax on the transfer of wealth and may be imposed upon certain events that constitute direct skips, taxable terminations or taxable distributions. The application of this tax was outlined in considerable detail in Chapter II, *supra,* and will not further be recapitulated here.

CHAPTER IV

DONATIVE INTENT AND CONSIDERATION

§ 23. Gift Tax: Donative Intent and Consideration

Donative intent (on the part of the transferor) is not an essential element in the application of the gift tax. See Regs. § 25.2511–1(g)(1). Application of tax is based on the objective facts of the transfer and the circumstances under which it is made rather than on the subjective intent or motives of the donor. Therefore, it will not avail the taxpayer to claim that a transfer otherwise constituting a gift was not a gift because he or she did not have the requisite intent; by the same token, it is not necessary for the Commissioner to prove that the taxpayer did have a donative intent in making the transfer in order to apply the tax.

A leading case standing for the proposition that donative intent is not necessary is Comm. v. Wemyss, 324 U.S. 303 (1945). There, the taxpayer transferred shares of stock in performance of the obligations of an antenuptial agreement. The Circuit Court of Appeals had held that the marriage agreement was an arms-length bargain, that donative intent was absent, that donative intent followed by a donative act was essential to constitute a gift, and hence the transfer was not taxable. In reversing, the Supreme Court said that Congress intended to use the term "gifts" in its broadest and most comprehensive sense, not in the common-law or colloquial sense, and chose not to require an ascertainment of an elusive state of mind. The transfer was taxable whether or not accompanied by "donative intent."

The Supreme Court went on to hold that for purposes of the gift tax Congress not only dispensed with the test of "donative intent" but also formulated an external or objective test: if property is transferred for less than an adequate and full consideration in money or money's worth, the excess of such money value shall, for the purposes of the gift tax, be deemed a gift. The adequate and full consideration rule is now embodied in I.R.C. § 2512(b). Whether the transferor receives something in return and the consideration received is worth less than the property transferred, or the transferor of property receives nothing in return, the excess value of the property transferred in deemed to be a gift.

In the *Wemyss* case, the Supreme Court further elaborated the consideration rule in holding that no consideration had been received by the transferor, for gift tax purposes, in the promise of his betrothed to marry him or, evidently, in the marriage itself. Thus the Court emphasized that consideration for contract law or other purposes is not the same as consideration that is "full and adequate in money or money's worth" for gift tax purposes.

The Gift Tax Regulations, § 25.2512–8, state that consideration that is not reducible to a value in money or money's worth (consideration such as love and affection, promise of marriage) will be wholly disregarded and the entire value of the property transferred shall be deemed to constitute the amount of the gift. The Regulations go on to say that relinquishment or promised relinquishment of dower or curtesy, or of a statutory estate created in lieu of dower or curtesy, or of other marital rights in the spouse's property or estate, shall not be considered to any extent a consideration "in money or money's worth." (Special rules are provided in I.R.C. § 2516 and the Regulations thereunder with respect to some transfers made in connection with divorce. See § 25, infra.)

In point of fact, not every transfer or unequal exchange will be treated as a taxable gift. To illustrate, the Regulations in § 25.2512–8 state that the gift tax is not applicable to ordinary business transactions and that a sale, exchange or other transfer made in the ordinary course of business will be considered as made for an adequate and full consideration in money or money's worth. A transfer made in the ordinary course of business is defined as a transaction which is "bona-fide, at arm's length, and free from any donative intent." Thus, many transactions in which an unequal transfer or exchange is made will not give rise to gift tax liability. Further, donative intent, which was held not to be an essential element of a taxable gift, is introduced as relevant to the question whether the transfer is a non-taxable transfer or exchange or a gift. Therefore, if a purchase or other exchange is made in the ordinary course of business and in a transaction where the parties deal at arm's length, if there is no attempt to disguise a gift in the form of a business transaction and if there is no evidence of an intent on the part of one party of the transfer to confer an unreciprocated benefit on the other, the transfer will not be taxable.

Many cases have demonstrated the principle that a transaction made in the ordinary course of business and at arm's length will not be taxed under the gift tax, even though the value of the property transferred is not equaled by the consideration in money or money's worth received. See, *e.g.*, Estate of Anderson v. Comm., 8 T.C. 706 (1947), involving senior executives who transferred some of their common stock in a corporation to its junior executives at a price lower than the value of the stock transferred. The transaction was bona-fide and conceded by the Commissioner to have been at arm's length and was part of a business plan to change the proportion of stockholdings among the management group, as responsibilities were shifted from the senior to the junior executives. The court, concluding that no gift had been made, relied heavily on the business context of the transaction and distinguished it from the kind of marital or family transaction involved in the *Wemyss* case and other leading gift tax cases.

The exception for business or arm's-length transactions makes eminent good sense, of course. Otherwise, every purchase or exchange would have to be examined to determine whether in fact there was an inequality in actual value in the exchange for purposes of gift tax liability. Any time a taxpayer made an ill-advised sale or found a bargain, there would be a serious question of transfer tax applicability. Such a state of affairs certainly would prove unworkable. Even under present law, however, difficult problems arise when a so-called business transaction arises in a family context, where one may suspect that the parties may not be dealing at arm's length, or when in a business context a transfer takes place that evidences a considerable difference in values exchanged and which cannot be explained simply on the ground that someone drove a hard bargain or found a good deal.

Under the broad definition of "gift" as used in the Internal Revenue Code and interpreted by the Supreme Court in the *Wemyss* case, and under the so-called "external test" of when a gift is present, a great variety of transactions have been deemed to constitute gifts. For example, payments by a wife, annually, of insurance premiums on policies of insurance on the life of her husband were held to constitute annual gifts to the extent of those premium payments, minus the present value of the rights of the wife under the policies and the trust in which they were placed. (Under the terms of that trust, the life insurance policies would provide benefits for the mother of the husband and in some contingencies would provide some benefits for the taxpayer wife. Thus, by her annual premium payments, the wife was conferring a benefit upon her husband and his mother and only partly upon herself.) Comm. v. Berger, 201 F.2d 171 (2d Cir. 1953). The court went on to say that the absence of donative intent is especially unimportant in family transactions where the eventual estate tax of the donor would be reduced by the inter-vivos transfer.

In another case, a taxable gift was found when a guardian, with the approval of a court, made payments from the estate of a well-to-do minor, the taxpayer, to the minor's mother. Evidently the minor was free of any legal obligation to support her mother, but the payments were made for the mother's personal support. So, the court said, since neither the minor taxpayer nor her estate received any benefit from any of the payments made that could be recognized as consideration, the payments were taxable as gifts. See Stokowski v. Pedrick, 52–2 USTC ¶ 10,861 (S.D.N.Y.1952); see also Comm. v. A. C. Greene, 119 F.2d 383 (9th Cir. 1941).

In some other cases, transactions between family members have been found to have been made at arm's length and thus to fall beyond the reach of gift tax under the doctrine stated earlier that a transaction which is bona-fide, at arm's length and free from any donative intent will be considered as made for an adequate and full consideration in money or money's worth. See, *e.g.*, Catherine S. Beveridge, 10 T.C. 915 (1948). The transaction need not take place in the business world or a commercial context to escape tax. However, a heavy burden rests on the taxpayers to demonstrate an absence of donative intent in a family transaction and to prove that the parties dealt at arm's length and "bona-fide." In some situations, a taxable gift has been found even though there were many indications of calculated and economically-determined behavior by the taxpayer. For example, see Comm. v. Siegel, 250 F.2d 339 (9th Cir. 1957) (exercise of the widow's election, discussed more fully at § 38 below.) (In other instances, the widow's election will not result in gift tax liability because she receives more than she gives up. See, *e.g.*, Zillah Mae Turman, 35 T.C. 1123 (1961) and Vardell v. Comm., 307 F.2d 688 (5th Cir. 1962). The Commissioner's acquiescence is to be found at 1964–2 C.B. 7.)

The "external test" has also led some courts to honor installment sales between relatives, with the subsequent yearly forgiveness of $3,000 of the debt qualifying for the pre-E.R.T.A. annual gift tax exclusion (which, beginning in 1982, amounts to $10,-000 per year). Thus the transfer is treated as a sale, in spite of the avowed intent of the "seller" to forgive each installment as it comes due, and thus, in the course of time, to forgive the entire debt. For example, Father sells property worth $30,000 to Son and Daughter, for $6,000 down, note and trust deed for the balance, with, suppose, $6,000 due on the note at the end of each of the four subsequent years. Under S. R. Haygood, 42 T.C. 936 (1964) the original sale is deemed to be for adequate consideration, *i.e.,* the down-payment plus the note. As each payment, including the down-payment, becomes due, its forgiveness constitutes a gift, but is excludable under § 2503, with the result that no gift tax is ever payable on the entire transaction. The Service has indicated strong dissatisfaction with this result, and will not acquiesce in *Haygood.* See Rev.Rul. 77–299, 1977–2 C.B. 343. Note, however, that under I.R.C. § 453B, any disposition of an installment obligation, even by gift or cancellation, will cause recognition of any gain inherent in the note. This makes the *Haygood* plan unworkable in many situations. A better plan would be to give away property, as contrasted with forgiving notes, in amounts equal to the annual exclusion. See Rev.Rul. 83–180, 1983–2 C.B. 169 (distinguishing Rev.Rul. 77–299).

Notwithstanding the objective test of whether a gift has been made, the motive or state of mind of the donor has been examined in some instances to determine whether a gift or a non-gift transfer was made. See, *e.g.,* Lillian Pascarelli, 55 T.C. 1082 (1971), involving the liability of a donee for gift tax. The donee lived with a man as husband and wife, although they were unmarried. The man gave her cash, opened a brokerage account in her name, and made improvements in her home. She rendered services in entertaining the man's business customers, but these were disregarded by the court. The court found that the transfers were motivated by affection, respect and admiration and held the donee liable for the tax as transferee of the property. These transfers would have been taxable as gifts if a purely mechanical formula such as that suggested by I.R.C. § 2512(b) had been employed; the only legitimate inquiry into the donor's state of mind was to determine that no transfer had been made in the ordinary course of business, bona-fide, at arm's length and without donative intent. To use the motivations of affection, respect and admiration as affirmative evidence of a gift seems inconsistent with the Supreme Court's approach in the *Wemyss* case and with many other authorities, unless—perhaps—such evidence merely serves to negative a suggestion that it was a business transaction at arm's length.

Some situations involve a mixed family and business context. For example, a gift may be found upon formation of a family business if disproportionate shares in the business are given to some members of the family (usually children) who contribute less in property or services than other members of the family (usually parents). See Gross v. Comm., 7 T.C. 837 (1946) (family partnership); Heringer v. Comm., 235 F.2d 149 (9th Cir. 1956), cert. den. 352 U.S. 927 (1956) (family corporation). (See §§ 2701–2704, discussed *infra* at § 48A, and the regulations at §§ 25.2701–0 through 25.2704–3 for special rules for valuing transfers of some business interests to a member of the transferor's family, transfers in trust, and transfers pursuant to options and purchase agreements.)

Until 1974, the status of political contributions or similar payments, either made in a business or a private context, was somewhat unclear. In an important early case, DuPont v. United States, 97 F.Supp. 944 (D.C.Del.1951), a contribution by the taxpayer to the National Economic Council, an organization formed for economic, political and lobbying purposes, was held taxable as a gift. In Revenue Ruling 59–57, 1959–1 C.B. 626, the Internal Revenue Service ruled that a contribution to a political party or to a candidate for public office is a taxable gift. However, the Service has also ruled that a transfer of property by local citizens to a manufacturing company in order to induce it to operate a manufacturing plant constituted a transfer in the ordinary course of business and not a gift. See Rev.Rul. 68–558, 1968–2 C.B. 415. In Stern v. United States, 436 F.2d 1327 (5th Cir. 1971), a political contribution to a citizens' group was held not to be a taxable gift. The court somehow concluded that the gifts were made in the ordinary course of business because they were bona-fide, at arm's length, and free from donative intent. The Internal Revenue Service then announced that it would not follow the *Stern* case, except in the 5th Circuit. See T.I.R. 1125 (Dec. 17, 1971).

Finally, in 1974, Congress mooted the entire issue by amending § 2501 to provide that all transfers to political organizations, for the use of such organizations, are exempt from the gift tax. See

§ 2501(a)(5). There is, it should be noted, no parallel "exclusion" for testamentary transfers under the estate tax.

In summary, the Supreme Court of the United States has taken I.R.C. § 2512(b) to provide a definition of the term "gift," even though the language and structure of the section might suggest a design merely to determine the value of property transferred in a transaction otherwise determined to be a gift. The Supreme Court has therefore held that the common-law concept of gifts and the requirement of donative intent will not be imported into the gift tax law. Thus the tax concept of a gift, for gift tax purposes, is given very wide scope, although a sale, exchange, or other transfer of property made in the ordinary course of business (a transaction which is bona fide, at arm's length and free from donative intent) will not be treated as a gift for gift tax purposes. The presence or absence of donative intent may be relevant in determining whether a transaction is a gift, although its presence is not required for there to be a gift taxable as such.

By defining a gift largely in terms of the adequacy of consideration in money or money's worth, the administration and courts have placed heavy pressure on the determination of what amounts to "consideration" for gift tax purposes. Obviously, by the descriptive phrase "in money or money's worth," consideration will be determined by economic values rather than by concepts drawn from the law of contracts, where a peppercorn may still suffice. A loss of wealth or income or some other detriment to the transferee is not consideration, since it does not benefit the transferor.

Underlying the definition of a gift for gift tax purposes are considerations related to the role of the gift tax as a backstop for the estate tax. Thus, a transfer which depletes the estate of the transferor is likely to be regarded as a taxable gift. However, that notion cannot safely be translated into a rule, for many consumption expenditures and other disbursements that do in fact deplete the wealth and hence the taxable estate of a person are not gift transfers for purposes of the gift tax. Support given to one whom the taxpayer is obligated to support, such as a minor child or spouse, is not a taxable gift. A transfer by an elderly person to his or her son or daughter will be scrutinized very carefully, even if it is cast in the form of a purchase or other business transaction, to determine whether it is a gift in disguise. While not every estate-depleting expenditure will be taxed as a gift, a transfer that confers a net benefit upon the recipient and is not offset by a receipt on the part of the transferor of the kind that will show up in his gross estate at death ("money or money's worth") is likely to be taxable as a gift unless it meets the exemption for transfers in the ordinary course of business, the consumption expenditure area or some other exception from the broad, "external" test laid down by the Supreme Court in determining whether a gift has been made.

One of the most important forms of consideration received in return for transfers that arguably are gifts is consideration in the form of a surrender or release or transfer of marital rights, the topic turned to next.

§ 24. Marital Property and Support Rights as Consideration—Estate Tax and Gift Tax

The gross estate of a married person survived by his or her spouse at death will include the value of all property to the extent the decedent had an interest in that property at the time of death. His or her gross estate will not be reduced by the extent of any interest in such property held by the surviving spouse at the time of the decedent's death as *dower or curtesy,* or by virtue of a statute creating an estate in lieu of dower or curtesy. See I.R.C. § 2034. The full value of the property is included in the decedent's gross estate, without any deduction for the interest of the surviving husband or wife and without regard to when the right to such an interest arose. See Regs. § 20.2034–1.

Consider, then, the situation of a taxpayer decedent who dies in a separate-property state with a net worth of $1,000,000 at his death. Suppose half ($500,000) of that wealth is held in the form of real property, and that under applicable state law his surviving widow has a dower interest equal to one-half the real property held by him at his death. (In many states, there will be found a statutory substitute for dower, providing that the widow can elect against the will no matter in what form the property is held at death). Assume also that the will of the decedent disinherits his wife but that under state law she is entitled to elect to take against the will and assert her dower right to the extent of one-half the decedent's real property, and that she successfully does so. For tax purposes, the gross estate of the decedent will consist of $1 million (not $1 million reduced by the dower interest held by the widow at his death and coming into effect by virtue of her election to assert it). In other words, the gross estate will be $1 million, not $750,000.

This rule (and the effect shown in the foregoing example) seems to make perfectly good sense. It treats equally the taxpayer involved in that example and a taxpayer who wills an equivalent amount of property to his wife or whose wife takes an equivalent amount of property under the laws of intestacy. In all three cases, the gross estate consists of the property held by the decedent at death, not reduced by the inchoate dower or curtesy or statutory substitute interest held by the surviving spouse.

To evaluate § 2034 further, however, compare the preceding example with the situation of a similar married couple in a *community-property* state. If the husband is the first to die and if the couple owns $1 million worth of (post-1927) community property in California, or community property of equivalent nature in another state, the gross estate of the husband will consist of only $500,000, not $1 million. This follows because the wife had a present and vested interest in one-half the community property; as a result the husband's interest, includable in his gross estate under I.R.C. §§ 2031 and

2033, consists of just one-half of the community property held at death. Thus the husband's gross estate is reduced by the interest of the surviving wife, which serves as a counterpart of the interest held by a surviving spouse in a separate property state in the form of dower or curtesy or a statutory substitute. It would seem, therefore, that very different tax treatment of the two decedents in the two states would result, although economically their positions are very similar.

Most disparity in treatment—between the community property decedent and the separate property decedent—is relieved by the *marital deduction* available to the decedent who makes a bequest or whose estate makes a transfer in compliance with state law as to dower, curtesy, or statutory substitute, under I.R.C. § 2056. See I.R.C. § 2056(c)(3). This is obvious in the case of post-1981 decedents, whose estates may take advantage of the new unlimited marital deduction, but was also true under the pre-E.R.T.A. rules. Thus, although the *gross* estates of the two pre-1982 decedents will be unequal, the marital deduction will reduce the gross estate in a separate property state from $1 million to $750,000 if the wife is entitled to and receives $250,000 worth of property. If she is entitled to one-half of all the decedent's property at his death, under a statutory substitute for dower or curtesy, the decedent's gross estate will be reduced from $1 million to a taxable estate of $500,000. In that event, the *taxable* estate of the separate property decedent will be no greater than the taxable estate of the community property decedent, for the marital deduction does not apply to the community property interest of a wife (since there was no transfer at death from the decedent to her).

Therefore, the rule of I.R.C. § 2034 (denying any reduction for dower or curtesy) makes sense not only when one compares the tax treatment of two decedents in separate property states, one of whom makes a bequest or devise to his surviving spouse and the other who does not do so but whose spouse makes a claim under state dower or curtesy or similar rules; the rule of § 2034 also makes sense when one compares the separate property treatment with that of spouses in a community property state. (But what will be the continuing purpose and role of § 2034, given the new unlimited marital deduction, equally available with respect to both community and separate property?)

To be distinguished from the marital rights that I.R.C. § 2043(b) decrees shall not be regarded as consideration in money or money's worth are rights to support and vested community property rights. For purposes of the gift tax, support rights will be regarded as consideration in money or money's worth. See Rev.Rul. 68–379, 1968–2 C.B. 414 (superseding E.T. 19, 1946–2 C.B. 166) and Rev.Rul. 60–160, 1960–1 C.B. 374. Consequently, an *inter vivos* transfer of property made in return for a release of rights to support will not be a taxable gift to the extent of the value of the support rights released in return. For estate tax purposes also, support rights are to be distinguished from the marital rights which I.R.C. § 2043 rules will not be treated as consideration in money or money's worth. Hence a deduction will be allowed under § 2053 for a claim founded on a promise or agreement given in return for a release of support rights.

Also, a spouse's vested rights in community property, such as the rights of a California wife in post-1927 community property, are not the kind of marital rights that I.R.C. § 2043(b) and the corresponding rule in the gift tax area decree not to be consideration in money or money's worth. Such vested community property rights or interests amount to "property" which will constitute consideration in money or money's worth for purposes of the gift tax under I.R.C. § 2512(b) or the estate tax. Hence, if a spouse or a person about to be married makes a transfer of property or promises to make a transfer of property in return for a conveyance, surrender or release of such vested community property rights, the transfer or promise will be deemed to have been made for an adequate and full consideration in money or money's worth up to the value of the community property or rights in community property conveyed or released by the other party to the transaction.

To regard the release of support rights as consideration and hence to refrain from applying the gift tax to a transfer made for equivalent value in the form of a release of support rights makes perfectly good sense. The transfer of property in exchange for the release of support rights is or can be viewed as an anticipatory lump-sum substitute for the pro-

vision of support during the lives of the husband
and wife. Actual provision of support, by husband
to wife over a period of years of marriage, for
example, would not be taxable as a gift, even if
there were no marital deduction. It is not taxed as
a gift because it is paid or provided in discharge of a
legal obligation. Even though the provision of that
support does reduce the gross estate and hence the
taxable estate of the provider, it is not the kind of
transfer sought to be taxed by either of the federal
transfer taxes. Similarly, if the spouse obligated to
provide support failed to do so and if the surviving
spouse had a claim against the estate for support
not forthcoming during the lifetime of the decedent,
that claim would give rise to a deduction under
I.R.C. § 2053 because it would not be founded on a
promise or agreement that in turn was not made for
adequate and full consideration in money or money's worth. Since the lifetime provision of support
would not be taxed as a gift and since the claim
against the estate for support wrongfully withheld
would give rise to a deduction from the estate tax, a
transfer made in return for a surrender or release
of the support obligation during life should not be
taxable as a gift.

Similarly, the rule that a spouse's vested interest
in community property is consideration in money or
money's worth (rather than the kind of marital
right which I.R.C. § 2043 provides will not be treated as consideration for tax purposes) produces correct results. To be sure, a transfer during life by a
husband to his wife in exchange for a conveyance by

her of her interest in community property (or a
release of her community property rights) does reduce the wealth of the husband which can be included in his gross estate at his death. However, it
does not artificially or unduly reduce that gross
estate since in return the husband gains the property conveyed to him by his wife or gains the opportunity to increase his estate by obtaining her release
of her community property interests so that future
accumulation becomes his property, rather than
half-his and half-hers.

In other words, underlying this entire area of the
law is a general policy of preventing wrongful depletion of the estate of the taxpayer such that the
death transfer tax is improperly avoided. Against
this policy lies a determination to allow those expenditures or transfers that are not themselves
wrongfully estate-depleting or substitutes for
wrongful estate-depleting to be made tax-free.
Thus a concept of "artificial" or "wrongful" estate
depletion may help explain the estate tax and the
gift tax rules. Another way of raising the matter is
to ask whether a promisee or the recipient of a
transfer inter-vivos gave something in return that
either augmented the transferor's wealth (and presumably will augment his or her estate at death) or
whether the transfer to the donee was of a kind
that is permitted to be made without transfer tax
and without stigma as a transfer-tax-avoiding dis-
bursement. This understanding of the law, however, is not a legal standard or a way in which the
I.R.S. or the courts generally frame the issue. At

best it can serve as a rationale and framework for
thinking about these tax issues.

§ 25. Transfers Pursuant to Divorce, Separation or Annulment—Application of the Gift Tax

Under the general rules about consideration in
money or money's worth, a transfer by one spouse,
to another (for example by a husband to his wife)
pursuant to a property-settlement agreement in
connection with divorce would be taxable to the
extent the property transferred by the husband
exceeded the value, in money or money's worth, of
anything he received from his wife in return. Marital rights (such as dower, etc.) in property would
not constitute consideration in money or money's
worth and thus there would be a gift by the husband except to the extent that the wife gave to him
an outright interest in property or released him
from a legal obligation of support.

I.R.C. § 2516 provides a special rule that is
broader and of greater protection to taxpayers than
the application of these general principles would be.
Under this section, if a husband and wife enter into
a written agreement relative to their marital and
property rights and if divorce occurs (or has occurred) within two years thereafter (or within one
year before), any transfer of property or interests in
property made pursuant to the agreement to either
spouse in settlement of his or her marital or property rights or to provide a reasonable allowance for
the support of issue of marriage during minority is

deemed to be a transfer made for a full and adequate consideration in money or money's worth. This is true regardless of whether the divorce agreement is approved by the divorce decree. Thus, for example, if the husband transfers property to his wife and otherwise complies with the terms of I.R.C. § 2516, it is not necessary for him to show that he received a discharge of support obligations equal in value to what he transferred in order to escape gift tax. The gift tax will not apply to his transfer, so long as it meets the terms of I.R.C. § 2516.

Note that under *revised* § 2516, the gift tax exemption for some transfers made pursuant to a marital property settlement is extended to agreements entered into within a *three*-year period, beginning on a date one year before the parties enter into an agreement and extending until two years afterward.

One may well ask why a transfer of property by a husband to his wife in connection with divorce should be exempted from gift tax even though the value of the property he transfers exceeds the value of the wife's support rights surrendered. One answer may lie in a view that his transfer is not a voluntary, gratuitous transfer of the kind the gift tax was designed to reach. His transfer is much like the transfer that he would make if no agreement had been reached and the divorce court ordered him to transfer property to his wife. In other words, the transfer has very substantial aspects of involuntariness about it. However, the involuntary, compelled nature of the transfer would not suffice to distinguish it from other transfers that are taxable as gifts under the general principles of the gift tax, in the absence of I.R.C. § 2516.

The additional justification for § 2516 lies in the estate tax *marital deduction*. To illustrate: If a man in a separate property state remains married to his wife until death and at that time transfers a large part of his wealth to her, the estate tax marital deduction of I.R.C. § 2056 would enable him to make that transfer free of estate tax on an unlimited amount of his wealth. In a community property state, by remaining married until death the husband and wife would accumulate half-interests in their property and thus, at the husband's death, the wife would have at least her one-half interest, which she received free of gift tax during the marriage.

When a marriage ends in divorce, it may be seen in some sense to suffer an early "death" and the property settlement transfers made at that time may be viewed as anticipatory substitutes for the death transfers to which the estate tax marital deduction would apply or which can be accomplished under a community property system without transfer tax to the extent of the wife's vested one-half interest in the community property.

Thus a property transfer in connection with divorce, whether made under compulsion of the divorce decree or under a property settlement agreement reached within two years before the divorce, may be viewed typically as an arm's-length bargain by which a spouse makes a transfer as a substitute for later transfers that, if the marriage had survived, would have discharged the obligation of support and as substitutes for death transfers which would have been partly or largely free of tax. Accordingly, the property settlement transfers are the functional equivalents of transfers which are permitted to be made without tax. They do not seem to be substitutes for a taxable testamentary disposition; they do not (prospectively) deplete the estate tax base.

Before I.R.C. § 2516 was enacted, the Supreme Court held (in a case that remains important for situations not covered by § 2516) that there would be no gift tax on a transfer made pursuant to a property settlement agreement that actually had been incorporated in the decree of divorce. See Harris v. Comm., 340 U.S. 106 (1950). The court held that the transfer was not founded so much on a promise or agreement as on the divorce decree and the divorce itself. The court pointed out that if the transfer were affected by court decree, there would be no promise or agreement. Hence, it reasoned, the transfer made pursuant to the property-settlement agreement that was incorporated in the decree of divorce similarly was free of any promise or agreement. It is difficult to understand why the freedom from promise or agreement should be the basis for saying the transfer is not taxable as a gift, since the gift tax itself does not say anything about "promise or agreement." The court, however, took the "promise or agreement" language from the estate tax statute that authorizes deductions from the gross estate, imported that language into the gift tax area and then concluded that the language did not apply to the facts before it. Whatever the strength of the reasoning, the result was clear—the transfer was not subject to the gift tax. That result was not changed even though the agreement was not conditional upon the entry of the divorce decree and even though the covenants in the agreement were expressly made to survive any decree of divorce that might be entered. Broadly speaking, the core of the *Harris* case was the idea that the transfer was made pursuant to a court decree rather than a promise or agreement.

I.R.C. § 2516 goes further than the *Harris* case and makes it unnecessary to show either consideration for the transfer, that it was in discharge of a legal obligation, that it was effected by a judicial decree or even that the agreement was incorporated in or approved by the divorce decree. Under § 2516 it is not necessary to allocate any part of the transfer to the discharge of support rights or to dower or curtesy rights or to show actual consideration for part of the transfer. And, the section shelters not only transfers to the spouse in settlement of marital or property rights but also transfers made to provide a reasonable allowance for the support of children.

If the facts of a given situation do not fit I.R.C. § 2516, for example because the divorce does not occur within the 3-year period (one year before or two years after the date of the written agreement), there is still some possibility for avoiding gift tax because I.R.C. § 2516 is not exclusive. If § 2516 does not apply, it is still possible that the *Harris* case can be used to avoid gift tax; the *Harris* case continues to have vitality in the area beyond the reach of I.R.C. § 2516.

When the *Harris* case but not the statute is applicable, for the gift tax not to apply, the agreement and settlement of property rights must have been incorporated in the divorce decree, although evidently it is not necessary that the contract be contingent on a decree and it will not be destructive if the contract is made to survive the decree. See, *e.g.*, McMurtry v. Comm., 203 F.2d 659 (1st Cir. 1953).

Under the unlimited marital deduction the incentives and plans will change, as taxpayers attempt to make full use of *that* deduction.

Interspousal Sales or Gifts and the Income Tax. In 1984, Congress enacted an income tax rule, new I.R.C. § 1041, that must be mentioned in connection with the gift tax. Section 1041 declares that a transfer of property from an individual to (or in trust for the benefit of) a spouse, or a former spouse (if the transfer is incident to the divorce), shall for purposes of "this subtitle" be treated as acquired by the transferee as a gift, and the basis of the transferee in the property shall be the adjusted basis of the transferor. This rule was designed to change the law of U.S. v. Davis, 370 U.S. 65 (1962), in which the U.S. Supreme Court held that the transfer by one spouse to another of appreciated property (such as his share of marital or jointly-owned property, as well as separate property) in a property settlement (in divorce) was an event of realization, such that the transferor had to realize gain as if he had sold the property for cash, or exchanged it for property (not of a like kind) of equal value in a taxable exchange. The recipient was presumed to have surrendered rights equal in value to the fair market value of the property received. Under *Davis,* the transferee spouse took a cost (FMV) basis (although she was not taxable on receiving the property in exchange for the surrender of her marital rights). See Rev. Rul. 67–221, 1967–2 C.B. 63.

Under this very broad rule of § 1041, the transferor is deemed to be making a gift even if he actually sells the property to his (or her) spouse for *cash,* and the transferee takes the transferor's basis even though she (or he) paid cash (or used property other than cash). These income tax non-inclusion and basis rules flow from the § 1041(b) characterization of the transfer as a gift. But that characterization certainly does not make the transferor taxable under the gift tax, at least if he (or she) receives fair and adequate consideration in return. The transferor then is not making a gift, for gift tax purposes, in the sense of a gratuitous transfer. Section 2516 of the gift tax deems qualified transfers pursuant to marital property settlement agreements to be made for a full and adequate consideration in money or money's worth. See § 25, *supra.*

As to similar rules in the estate tax, see I.R.C. § 2053 and § 2043, and § 26 of this text. Section § 2043(b)(2), as of 1984, incorporates the § 2516 exemption into the estate tax. Moreover, § 1041 itself limits its "gift" characterization to the "purposes of this subtitle", meaning "Subtitle A" of the Internal Revenue Code, which includes only the *income* tax, §§ 1–1561, not subtitle B, which contains the estate and gift taxes. Treating the property settlement transfer as a "gift" in § 1041 is a shorthand way of producing the desired income tax consequences or some interspousal transfers (nonrecognition of gain or loss and carryover of basis), not a conclusive legal label with automatic gift tax consequences. Whether a taxable gift *is* involved when property is transferred by one spouse to another must be analyzed under normal gift tax principles, not under § 1041 of the income tax.

§ 26. Transfers Pursuant to Divorce, Separation or Annulment—Application of the Estate Tax

Transfers or agreements to transfer property in connection with divorce sometimes give rise to estate tax questions. For example, suppose that a husband during his life signs a property settlement agreement with his wife and that agreement is ultimately incorporated in or approved by the divorce decree so that I.R.C. § 2516 would relieve the transfer under that agreement from gift tax if the transfer were made. Then suppose the husband dies before making the transfer. As a result, his

estate will still include the property to be transferred, even though his contract binds the estate,
which will then have to make the promised payment. Will any relief from the estate tax be available under these circumstances?

Some relief from estate tax is provided by I.R.C.
§ 2053(a)(3) which declares that the value of the
taxable estate shall be determined by deducting
from the value of the gross estate such amounts for
claims against the estate as are allowable by the
laws of the jurisdiction under which the estate is
being administered. The widow's claim under the
property settlement agreement qualifies and thus
can be deducted in arriving at the taxable estate.

However, I.R.C. § 2053(c)(1)(A) adds an additional barrier. As noted earlier, it requires that the
deduction allowed for claims founded on a promise
or agreement shall be limited to the extent that the
claims were contracted bona-fide, and for an adequate and full consideration in money or money's
worth. This qualification prevents escape from the
estate tax by collusive agreements by taxpayers who
promise to transfer property or funds and do not
make the transfer before death, but attempt to
arrange for a deduction from the gross estate for
what amounts to a simple testamentary transfer.
The difficulty with this limitation results from
I.R.C. § 2043, also noted earlier, which bars marital
rights in the decedent's property or estate as consideration in money or money's worth. The question then arises whether the promise by the husband during his life to make a transfer of property

in connection with divorce is a promise contracted bona-fide and for an adequate and full consideration in money or money's worth, if the consideration involved is the surrender by the wife of rights of support and rights in his property.

This question was resolved in 1984 by the introduction of I.R.C. § 2043(b)(2). Transfers meeting the requirements of I.R.C. § 2516(1) are deductible under I.R.C. § 2053. If the facts of a given situation do not fit this exception, an I.R.C. § 2053 deduction remains a possibility.

It has been held and ruled that a deduction from the decedent's gross estate will be allowed for a claim against the estate arising out of a contractual promise incorporated in a divorce decree. See Comm. v. Watson, 216 F.2d 941 (2d Cir. 1954). The *Watson* case allowed the deduction even though the contractual promise was not contingent on divorce and was made to survive the divorce. In a sense, then, the rule of the *Harris* case, see § 25 *supra,* governs in this area just as it governs in the gift tax area when the conditions of I.R.C. § 2516 are not met. The claim is deemed not to be founded on a promise or agreement for § 2053 deduction purposes, but rather on the divorce decree. See Rev.Rul. 60–160, 1960–1 C.B. 374; Rev.Rul. 68–379, 1968–2 C.B. 414, superseding E.T. 19, 1946–2 C.B. 166. Cf. Rev.Rul. 67–304, 1967–2 C.B. 224.

The deduction under the rule of the *Watson* case and the Revenue Rulings cited depends on power in the divorce court to decree a settlement of all property rights or to vary the terms of a prior settlement agreement. If the divorce court does not have such power, as a matter of local law, then the indebtedness is considered to be founded on a promise or an agreement, not a decree, in which event the estate tax deduction will be allowable only to the extent of the reasonable value of support rights of the wife or other consideration in money or money's worth given by her in return.

Once again, the unlimited marital deduction alters the planning efforts and litigation troublespots.

CHAPTER V

TRANSFERS DURING LIFE—
APPLICATION OF THE
ESTATE AND GIFT TAXES

§ 27. Introduction

Some transfers made during life will not only produce gift tax consequences, but estate tax consequences as well. More specifically, the gross estate of the decedent at death sometimes includes property actually transferred by the decedent during life and not owned by him or her at death. Loosely speaking, previously transferred property will be included if the decedent retained too much interest or power and control over it or if the transfer was made to avoid the death tax or to substitute for a death transfer.

The gift tax will apply to an inter-vivos transfer that is complete for gift tax purposes. But even though gift tax rates are no longer lower than those of the estate tax, it is necessary that the estate tax itself apply to a transfer made during life if that transfer is the functional equivalent of a death transfer and too easily would provide a means of avoiding the estate tax. This potential avoidance results from the gift tax exclusion of $10,000 per year per donee, from the different valuation dates under the two taxes, and from the fact that the estate tax base, but not the gift tax base, includes the assets used to pay the tax. These continuing advantages (even after the 1976 "unification" of the gift and estate taxes) of making a gift that is not included in the gross estate will be discussed and critiqued in § 76, *infra*.

The Internal Revenue Code contains a number of estate tax rules which will cause the gross estate of the decedent to include property transferred by him during life. A prime example is the rule applicable to transfers made within three years of death (formerly called gifts "in contemplation of death"). Other rules apply to a transfer with a retained life estate, a transfer that is revocable or over which the transferor retains a power to alter or amend the disposition or to designate the persons who shall possess or enjoy the property or its income. Also, certain transfers that take effect at death, even though made during life, will cause inclusion in the decedent's gross estate of more than just the property he or she held at death.

§ 28. Transfers Within Three Years of Death—Application of the Estate Tax

Introduction. Since a transfer tax solely on property owned at death is easily avoided by making gifts shortly before dying, the Federal Estate tax, ever since its enactment in 1916, has contained a provision to bring some such gifts into the estate tax base. The Federal Gift tax, enacted in 1932, although limiting the avoidance possible, still made special treatment of deathbed gifts necessary, because of its lower rates, separate deductions and its new start up the rate scale. Although the 1976 Amendments largely equalized the tax burden on *inter vivos* and testamentary gifts, still, enough difference remains (see § 76, *infra*) to warrant inclusion of some deathbed gifts in the gross estate.

Until the 1976 amendments, the operative element causing inclusion in the gross estate under § 2035 was the subjective intent of the decedent, *i.e.*, that the gift was made "in contemplation of death". This was, of course, very difficult to ascertain, and the statutory presumptions of old § 2035 did not greatly alleviate the difficulty.

The 1976 amendments to § 2035 therefore substituted a rule of automatic inclusion in the gross estate for *all* gratuitous transfers within three years of death. E.R.T.A. (1981) subsequently greatly reduced the scope of this automatic inclusion rule, effective for gifts made by decedents who die after 1981.

Before the automatic inclusion rule adopted in 1976, even apart from difficulties in ascertaining the exact meaning of the statutory phrase "in contemplation of death," the Commissioner had encountered problems in administering the statute and in getting results that were fair, reliable and evenhanded. A number of cases involved optimistic octogenarians who made transfers within three years of death and yet survived the contemplation-of-death rule because of evidence that, though elderly and perhaps even not in the best of health, the transferors were vigorous and life-motivated in their thinking and did not have imminent death on their minds as a controlling reason for their transfers. A leading example of this judicial phenomenon is the case involving Frank L. Felix, who made gifts at the age of 99 and died within three years, when over 100 years old. Nevertheless, the court held that his transfers were not made in contemplation of death and were not includable in his gross estate. See C. B. Kniskern, Jr., Executor v. U. S., 232 F.Supp. 7 (S.D.Fla.1964).

Pre-E.R.T.A., Post-1976 Law. Even before 1976 the difficulties in administering the "contemplation of death" rule had caused much dissatisfaction. Since the burden of proof was on the taxpayer, and since the factual question was so hard to prove, it was very costly to fight the 3-year presumption. The result was that most small gifts made within 3 years of death were included in the estate, while most large gifts escaped inclusion after a costly trial. Congress, unhappy with these results, as long ago as 1926 experimented with a statute that provided a *conclusive presumption* that gifts made within two years before death were made "in contemplation of death." That statute was held unconstitutional on due process grounds. Heiner v. Donnan, 285 U.S. 312 (1932). (Later, until 1976, the *rebuttable* presumption that gifts within 3 years of death were made "in contemplation of death" was employed, instead.)

The 1976 Amendment of § 2035(a) provided for *automatic inclusion* in the gross estate of any gift made within 3 years of death, thus eliminating both the old 3-year rebuttable presumption, and the old irrebuttable presumption that gifts *before* 3 years before death were *not* "in contemplation." Since there was no conclusive presumption, nor any presumption at all, the statute appeared not even to raise any due process question. It should be noted that the amendments to § 2035(a) affected only the condition of *inclusion* of gifts in the gross estate. They changed no other substantive law.

Since 1976, I.R.C. § 2035(c) has provided for the "grossing-up" of gifts falling within § 2035. That is, not only is the value of the includable gift (as of the date of death, or alternate valuation date) made within three years of death included in the gross estate, but so is the amount of any gift tax paid or payable on such a gift. However, a credit for the tax paid is provided for under § 2012(a). See § 29, *infra*. The import of this gross-up rule is discussed in § 76, *infra*. Prior law had provided for no such "gross-up," and therefore never completely eliminated the tax advantages of making deathbed gifts, since the amount of gift tax paid by the donor/decedent escaped estate taxation, even if the gift itself were drawn into the estate by § 2035.

Section 2035 interactions. Section 2035 may interact with other sections of the Code, such as I.R.C. §§ 2036–2038, to bring about inclusion in the gross estate of more than the property or interest actually transferred in contemplation of death. For example, if a person transfers property and retains a life estate such that under I.R.C. § 2036(a)(1), all the property in which the life estate was retained could be included in the gross estate of the transferor on his death and if within three years of death he or she releases or otherwise transfers the life estate earlier retained, the combination of I.R.C. § 2035 and § 2036 will result in inclusion of the entire property in the gross estate. Inclusion will follow even though at the time of death taxpayer neither owns the property itself nor then has the life estate he or she retained. Because the retained life estate was transferred or released within three years of death, without consideration in money or money's worth, he will be taxed as though he had retained the life estate until death. Regs. § 20.2035–1(b) explicitly state that if a decedent transfers an interest in property or relinquishes a power in contemplation of death, the decedent's gross estate includes the property subject to the interest or power to the extent that it would be included under §§ 2036, 2037, or 2038 if the decedent retained the interest or power until his death. If the decedent exercises or releases a power of appointment within three years of death, the property subject to the power will be included in the decedent's gross estate to the extent provided in I.R.C. § 2041 and the regulations under that section. See § 2035(d)(1) & (2), discussed after the next paragraph.

The valuation of property included in the gross estate under § 2035 is to be determined as of the applicable valuation date. See § 48, *infra*. But it is only the transferred property itself which is includable at such value. Therefore, if the transferee has made improvements or additions to the property, any resulting enhancement in value is not considered as part of the gross estate. Also, income received from the property after its transfer or property purchased with such income is not included in the gross estate. See Regs. § 20.2035–1(e).

Post-1981 law. E.R.T.A. (1981) drastically limited the types of gifts subject to inclusion under I.R.C. § 2035(a). Section 2035(d)(1), as to decedents dying after 1981, makes the general, automatic inclusion rule of § 2035(a) for all gratuitous transfers within 3 years of death *inapplicable*, except as § 2035(d)(2) otherwise provides. There are now only two types of gifts within three years of death that will be drawn into the gross estate of decedents dying after 1981. The first consists of gifts of an interest in property which is otherwise includible under one of the estate tax provisions governing "constructive ownership", *i.e.,* I.R.C. §§ 2036–2038, 2041 or 2042. The second includes gifts of an interest in property which would have been included thereunder had the decedent retained the interest until death. See I.R.C. § 2035(d).

It might appear that there was no need to include the first type of transfer within the coverage of the new three-year rule, since such gifts would in any event be included in the gross estate under the relevant constructive ownership section, *e.g.* § 2036, *et al.,* and the § 2035(c) "gross-up" continues to apply to all gift taxes paid with respect to all gifts within three years, whether or not the gifts themselves are included in the gross estate under § 2035(a). § 2035(d)(2) makes it clear that nothing in § 2035 was designed to change that result.

The inclusion of the second type of gift also bears further analysis. As an example, assume that F owns two pieces of real estate, Blackacre and Whiteacre. In 1992 F gives away Whiteacre, but retains a life estate therein. In 1988 F unconditionally gives away Blackacre, and also gives away the life estate he had retained in Whiteacre. When F dies in 1994, the value of Whiteacre, but not Blackacre, will be included in his gross estate under I.R.C. § 2035, because the value of Whiteacre would have been included in his gross estate under I.R.C. § 2036(a) had he retained the life estate until death.

One may be inclined to wonder just what difference between the two transactions justifies the disparity in treatment. One answer would appear to lie in the fact that the valuation date for gifts is the date of the gift, while property drawn back into the estate will be valued for transfer tax purposes as of the date of death (or alternate valuation date). Assume now that F had given away Whiteacre, retaining a life estate, not in 1992, but in 1960. In the absence of the special rule of inclusion, *i.e.*, if the property were not drawn back into his estate, F would have succeeded in enjoying the property for many years, until shortly before his death, and yet a transfer tax would have been paid upon only the property's 1960 value, and not on the possibly much larger date of death value. It is this type of abuse which is prevented by the special rule of § 2035(d)(2). Note, however, that even assuming that inclusion is proper in the case of gifts of constructive ownership interests even though outright gifts are no longer so included, the E.R.T.A. changes created a very complex statutory tangle in this area. Note above all, that one of the constructive ownership statutes itself contains a three-year rule (§ 2038), while others do not, *e.g.,* § 2036. The interrelations among all these rules are certain to create very difficult problems in an area already overly complex and already governed to an unacceptable degree by arguments from analogy.

The puzzling differentiation in § 2035(d) between outright gifts, not included in the gross estate under § 2035(a) because of § 2035(d)(1), and transfers involving §§ 2036–2038 and § 2042 may better be explained by a Congressional view that a §§ 2036–2038, or §§ 2041–2042 transfer is "inherently" testamentary, even if made many years before death. So, Congress sought to prevent escape from these other sections by a "last minute" (within three years) disposition of the testamentary "string." In contrast an outright gift of the property itself, with no strings attached, even if within 3 years of death may seem less "testamentary" to Congress than the (above) two-step dispositions. As the Senate Finance Committee put it, it may not be "appropriate to tax appreciation that accrues after a gift has been made under the unified estate and gift taxes merely

because the donor died within 3 years of the gift."
Sen. Rep. No. 97–144, p. 138.

There remains the question how to reconcile the
two inclusion rules contained in § 2035(d)(2). It
seems that the *first* one was intended to cover the
underlying transfer of property, within 3 years of
death, when inclusion is required under §§ 2036–
2038 or §§ 2041–2042. That is, § 2035(d)(1) will
not apply so as to countermand any inclusion made
under §§ 2036–2038 or § 2042.

The second rule seems to contemplate a case
[such as C. Allen, Exr., 293 F.2d 916 (10th Cir.
1961)] in which taxpayer makes a gift more than
three years before death but retains a "string"
under §§ 2036–2038, §§ 2041–2042 that, if retained
until death would cause inclusion and then, within
3 years of death, relinquishes that string (other
than in a bona-fide sale for an adequate and full
consideration in money or money's worth). The
second rule of § 2035(d)(2) says that the rule of
§ 2035(d)(1) will not pre-empt § 2035 as combined
with §§ 2036–2038, §§ 2041–2042. So, giving away
the "string," the interest or power whose retention
or acquisition produces inclusion in the gross estate,
will not prevent such inclusion (if it is given within
three years of death).

As before, gifts excludable under § 2503 are not
subject to § 2035, unless a gift-tax return had to be
filed with respect to that year's gifts to that donee.
(See § 2035(b)(2)). Thus gifts of any size with
respect to life insurance, gifts with respect to which

gift-splitting was elected, and gifts under $10,000 to a donee to whom the decedent/donor gave over $10,000 in the relevant year will all be drawn back into the gross estate.

It should also be noted that the application of certain relief provisions, *e.g.*, special-use valuation, are dependent upon the relative sizes of the property involved and the gross estate. In order to prevent the manipulation of these provisions by the making of death-bed gifts, the value of all gifts within three years of death, other than those qualifying for the § 2035(b) exclusion, are to be included in the gross estate solely for the purposes of qualification under those specialized provisions. I.R.C. § 2035(d)(3).

A Section 2035 Overview. The need for the former rule of § 2035, which swept deathbed transfers into the gross estate, waned when the gift tax became more fully integrated with the estate tax in 1976. Since all post-1976 transfers in principle affect the final estate tax return, whether they were made during the full flower of life, near death or at death, Congress came to accept the idea that § 2035 could largely be declawed without a serious loss to the transfer tax system. So, while § 2035(a) still declares the broad inclusionary rule, § 2035(d) makes it inapplicable except in limited instances. So the synthesized general rule has evolved into one of *non*-inclusion, with some exceptions. [(The deathbed transfers *not* included in the gross estate by § 2035(a) & (d) will, however, fall subject to the gift tax and will enter into the final estate tax return and tax computation as lifetime transfers that influence the tax rate for (other) property that *is* included in the taxable estate. The transfers not included under new § 2035 will, however, be valued as of the date of gift and not, as when they were includable under § 2035, at the date of death (or alternate valuation date)]. So, interim appreciation will now escape the transfer tax. It is this appreciation that does seem to be the target of § 2035(d)(2) when it does require inclusion of property transferred with a §§ 2036–2338, or §§ 2041–2042 string attached which string, in turn, has been relinquished within three years of death.

And, the § 2035(c) "grossing up" rule draws the gift tax paid on transfers within three years of death back into the gross estate.

For income purposes, property transferred within three years of death, but no longer drawn back into the estate by retracted § 2035, will not get a fresh start basis under § 1014.

And the income tax basis rule of § 1014(e), denying fresh start basis for property transferred *to* a decedent within one year of death and bequeathed back to the transferor, might be said to be a "contemplation of death" rule of its own.

When all is said and done, § 2035—after being substantially restricted in 1981 (so that it no longer includes in the gross estate all property simply transferred during the three-year pre-death period)—plays two principal functions. One is that it increases the gross estate by the amount of any gift tax paid on a transfer by the decedent or his or her spouse within the 3-year pre-death period. See § 2035(c). This is a "gross-up requirement" that does not, though perhaps it ought to, extend to gift taxes paid on §§ 2036–2042 "incomplete" transfers. It is designed to erase the benefit of deliberately making death-bed transfers to remove the amount of gift tax resulting therefrom from the estate tax base. Section 2035 also, as mentioned, guarantees that if a taxable "string" under §§ 2036–2038 or § 2042 is released within the three-year period, presumably to prevent inclusion under one or more of those sections, the decedent will be treated as if the string had been retained until death.

Also, § 2035(d)(3) and (4) block the use of last minute gifts to take property out of the gross estate to qualify for special statutory benefits. Such benefits are: (a) favorable income tax treatment for § 303(b) redemptions of stock to pay death taxes; (b) special estate tax valuation for qualified real property under § 2032A, and (c) an extension of time under § 6166 to pay the estate tax resulting from inclusion of a closely held business.

And § 2035(d)(3)(C) makes property transferred during the 3-year pre-death period subject to liens for taxes under §§ 6321–6324B.

Even when otherwise applicable, the § 2035 inclusion rule does not cover a transfer that is a bona-fide sale for adequate and full consideration, nor to a gift with respect to which the decedent was not obliged by § 6019 to file a gift tax return, such as many gifts that fall below the $10,000 annual exclusion.

§ 29. Transfers Within Three Years of Death—Application of the Gift Tax and the Gift Tax Credit

If an inter-vivos transfer of property is completed, the gift tax will apply, pursuant to its own rules, even though later the estate tax also be deemed applicable, by virtue of I.R.C. § 2035 or any of the sections pertaining to transfers not complete for estate tax purposes. Since the imposition of both taxes would put an unreasonable burden on such transfers, the estate tax provides a credit against estate taxes for gift taxes paid on such transfers. For pre-1977 transfers, the basic rules of the credit for gift tax paid are spelled out in I.R.C. § 2012 and the regulations under that section. The amount of credit is limited so that it cannot exceed the amount of the gift tax deemed to have been paid on the transfer of property later brought into the estate and also so that it cannot exceed that part of the estate tax which is paid with respect to the gift property when it is later included in the gross estate. The statute and regulations should be consulted for more detailed rules pertaining to the credit.

For gifts made after 1976, the gift tax credit of § 2012 is unavailable [see § 2012(e)]. This is because the new method for calculating the estate tax payable automatically provides for a credit for any gift tax payable on post-1976 gifts. [See

§ 2001(b)(2)]. And see § 2001(e), which provides a special rule for split gifts and § 2035 inclusion.

§ 30.   Incomplete Transfers—Estate Tax—Introduction

The present statutory sections providing estate tax rules to include in the gross estate property transferred before death, but not deemed completely transferred until death for estate tax purposes, are I.R.C. §§ 2036, 2037 and 2038. These sections have their roots in a more general statutory rule which, formerly, asked simply whether a transfer was one "intended to take effect in possession or enjoyment at or after the grantor's death." This general section later was broken out into more specific rules which cover several kinds of intervivos transfers that are substitutes for death transfers because of a retained interest or power which makes the transfer not complete until death. The present statutory rules cause inclusion in the gross estate of property transferred during life where the transferor retained the economic benefit of the property, in the form of possession or enjoyment or right to the income, for his life and until his death. See § 2036(a)(1). Also included is property transferred but with possession or enjoyment by the transferee postponed until the death of the transferor, contingent in some ways on his death. See § 2037. The gross estate also includes property transferred during life if the transferor reserved significant powers over the possession or enjoyment of the property. Such a power might consist of a power to revoke the transfer, a power to alter or amend it in significant ways or a power to designate who would possess or enjoy the property. See § 2036(a)(2) and § 2038.

Sections 2036 through 2038 are in some ways not coherently drafted, with the result that they sometimes overlap or conflict. A given disposition of property may be governed by more than one and, still more troublesome, the tax results of applying one section may differ from the tax results of applying another. Dependably, the Internal Revenue Service will assert all applicable sections and will strive for inclusion of the largest amount in the decedent's estate. The representative of the estate, in contrast, will urge the application of only that section which produces the smallest inclusion. If it is unmistakable that two or more sections apply, the greatest possible inclusion will result. However, in some instances it is uncertain whether more than one section applies and there is room for real controversy about the amount to be included in the decedent's gross estate.

Sections 2036 through 2038 have in common the effect of including in the gross estate some property not owned at the death of the decedent. In this respect, they resemble § 2035 and other statutory rules to be encountered. In another respect, they share a more unique characteristic.

Sections 2036–2038 are called the "grantor sections" because they apply to decedents who earlier transferred the property (in trust or otherwise) and

retained or reacquired the powers or interests specified in the statutes. In other words, I.R.C. §§ 2036
through 2038 will *not* apply when a decedent, at
death, held a power or interest in property *not*
earlier transferred by him or her. They will not
apply, for example, to a power or interest given to
the decedent by someone else in property never
transferred by decedent.

In considering the statutory sections more particularly, it is important to understand the kinds of
dispositions to which each is addressed, to understand the policy and logic behind the rule of inclusion and its limitations, to ask whether some other
statutory section would also cover the disposition
presented, and finally to think about whether some
or all of these statutory sections could be repealed
without significantly changing the law because
I.R.C. §§ 2031 and 2033 could cover the same
ground. (Also, it may be useful to ask whether a
single general rule, encompassing "transfers taking
effect in possession or enjoyment at or after the
grantor's death," could be substituted for the present complexities of §§ 2036 through 2038.)

Sections 2036 through 2038 present many questions as to the scope and meaning of their terms.
The statutes will be examined in greater detail in
the following sections of this book. While examining the statutes and regulations in greater detail, it
is helpful to keep in mind the general thrust of the
rules. They are designed to tax *inter vivos* transfers having the character of will-substitutes. They
apply to transfers *other than* a bona-fide sale for an

adequate and full consideration in money or money's worth. They cause inclusion in the gross estate of property *not owned* by the decedent at death. They may cause *inclusion* of all the property transferred or of some lesser amount, namely the amount subject to the described power or the amount in which the decedent had the described interest. As "grantor sections," they apply only to powers in *property transferred* by the decedent. In some instances they apply only to *powers retained* by him, but in others they apply to powers reacquired or obtained in any way. They apply to powers held at death, even if not actually exercised. Also, some of the sections contain different rules for transfers made at different times, geared to changes in the law and to prevent unfair surprise by a retroactive application of new legal rules.

All in all, they apply to inter-vivos transfers, whether or not complete for gift tax purposes, which are regarded as incomplete for estate tax purposes.

§ 31. Transfers with a Retained Life Estate—
I.R.C. § 2036(a)(1)

If a person transfers property and retains a life estate in that property, either by a transfer in trust or by retaining a legal life estate, the value of the entire property transferred will be included in the gross estate at the transferor's death. I.R.C. § 2036(a)(1) (cumbersomely) provides that the value of the gross estate "shall include the value of all property to the extent of any interest therein of which the decedent has at any time made a transfer (except in case of a bona-fide sale for an adequate and full consideration in money or money's worth) by trust or otherwise, under which he has retained for his life, or for any period not ascertainable without reference to his death, or for any period which does not in fact end before his death, the possession or enjoyment or the right to the income from the property." By its terms, this section is a "*grantor* section" and thus will apply only when the decedent's life estate is held in property which he himself formerly owned and transferred. Therefore, if grandmother transfers property in trust with income to her son for life and remainder at the son's death to granddaughter, there will not be any inclusion in the gross estate of the son at his death under § 2036(a)(1) because the son, the decedent for purposes of present concerns, was not the transferor or grantor. He did not make a transfer in the terms of § 2036. (Of course, a termination of the son's interest may well incur a generation-skipping transfer tax.)

Section 2036 applies when there has been a *retention* of a life estate or similar interest, but not when there has been an acquisition or reacquisition of such an interest. Therefore, if the transferor of property disposes of all his interests in the property and then reacquires a life estate in the property which remains in effect until his death, there will not be inclusion under § 2036(a)(1), because the life estate was acquired or reacquired, not retained.

Although the language of § 2036 requires a retention of a life estate "under" the transfer, the life
estate need not be reserved by the very instrument
of transfer itself. For example, if the retention of
the life interest occurs by simultaneous agreement
on the part of the transferee, or if such an agreement can be inferred from objective evidence,
§ 2036(a)(1) will apply.

If the transferor of property retains a life interest
in only a portion of the property transferred, only
the portion in which the interest was retained will
be included in his or her gross estate under
§ 2036(a)(1). Similarly, if a decedent had earlier
transferred community property into a trust and
retained a life estate in the transferred property,
only the decedent's community share of the property will be includable under § 2036. See Katz v. U.
S., 382 F.2d 723 (9th Cir. 1967).

Under I.R.C. § 2036, the decedent is considered
to retain the equivalent of the use, possession or
right to the income or other enjoyment of the
transferred property to the extent that the income
is to be applied toward the discharge of his or her
legal obligations, including, of course, a legal obligation to support a dependent during the lifetime of
the transferor. See Regs. § 20.2036–1(b)(2).

Under the language of the statute, the period for
which the possession or enjoyment or right to the
income must be retained is a period for the transferor's life or for any period not ascertainable without reference to his death or for any period which

does not in fact end before his death. Consequently, § 2036(a) covers more ground than that occupied solely by dispositions with a retained life estate, strictly defined. To illustrate, if a grantor transfers property in trust and retains a right to the income from that property for his life but provides that no installment of the annual income shall be paid for the calendar quarter or half year or year preceding his death, § 2036(a) will apply even though the grantor does not receive all the income earned during his lifetime. Since the period for which he has a right to the income cannot be ascertained without reference to his death, the statutory terms apply.

Suppose a grantor transfers property in trust and provides that the income shall be received by her for ten years with the remainder to be distributed to a named remainderman. If the grantor dies before the expiration of the ten year period, § 2036(a)(1) will cause the property to be included in her gross estate. However, if she lived longer than the ten year period, there would be no inclusion because the period then in fact would end before her death.

I.R.C. § 2036(a)(1) also applies to a retained *secondary* life estate in the grantor. Thus, if the grantor transfers property in trust and provides that the income is to be paid to his wife for her life and then at her death the income to be paid to him for his life and remainder at his death to their children, and if the grantor survives his wife, at his death the value of the remainder, i.e., the transferred property, will be included in his gross estate.

Suppose, however, that the grantor in the preceding example had died during the life of his wife, the first life tenant. In that event, although the grantor retained a right to trust income, that right had not yet taken effect in enjoyment at the time of his death. Moreover, since it was contingent on the grantor surviving his wife, that interest will never take effect in possession or enjoyment. Nevertheless, I.R.C. § 2036(a)(1) does require inclusion as a result of such a transfer. Marks v. Higgins, 213 F.2d 884 (2d Cir. 1954); Comm. v. Estate of Nathan, 159 F.2d 546 (7th Cir. 1947). However, the interest that will be included in the grantor's estate must be reduced from the total value of the transferred property by the value of his wife's life interest remaining outstanding at his death, since that interest precedes and is, therefore, unaffected by the grantor's rights in the property. See Regs. § 20.2036–1(a). In other words, the interest that is shifting at his death is not the entire property, because the wife's life interest in that property was transferred earlier by a completed *inter vivos* transfer. The interest that is shifting at his death is the remainder which will take effect in possession or enjoyment only after the surviving wife dies. Thus, the amount to be included is the present value of that remainder interest, which is determined by taking the value of the property and subtracting an amount determined by the life expectancy of the surviving wife.

If a grantor who has retained a life estate or other interest which will produce inclusion under I.R.C. § 2036(a)(1) gives away that retained interest within three years of death, as determined under I.R.C. § 2035, the entire amount of the trust property will be includable in the decedent's gross estate. See § 2035(d)(2). Thus, the grantor cannot escape the impact of § 2036(a)(1), which is designed to require inclusion of property given in a way that amounts to a substitute for a testamentary transfer (and one that takes effect in possession or enjoyment only at or after the grantor's death) by another gift (of the life-interest) in contemplation of death, a gift which itself is a life-time substitute for a testamentary transfer.

Section 2036 contains an exception for a transfer that would otherwise fit the terms of the section but which is a bona-fide sale for an adequate and full consideration in money or money's worth. As a result of this section, a transfer of property by a grantor who in return receives other property equal to the transferred property in money or money's worth will not result in inclusion under § 2036. This result makes sense if the property received is equally likely to be included in the gross estate of the transferor at his death. In that event, there has been no depletion of the prospective estate tax base.

The measure of adequate consideration in a § 2036 situation can prove tricky. By way of illustration, suppose that a grantor makes a transfer of property but retains a life estate such as to require inclusion under I.R.C. § 2036. Then, at a later time and before his death, the transferor releases or transfers the retained interest for value and receives in return an amount equal to the value of the retained life estate, but not equal to the value of the property in which the life estate was retained. The question then arises whether the surrender or transfer of the retained life estate for full and adequate consideration in money or money's worth in a bona-fide sale is sufficient to take the entire matter beyond the reach of § 2036.

This adequacy-of-consideration problem was notably presented in the case U. S. v. Allen, 293 F.2d 916 (10th Cir. 1961). In that case, the decedent Maria created an irrevocable trust and reserved in herself an interest consisting of three-fifths of the income for life, the remainder to pass to her two children who were also the beneficiaries of the other two-fifths interest in the income. At the age of 78 and anticipating that the retention of her life estate would cause the attributable share of corpus to be included in her gross estate, the decedent sought to diminish her estate tax by selling her retained life estate. She found a buyer in her son, Wharton. The actuarial value of her retained life estate, based on her life expectancy, was $135,000. The attributable share of the corpus, that is to say three-fifths of the corpus, was valued at approximately $900,-000. Maria's son Wharton agreed to pay her $140,-000 for her retained life estate and the court agreed that he acted as a bona-fide, third party purchaser. Shortly after the transfer was completed, Maria was

discovered to have an incurable disease which resulted in her death soon afterward. As a result, the
son received less income than expected and suffered
a considerable loss on his investment.

The Commissioner argued that § 2036(a)(1) required that Maria's gross estate include three-fifths
of the corpus of the trust minus the $140,000 pur-
chase money. The executors of the estate argued
that the sale of the life interest was for an adequate
consideration and hence no part of the trust corpus
was properly includable in the gross estate. So the
question was presented whether the adequacy of
the consideration must be measured against the
interests transferred or against the interest which
would otherwise have been included in the gross
estate. The court concluded that Congress meant
the estate to include the corpus of the trust or, in
its place, an amount equal in value. Thus, a grant-
or cannot easily avoid the application of
§ 2036(a)(1) by selling the retained power in contemplation of death even if he or she receives consideration in money or money's worth equal to the
value of that retained power. For more on the
question of adequacy of consideration in the case of
lifetime transfers to which the estate tax may apply,
see § 37 *infra*.

Two specific applications of § 2036 in the family
context have presented problems resulting in important court decisions. One is the problem that
arises when a spouse transfers the family residence
to his or her spouse and then continues living in the
house, with the owner, until death. In such event,

the Commissioner has argued that the owner of the house transferred it with a retained life estate in the form of retained possession or enjoyment. This argument did not prevail in Gutchess' Estate v. Comm., 46 T.C. 554 (1966), where the court refused to infer an agreement between the transferor and the transferee that the transferor would be allowed to live in the home. The Commissioner later acquiesced in the decision in the *Gutchess* case. See Acquiescence, 1967-1 C.B. 2.

Since acquiescing in the *Gutchess* case, the Commissioner has stated that continued occupancy by the donor *will* be evidence of an agreement in cases where donor and donee are not husband and wife. (Since the advent of the unlimited marital deduction, these are the only cases that matter.) See Rev.Rul. 70-155, 1970-1 C.B. 189. The Commissioner's position was recently upheld in Estate of Maxwell v. Comm., 3 F.3d 591 (2d Cir.1993). In *Maxwell,* mother sold her personal residence to her son and his wife, forgiving $20,000 of the purchase price and accepting a $250,000 mortgage note for the balance. Mother leased the home until her death, paying a monthly rental that was close to the amount of interest due on the note. Each year, mother forgave another $20,000 on the note, and any unpaid balance at her death was forgiven in her will. The court held that there was an implied agreement that mother would live out her life in the residence. Furthermore, the exchange was not made for adequate consideration because of an implied agreement that the note would never be enforced. Therefore, the transaction was a transfer with a retained life estate, not a sale, and the full value of the residence was includable in mother's estate. See also Guynn v. U.S., 437 F.2d 1148 (4th Cir.1971), and Linderme's Estate v. Comm., 52 T.C. 305 (1969).

For a brief period, some tax planning enthusiasts believed, or sought to persuade others, that an arrangement called a "Family Estate Trust" would produce wonderful estate tax savings. This concoction involved grantor (or grantors, husband and wife) putting all his (their) property (including the family home) and his or her "lifetime services" into an irrevocable inter-vivos trust, while continuing to live in the home, and continuing to enjoy the benefits of the paychecks and investment income "in" the trust. To the surprise of few, the I.R.S. ruled that the property was fully taxable in the estate of the grantor-decedent under § 2036, § 2038 and § 2033. See Rev.Rul. 75–259, 1975–2 C.B. 361. And see Estate of McCabe v. U.S., 475 F.2d 1142 (Ct.Cl.1973).

Another intra-family application of § 2036(a)(1) lies in the so-called private or family annuity transaction. Such a transaction involves a transfer, not in contemplation of death, to another person (usually a member of the same family) in return for a promise to make periodic payments to the transferor for his or her lifetime. In such an event, courts sometimes have held that the payments are not income from the transferred property so as to include the property in the estate of the decedent under § 2036. See, *e.g.,* Estate of Sarah A. Bergan, 1 T.C. 543 (1943), Acq., 1943 C.B. 2. In other instances, for example a transfer in return for promised payments that are geared to the income from the property or in which the transferred property stands as security for annuity payments, inclusion in the gross estate of the transferor has been required. See *e.g.,* Estate of Fry, 9 T.C. 503 (1947); Tips v. Bass, 21 F.2d 460 (W.D.Tex.1927). The principles to be applied in determining the tax consequences of the transfer of appreciated property for a private annuity contract in an intra-family exchange have been set forth in a Revenue Ruling. See Rev.Rul. 69–74, 1969–1 C.B. 43. See also §§ 43, 44, *infra.*

One last § 2036 annuity problem remains to be mentioned. If a person transfers cash or other property to a commercial insurance or annuity company in return for a combination single-premium life insurance and annuity package, the question may arise whether the proceeds of the insurance policies on the life of the decedent, although payable to named beneficiaries and irrevocably assigned by the insured, should be included in the estate of the decedent under § 2036. The Supreme Court of the United States, in Fidelity-Philadelphia Trust Co. v. Smith, 356 U.S. 274 (1958), held that the insurance proceeds payable to the named beneficiaries were not includable in the estate of the decedent. The court held that the annuities arose from the personal obligations of the insurance companies which were in no way conditioned on the continued existence of the life insurance contracts. The court said that the Commissioner could not, by aggregating the two types of policies in one investment, conclude that by receiving the annuities the decedent had retained income from the life insurance contract, for § 2036 purposes.

The amount to be included in a gross estate under § 2036(a)(1) has been determined by the Supreme Court to include not only the original property constituting the trust corpus but also accumulated income. U. S. v. O'Malley, 383 U.S. 627 (1966). This rule contrasts with that applicable under old § 2035, where income accumulated between the date of the gift and the grantor's death is not includable in the gross estate, Comm. v. Gidwitz' Estate, 196 F.2d 813 (7th Cir., 1952), apparently since decedent retains no power over income in a plain § 2035 transfer. Perhaps, however, the Supreme Court's decision in *O'Malley* casts a shadow over the § 2035 rule previously established in Circuit Courts of Appeal.

§ 2036(c) and "Estate Freezes". One objective in planning the estate of a wealthy taxpayer often is to minimize the growth in value of assets retained by the client until death, while passing interim appreciation to the next generation free of transfer taxes. Sometimes this principle simply suggests that the elderly parent retain income producing bonds but give growth stock from his or her portfolio by inter vivos transfers to children to "get the growth out of the estate".

A well-known estate freezing technique for a person who owns all, or a large portion, of the stock of a corporation is to divide the equity ownership into voting preferred shares (representing most of the corporation's net or equity value) and non-voting common shares (having little present value but standing in a position to appreciate rapidly if the corporation enjoys future success). This is sometimes termed an "old-to-young recapitalization" when coupled with the next step, a gift of the common shares to one or more of the children or grandchildren. The senior generation would keep the voting control (at least for a while) and the preferred dividend and liquidation rights. It would give away the chance for big growth in value of the shareholders' interests.

The I.R.S. had attacked these techniques and limited their effectiveness, by rulings, but the technique remained essentially viable.

Section 2036(b), added in 1976, moved in a cognate way to support the I.R.S. See § 33 of this text, *infra*. It provided, in § 2036(b)(1), that retention of the right to vote shares of stock of a controlled corporation shall be considered to be a retention of the transferred property. Section 2036(b)(2) defines a controlled corporation and § 2036(b)(3) announces that, for purposes of applying § 2035 as to § 2036(b)(1), the relinquishment or cessation of voting rights should be treated as a transfer of property made by the decedent. But these rules focussed not on the estate freeze by recapitalization and gift, but rather the retention of voting power of stock itself transferred to the founder's children, through a trust, voting trust or shareholders' voting agreement. Section 2036(b) applies only to a retention (or later release) of voting rights *in the transferred stock*. The division between voting preferred stock and non-voting common (growth) stock was not directly addressed.

In 1990, Congress enacted §§ 2701–2704 to deal with valuation problems created, in part, by estate-freeze schemes. Section 2701 attempts to thwart the recapitalization-and-gift variety of estate freeze by valuing the retained interest of distribution rights at zero, thus subjecting the donor to a gift tax on the full value of the stock transferred. Section 2701 applies only to a transfer of an interest in a corporation or partnership, to or for the benefit of the transferor's family, that is made after October 8, 1990. This section is very complex and should be consulted directly, along with the regulations at § 25.2701, for further detail. See also the discussion at § 48A *infra*.

Section 2702 prescribes valuation rules for retained interests resulting from transfers of interests in trust to or for the benefit of the transferor's family. Sections 2703 and 2704 provide for treatment of options, agreements, and lapses in voting rights.

[Sections 2701–2704 replace former § 2036(c), which was enacted in 1987, amended in 1988, and retroactively repealed in 1990 [P.L. 101–508, § 11601(c)]. Former section 2036(c) provided that if a person who held a substantial interest in an enterprise transferred property having a disproportionately large share of the potential appreciation in such person's interest while retaining an interest in the income of, or rights in the enterprise, the retention interest would be considered to be a retention of the enjoyment *of the transferred property.* Consequently, it (the transferred common stock) would be includable in the gross estate of the transferor.]

Some room may remain for creative estate freezes. See Kasner, Reverse Recapitalizations and Other Planning Techniques Available Under The Chapter 14 Regulations, 45 Major Tax Planning, p. 11–1 (1993); and see Coplan and Gerson, Estate Freeze Transactions Not Covered By Chapter 14, The Tax Adviser, Jan. 1992, pp. 32–33.

§ 32. Revocable Transfers and Powers to Alter, Amend, Terminate or Affect Enjoyment—§§ 2038 and 2036(a)(2)

If a property owner makes a transfer during his life and if at the time of his or her death the enjoyment of the property remains subject to a change through the exercise of a power held by him to alter, amend, revoke, or terminate the transfer, or where any such power is relinquished within three years of his death, the property subject to such power will be included in the decedent's gross estate. See I.R.C. § 2038(a). Here too, the decedent has kept too many "strings attached" to be allowed to avoid the estate tax. I.R.C. § 2038(b) provides that the described power shall be considered to exist on the date of the decedent's death even if the exercise of that power is subject to some precedent giving of notice or even though the alteration or amendment will take place only after the expiration of a stated period after the exercise of the power, whether or not before the date of the decedent's death notice has been given or the power has in fact been exercised. If a power applies only to a portion of the trust corpus, such as a right to accumulate income from a given percentage of the trust corpus, only that percentage of the corpus will be included in the gross estate. See Industrial Trust Co. v. Comm., 165 F.2d 142 (1st Cir. 1947).

Section 2038, like § 2036(a)(1), is a "*grantor* section" and applies only where the property whose enjoyment is subject to the power was at some point owned and transferred by the decedent. Unlike the language of other grantor sections, however, § 2038 does not require that the power over the enjoyment be *retained* by the decedent; it is enough that the power be *held* by him at his death. The purpose and policy of this rule is evident; if the transferor can get the property back by revoking or terminating the transfer, he is for all practical purposes the owner of the property until his power disappears at his death. The section goes further than that, however, and includes a power to alter or amend the transfer in such a way as to affect the enjoyment of the property. Again the theory seems to be that such power is an important attribute of ownership and for tax purposes should be treated as tantamount to ownership of the property at death.

The estate tax should not be subject to avoidance by a transfer inter vivos when substantial ownership rights have been retained or reacquired by the decedent.

Reservation of a power to alter or amend a transfer of property will result in inclusion of the property in the gross estate even though the power could not be exercised in favor of the decedent or his estate. See, *e.g.,* Porter v. Comm., 288 U.S. 436 (1933). Therefore, under § 2038, a power to name new beneficiaries of a trust or to change the beneficial interest among a limited class of beneficiaries, or to shift the proportionate income shares among persons enjoying the income, or the power to accumulate income even though the named beneficiaries have a vested right to the ultimate receipt of the income, will produce inclusion in the gross estate.

If, however, the power is governed by some objective, ascertainable external standard, such as a power to invade principal for the benefit of an income beneficiary only in the event of prolonged illness, the estate tax can be avoided. The standard limits the holder of the power and makes him or her less than substantially the owner of the property.

For example, in Estate of Wilson v. Comm., 13 T.C. 869 (1949), affirmed 187 F.2d 145 (3rd Cir. 1951), no inclusion under §§ 2038 and 2036(a)(2) resulted because of the standard applicable. Although payments of interest or principal could be accelerated in the event of need for educational purposes or because of illness or for any other good reason, the court held that this provision did not give the decedent the kind of power contemplated by §§ 2038 and 2036(a)(2). Similarly, in Estate of Wier v. Comm., 17 T.C. 409 (1951), Acq., 1952–1 C.B. 4, the court held that there would not be inclusion under § 2038 [or under § 2036(a)(2)] since the decedent was limited by an external standard in connection with the power to invade corpus. The language of the trust instrument referred to the intent that the daughter (of the transferor) should be properly maintained, educated, and supported in the manner appropriate to her station in life and that if, in the discretion and judgment of the trustees (including decedent), it were necessary for that purpose to use all of the income or even all of the corpus, it should be their duty to see that the daughter of the transferor was properly maintained, educated and supported. So, in general it can be said that when the power is limited by an external standard which restricts the power to definite amounts or uses which a court could enforce, the power is not deemed to be one which requires inclusion of the property in the decedent's gross estate. Many cases have dealt with the question whether a particular standard is sufficiently specific and enforceable to satisfy this test.

Under § 2038, inclusion will result whether the grantor holds the forbidden power alone or with another person, whether adverse, friendly or independent. One exception is specified by the Regulations which provide that § 2038 does not apply if the grantor's power is exercisable only with the consent of all parties having an interest (vested or contingent) in the transferred property and if the power adds nothing to the rights of the parties under local law. See Regs. § 20.2038–1(a)(2). (The Supreme Court decided, in Helvering v. Helmholz, 296 U.S. 93 (1935) that a § 2038 power held jointly with all persons having a beneficial interest in the trust was exempt from the reach of the federal estate tax. This decision accounts for the Regulations to the same effect, but is hard to reconcile with the statutory language which applies to powers to revoke held "in conjunction with any other person.") A § 2038 power held by a third person alone, of course, will not result in application of § 2038 to the decedent.

Section 2038 will require inclusion in the gross estate of a decedent who has made a transfer of property in trust during his life and provided for the income to be paid to his wife for her life, remainder at her death to their children, if the grantor retained a power to invade the corpus of the trust for the benefit of the wife (and income beneficiary). Similarly, § 2038 will produce inclusion if he retained a power to cause the income to be accumulated during the wife's life and distributed at her death to the remainderman. In fact, § 2038 would cause inclusion in the event of such power even if the income beneficiary and the remainderman were one and the same person. In other words, a power to affect the time of possession and enjoyment of the property and the nature of that possession and enjoyment will be regarded as a

§ 2038 power with the result that the property subject to that power will be included in the gross estate of the grantor or transferor. Such powers include, for example, a power to terminate a trust and thus give the income beneficiary an immediate fee interest, or a power to accumulate income and have it distributed to the one person who is both income beneficiary and remainderman at the expiration of a period of time. See Regs. § 20.2038–1(a).

§ 33. Powers to Designate the Persons Who Shall Enjoy or Possess Property or Income—§ 2036(a)(2)

I.R.C. § 2036(a)(2) contains rules that much resemble and often overlap with the rules of § 2038. Under § 2036(a)(2), the gross estate shall include the value of all property to the extent of any interest of which the decedent has made a transfer under which he has retained for his life or a similar period the right, either alone or in conjunction with any person, to designate the persons who shall possess or enjoy the property or the income therefrom. This power, to determine who will actually possess or enjoy property earlier transferred or the income from it is much like a § 2038 power to affect the enjoyment of the property through an exercise of a power to alter or amend, revoke or terminate.

Thus it may generally be said that these two statutory sections draw into the gross estate the value of any interest in property which the decedent has transferred during his life if the enjoyment of that property or its income is subject to a substantial measure of control by him at the time of his death. In State Street Trust Co. v. U. S., 263 F.2d 635 (1st Cir. 1959), § 2036(a)(2) was held to include property transferred in trust because there was a very broad investment management power in the trustees and the grantor was one of the co-trustees. The Court found that this broad power allowed the trustee to shift enjoyment between the life beneficiary and the remainderman through its choice of high-income yield investments or no-income investments. However, the Commissioner has not had great success in pushing the broad doctrine of this case very far, and the 1st Circuit has overruled its prior *State St.* decision, in Old Colony Trust Co. v. U. S., 423 F.2d 601 (1st Cir. 1970), but because the settlor-trustee had also retained the power to allocate receipts and expenditures between income and principal accounts, inclusion was required. The Court held that purely administrative powers are not sufficient retention of dominion and control to warrant inclusion in the grantor's gross estate. It went on to say, however, that an express power to distribute income, not limited to an ascertainable standard, would cause inclusion. More recently, in Byrum v. U. S., 408 U.S. 125 (1972), the Supreme Court held that the decedent did not hold a § 2036(a)(2) power (over corporate stock transferred in trust for his children) by virtue of retaining voting and other control over the corporation and hence over its dividend policies or by retaining a power to vote the transferred shares, veto their

sale by the trustee, approve or disapprove investment decisions or remove the trustee.   Compare
Rev.Rul. 67–54, 1967–1 C.B. 269 (involving non-
voting stock; result contrary to *Byrum*; revoked by
Rev. Rul. 81–15, 1981–1 C.B. 457.

The Tax Reform Act of 1976, in response to the
Byrum decision, amended § 2036 to include in the
decedent's gross estate the value of transferred
stock in a "controlled corporation," if the decedent
retains the right to vote such stock.   For the purpose of § 2036, a corporation is controlled only if,
after the transfer and within three years of his
death, the decedent had the right (alone or in
conjunction with any other person), to vote 20% or
more of the total voting stock of the corporation, or
the decedent or his family (*i.e.,* using the constructive ownership rules of I.R.C. § 318) owned 20% or
more of the total voting stock.   In addition, the
cessation or relinquishment of the right to vote the
transferred stock is a "transfer" of property for
purposes of § 2035.   Thus if the decedent gives up
the voting rights within three years of death, the
stock may nonetheless be included in his gross
estate.   See § 2036(b).   This "*Byrum* amendment"
to § 2036 has its own special effective date; it
applies to all transfers after June 22, 1976.   It
should be noted that this amendment did not fully
adopt the position taken by the Service in *Byrum*.
Section 2036 only applies explicitly if the decedent
keeps voting rights in the *transferred* stock.   Where
he, for example gives up those rights, even though
still controlling the corporation and therefore its

dividend policy, and therefore the "enjoyment" of the income from the stock, § 2036(b) does not apply. It is, however, possible that the fact that Congress has now shown itself sensitive to these subtle manifestations of control will compel courts in the future to be more solicitous of the Service's attempts to bring such arrangements within the scope of § 2036 generally.

Another "strings attached" transfer consists of a "preferred stock estate freeze" (or similar technique) in which the owner of an enterprise transfers, for example, common stock in the corporation to his adult children while he is alive but retains preferred stock for its income. By doing so, he may seek to transfer most of the future appreciation and growth in value of the enterprise to his children and remove it from his estate while it has relatively low current market value for transfer tax purposes, but retain a disproportionately large share of income or rights and control for himself. See § 31, on § 2036(c) and "Estate Freezes", above. Former § 2036(c) tried to reach such dispositions by an inclusion rule; the result was unsatisfactory. Now this estate planning device is met by the special valuation rules of I.R.C. §§ 2701–2704. These rules discourage or counteract such transfers by placing little value on some retained interests and high (taxable) value on the transferred interests, for gift tax purposes. See § 48A, below, for an explanation of these rules.

Neither § 2038 nor § 2036 will require inclusion in the case of a transfer made for an adequate and full consideration in money or money's worth. Section 2036(a)(2), like § 2038, applies as a "grantor section" and only when the power to designate covers property transferred by the decedent. Unlike § 2038, § 2036(a)(2) applies only when the decedent has transferred property and under the transfer has *retained* the described power; § 2036(a)(2) will not apply to an acquired or reacquired power. However, under the Regulations, an interest or right is treated as having been retained or reserved if at the time of the transfer there was an understanding, express or implied, that the interest or right would later be conferred. See Regs. § 20.2036–1(a)(ii).

§ 34. §§ 2038 and 2036(a)(2)—Overlaps, Conflicts and Congruence

Much the same kinds of power that fall under § 2038 will also be taxable under § 2036(a)(2). A power to accumulate income for the benefit of remaindermen or to invade corpus for the benefit of the income beneficiary will constitute a power "to designate the person who will possess or enjoy the property or the income therefrom" under § 2036(a)(2). A power to revoke a trust set up for the grantor's spouse for life, remainder to their child, would produce inclusion to the same extent under § 2038 or § 2036(a)(2).

It is not clear, however, whether a power to affect only the timing of possession or enjoyment, for example by accumulating income for distribution to the income beneficiary at a later time, or a power to invade corpus for the benefit of those who ultimately will enjoy it if it is not invaded, will be treated as a taxable power over some or all the property for purposes of § 2036(a)(2). Since those powers will be regarded as taxable powers under § 2038, it would seem to make little difference whether they also are regarded as powers also fitting the description of § 2036(a)(2). The additional application of a second statutory rule can make a difference, however, if the interest or amount of property to be included under the second rule of inclusion is greater than the amount to be included under the first rule. This problem leads us into difficult intricacies of §§ 2038 and 2036(a)(2).

Under the terms of § 2038, the decedent's gross estate shall include the value of all property to the extent of any interest of which he has made a transfer where the enjoyment "thereof" was subject at his death to one of the described powers. This statutory language suggests that only the interest whose enjoyment was subject to the described power will be included in the gross estate. The Regulations support this interpretation, in saying that "only the value of an interest in property subject to a power to which § 2038 applies is included in the decedent's gross estate under § 2038." See Regs. § 20.2038–1(a). Thus, if the transferor retains a power to affect the enjoyment only of the life estate but not the remainder, it would seem that only the value of the life estate will be included in his gross estate, not the remainder. Similarly, if his power extends only to the remainder interest or interests, it would seem that under § 2038 only those interests will be included since only they are subject to his § 2038 power.

The language of I.R.C. § 2036 arguably is somewhat broader. It requires inclusion of all property to the extent of any interest therein of which the decedent has made a transfer under which he has retained the prohibited power. This language suggests that it is not just the property subject to the prohibited power but rather the entire property transferred that will be included in the gross estate.

The Regulations under § 2036 say that if a decedent retained or reserved an interest or right with respect to a part only of the property transferred by him, the amount to be included in his gross estate under § 2036 is only a corresponding proportion of the amount described "in the preceding sentence." Regs. § 20.2036–1(a)(ii). The preceding sentence of the regulations specifies that if the decedent retained or reserved an interest or right with respect to all of the property transferred by him the amount to be included under § 2036 is the value of the entire property, less only the value of any outstanding income interest which is not subject to the decedent's interest or right and which is actually being enjoyed by another person at the time of the decedent's death. See Regs. § 20.2036–1(a)(ii). However, this language in the regulations is susceptible to an interpretation that would make it refer only to different "parts of the property" described in physical terms. In other words, if both Blackacre and Whiteacre are conveyed in trust by a husband whose trust provides that income shall be paid to his wife for life and remainder to his children at her death and if he retains a power to designate who shall possess or enjoy the property or the income only from Blackacre, not from Whiteacre, the language of the regulations suggests that only the value of Blackacre is to be included in the gross estate of the husband under § 2036. Suppose, in contrast, that the husband has retained a power to cause the trust to accumulate income from both Blackacre and Whiteacre and add to corpus, such that the accumulated income will be paid over to the remainderman, the children, at the death of the wife. An argument can be made that under § 2036(a)(2) the entire property would be includable but that under § 2038 only the value of the income beneficiary's interest is includable, because the interest of the remainderman cannot be diminished and therefore is fixed as to time and enjoyment and amount.

The Commissioner has given some indication of his interpretation of the inclusion problem under § 2038. In Rev.Rul. 70–513, 1970–2 C.B. 194, the Commissioner ruled that the amount includable in the decedent's gross estate was limited to the remainder interest in the following situation: Transferor created a trust and gave his son a life estate with the corpus to be distributed to the beneficiaries of the son's estate. Trustees were given discretionary power to terminate the trust at any time and pay the corpus over to the income beneficiary, but they could not exercise that power without the decedent's consent. (Therefore, the decedent is viewed as holding that power for purposes of § 2038). The ruling determined that only the remainder interest would be included under § 2038 because inclusion under that section is limited to the value of the property interest that was subject to the decedent's power. Therefore, since the enjoyment of the life estate was not subject to change through the exercise of the decedent's power, only the value of the remainder interest was held includable. One might say, however, that the enjoyment of the life estate was subject to change because it would be ended if the power to terminate the trust were exercised. To be sure, the same person who was the life beneficiary would then enjoy the property as its outright owner, rather than its life tenant, but he would enjoy the property then through a different interest.

It is not possible at this time finally to state a single broad principle to settle the controversy whether the includable interest under § 2038 can differ from the interest includable under § 2036(a)(2). One Supreme Court case, Lober v. U. S., 346 U.S. 335 (1953), suggests that the inclusion would be the same. A similar inference can be made from other cases. See *e.g.*, Struthers v. Kelm, 218 F.2d 810 (8th Cir. 1955). However, there is not a sufficient supply of authoritative decisions squarely on point to provide a definite answer. In light of the fact that inclusion required by §§ 2038 and 2036 may not be identical and that the Commissioner will seek to apply both sections in order to make sure to include the larger amount, representatives of the taxpayer must look forward to the necessity to argue or negotiate with respect to both statutory sections and to fight the claim that the larger amount should be included.

One very important limitation on the reach of § 2036(a)(2), compared to § 2038, is a statement in the regulations to the effect that the phrase "right to designate the person or persons who shall possess or enjoy the transferred property or the income therefrom" does not include a power over the transferred property itself which does not affect the enjoyment of the income received or earned during the decedent's life. But, the regulations note that § 2038 may require inclusion of property in the gross estate on account of such a power. See Regs. § 20.2036–1(b)(3).

An important application of § 2036(a)(2) and § 2038 is in the area of gifts to minors under the Uniform Gifts to Minors Act. See Rev.Rul. 59–357, 1959–2 C.B. 212. The foregoing ruling indicates that the value of property transferred under these acts will be included in the gross estate of the donor for federal estate tax purposes if the property is given in contemplation of death (within three years of the donor's death) or the donor appoints himself custodian and dies while serving in that capacity. Citing Regs. § 20.2038–1(c), the Service reasoned that the powers of the custodian under the Act were sufficiently broad to give the grantor/custodian power to withhold or alter enjoyment of the custodial property. When read with the cases discussed in

§ 33, *supra,* it becomes obvious that a grantor cannot hide from the far-reaching inclusionary rules of § 2036(a)(2) and § 2038 behind the mask of a fiduciary. This is important to remember, when deciding between a neutral fiduciary and the grantor as a fiduciary for gifts made in trust or under the Uniform Act or in deciding what powers to give to a grantor/fiduciary. The authorities agree that purely administrative powers or powers limited by an ascertainable standard will not trigger the inclusionary rules, while broad discretionary powers to accumulate or expend trust property for the beneficiaries is a "right" under § 2036(a)(2) or "power" under § 2038. In all other circumstances, the ruling states, the custodial property is includable only in the gross estate of the donee.

When property is to be included in the gross estate under § 2038 or § 2036(a)(2), the property to be included is valued at the date of the death of the decedent, under I.R.C. § 2031(a), unless the executor elects, under I.R.C. § 2032, to apply the value of the property at the alternate valuation date, usually a date six months after the decedent's death.

Many problems of valuation result if the property transferred during life has been squandered, converted, depreciated, improved, or transferred by the donee between the time of the transfer and death or if income earned in the interim has been accumulated. In general, the problem becomes whether to apply the statute literally so as to include in the gross estate only the value of the physical property actually transferred or whether accumulated income, stock dividends, property into which the transfer property has been converted, and improvements should also be included in the valuation. The answers to many of these questions remain uncertain; answers to some can be found in various rulings and cases too voluminous and variegated to summarize here. See § 51, *infra*.

§ 35. Transfers Taking Effect at Death— § 2037

Section 2037 of the Internal Revenue Code is captioned "Transfers Taking Effect At Death." Under this statute, property transferred during life by the decedent will be included in his or her gross estate if two conditions are met. The first condition is that possession or enjoyment of the property, through ownership of an interest transferred, can be obtained only by *surviving* the decedent. Secondly, decedent must have retained some form of *reversionary* interest in the property which, immediately before the death of the decedent, exceeded 5% of the value of such property. A "reversionary interest" includes the possibility that the property will return to the decedent's estate or may be subject to a power of disposition by him or her. See I.R.C. § 2037(b).

An example of a § 2037 transfer will help explain its rules. Alice transfers property in trust during her life; the trust's terms provide that income shall be paid to Ben, annually, for as long as Alice lives, the remainder at her death to be paid to Charles if he is then living; if Charles is not then living, the property is to revert to Alice (meaning Alice's estate). Another example would be: Alice transfers property in trust, income to be accumulated for Alice's life and at her death corpus and accumulated income to be paid to Charles if he is living; if not, all property and income to revert to Alice. In each of these examples, the survivorship test of § 2037 is met. Charles can take possession and enjoyment of his interest only by surviving Alice. If the value of her reversionary interest exceeds 5% of the property transferred, § 2037 will cause inclusion in her gross estate. To sum it up, her transfer to Charles will take effect only at her death; until then, it remains uncertain whether Charles will ever possess and enjoy his interest. Alice's heirs may "get it back," to the disappointment of Charles' heirs. Alice's transfer of the interest to Charles has not been completed during her life and remains incomplete until her death.

In contrast with the foregoing dispositions covered by § 2037, consider the following situation, which does not satisfy all the tests of § 2037. H creates a trust to pay the income to W for life, remainder to S if S is then living; if S fails to survive W, reversion to H or his estate. Suppose also that H dies while W is still living. Even if the reversionary interest in H is worth more than 5% of the property, § 2037 will not require inclusion of anything in H's gross estate. S need not survive H in order to come into possession of his interest. All S has to do is survive W, in order to take possession or enjoyment of the property through his remainder interest.

Now consider the rules of § 2037 as applied to this example. H places property in trust, the income to be accumulated during H's life, with principal and accumulated income to be distributed to his children at his death, but if none has survived, then to his wife. Section 2037 will *not* require inclusion in H's gross estate because he has retained no reversionary interest. If none of H's children are alive at his death the property will pass to his wife or her estate, not to H's estate.

The purpose of § 2037, a purpose that can sometimes be lost in the intricacies of its rules, seems clear. When a transfer will take effect only at the death of the decedent because only at that time can someone be sure that he or she will possess or enjoy the property and if, all along, there existed a material likelihood that the interest transferred would return to the decedent or his estate, the decedent had not fully parted with the property (to the extent of the interest transferred) before death and the property should be included in the gross estate. Such a transfer resembles a testamentary transfer, under which a named beneficiary cannot be sure he or she will possess or enjoy the property until the death of the decedent, since the decedent might tear up the will and transfer the property to others by will or intestacy. In other words, an inter-vivos transfer with the retained reversionary interest and the survivorship condition is not a completed lifetime transfer but amounts to a substitute for a death transfer. Historically, § 2037 is the residuum, after § 2036 and § 2038 had been carved out, of the original, broad rule in the 1916 statute which attempted to encompass all transfers where 'possession or enjoyment of the property could take place only at or after the death of the decedent.'

If either the survivorship or the reversionary interest requirement is not met, § 2037 will not include the property or any interest in it in the gross estate of the decedent. In that event, however, some other section may include the property or some interest in it in the gross estate. For example, if the reversionary interest is present but the survivorship requirement is not met, § 2037 will not produce any inclusion, but § 2033 will cause inclusion of the decedent's remainder or other reversionary interest, if that interest survived the death of the decedent and transferred then to someone else. See Regs. § 20.2037–1(e) Example (1), and discussion of the requirements of I.R.C. § 2033, *supra,* § 16.

Section 2037 is a *"grantor* section" and applies only to the decedent who earlier transferred the property, *retaining* the necessary reversionary interest.

I.R.C. § 2037 can apply when the measuring life which measures the interest in question is the life of the donor or grantor. To detect the application of § 2037 when the grantor's life is the measuring life proves relatively easy. In that event, the grantor's death is the occasion for a shift of possession or enjoyment or a new certainty about the possession or enjoyment of the property.

The survivorship requirement can also be met even if the grantor's life is not the "measuring" life. To illustrate, suppose Harold places property in trust during his life and the trust terms grant income to Wilma for as long as she shall live; at Wilma's death, the trust shall terminate and be distributed to Harold if he is then living; if not, everything shall be paid to Samuel and his heirs. To take possession and enjoyment of the property through ownership of his interest, Samuel must survive Harold, whether Harold dies before Wilma or not. If Samuel does not survive Harold, Samuel's heirs, rather than Samuel himself, will take the property if Harold does not outlive Wilma. In this example, the donor's life is not the measuring life and his death is not the time of shifting of interests. Nevertheless, § 2037 will apply since the survivorship test is met and the reversionary test too, if Harold's reversion exceeds 5% of the property's value.

If someone can take possession of the interest that is being tested under § 2037 either by surviving the decedent or if some other condition is met, there will not be inclusion under § 2037 (unless the other event is unreal and the decedent in fact dies before the other event occurs). See Regs. § 20.-2037–1(b). No interest shall be included in the decedent's gross estate under § 2037 if possession or enjoyment of the property could have been obtained by any beneficiary during the decedent's life through the exercise of a general power of appointment that was in fact exercisable immediately before the decedent's death.   See I.R.C. § 2037(b)(2).

If possession under an interest has commenced during the life of the decedent but might terminate and if that possibility of termination will not end until the death of the decedent, the survivorship test of § 2037 will be deemed to have been met. See, *e.g.,* Thacher v. Comm., 20 T.C. 474 (1953), Acq., 1954–1 C.B. 7.

Like the other incomplete transfer sections of the estate tax, § 2037 contains an exception for a transfer that is a bona-fide sale for an adequate and full consideration in money or money's worth.   Section 2037 also contains some special rules.   Under § 2037(b), the term "reversionary interest" includes a possibility that property transferred by the decedent may return to him or to his estate or may be subject to a power of disposition by him, but the term does not include a possibility that the income alone from such property may be returned to him or become subject to a power of disposition by him. [I.R.C. § 2036 might include property in the gross estate by reason of such rights.   See Regs. § 20.-2037–1(c)(2).]   As the Regulations state, the term "reversionary interest" is not used in a technical sense but refers to any reserved right under which the transferred property shall or may be returned to the grantor.   Thus, it encompasses an interest arising either by the express terms of the instrument of the transfer or by operation of law.   The term "reversionary interest" does not include the possibility that the decedent during his lifetime might have received back an interest in transferred property by inheritance from the estate of another person or under the statutory right of a spouse to receive a portion of the decedent's estate. See Regs. § 20.2037–1(c)(2).

Under § 2037, the important question is not one about the vesting of an interest but rather is one of deferred or uncertain possession and enjoyment of property through the ownership of an interest. Therefore, even if a beneficiary can get a vested interest before the decedent's death, that is to say without surviving him, it will be a § 2037 transfer if the beneficiary cannot get possession or enjoyment until the death of the decedent. If possession and enjoyment will shift from the decedent himself, § 2037 can apply (and § 2036(a)(1) or other sections may also apply). If possession and enjoyment will shift from someone else at the death of the decedent or because the beneficiary survived the decedent, then § 2037 also may apply.

The 5% rule of the statute refers to the value of the reversionary interest, not to the amount that is to be included in the gross estate. Thus, if the survivorship test is met and if a reversionary interest exceeds 5% of the value of the property, much more than the value of the reversionary interest alone can be included under § 2037. As another example of the difference between the 5% rule and the rule of inclusion, the value of a preceding life estate would be taken into account when comparing the reversionary interest with the value of the property transferred, but the value of that preceding life estate would be excluded when ascertaining the interest to be included in the gross estate under § 2037.

The question of what interest is to be included under § 2037 is not an easy one, but can be outlined by several examples. Suppose, for example, that A transfers property in trust providing that the income from the property shall be paid to W for A's life and at A's death the corpus to be paid to W if she is then living and if not to A's estate. Assume that W, the wife of A, survives A and that A's reversion was worth 5% or more of the transferred property. In that event, the entire value of the trust property will be includable, since all of it is the value of the interest transferred by the decedent to take effect in possession or enjoyment at his death. No subtraction is made for the wife's outstanding interest at the death of A since at A's death her interest is no longer outstanding. One must view and value the interest at A's death.

Suppose, however, that A transfers property in trust and provides that all the income shall be paid to W, his wife, for her life and at her death the corpus shall be paid to A, the grantor, if he is then living and if not to his son or his son's estate. Assume that the son and the wife survive A. In that event the wife's interest is not dependent on A's death; she got immediate enjoyment of the property for her life, whether A, the grantor, lives or dies. Therefore, the value of her interest would not be included in A's gross estate under § 2037.

However, the son or the beneficiary of the son's estate must survive the decedent to take possession or enjoyment of their interests. Therefore, those interests will be included in the gross estate of the decedent.

Further examples demonstrating the reach of § 2037 can be found in the Regulations. See Regs. § 20.2037–1(e).

The value of the retained reversionary interest is to be determined immediately before the death of the decedent by the usual methods of valuation, including tables of mortality and actuarial principles.

In W. S. Hall v. U. S., 353 F.2d 500 (7th Cir. 1965) the court ruled that the valuation of a reversionary interest under § 2037 should include not just mortality tables but also evidence of the individual health of the decedent. Thus it may be possible, for example, to show that a holder of a reversionary interest was in poor health prior to death so that his or her actual life expectancy was markedly shorter than would be indicated by actuarial tables. In determining the value of a possibility that property may be subject to a power of disposition by the decedent, that possibility is to be valued as if it were a possibility that such property would return to the decedent or to his estate.

Because the logic of the operation of § 2037 is not as easy to grasp or keep in mind for someone who is not working with such material frequently, it may prove desirable to test the application of § 2037 in a somewhat mechanical fashion, under its own rules, whenever a lifetime disposition of property has been made and the question is raised whether any estate tax consequences are presented. In this connection, it is most important to remember that the section employs two principal tests, the *survivorship* condition and the *reversionary interest* requirement, both of which must be satisfied for § 2037 to cause some property or interest to be included in the gross estate.

§ 36. Reciprocal Trusts—Who Is the Grantor?

For purposes of §§ 2035–2038, decedent must have been the grantor, donor, or transferor of property to be included in his gross estate. However, substance will override form in this matter and some possibility exists that a person will be treated as the grantor of a trust or the transferor of property for purposes of §§ 2035–2038 even though he is not apparently or technically the transferor. For example, if one person transfers property or pays money to a third party to cause that third party to make a transfer in trust with income to be used for the benefit of the first person for life, remainder at death to someone else, the first person would be viewed, quite properly, as the grantor or transferor of property with a retained life estate. Use of a "dummy" or a "straw man" or a "conduit" will not permit someone to escape I.R.C. §§ 2035–2038.

A particular example of the attribution of transfers or trusts to someone other than the apparent transferor involves the estate planning technique called "reciprocal trusts." A simple example of this technique would be the following. Husband and wife, each owning separate property, each establishes a trust and transfers the property under terms such that the income from the property he or she transferred would be paid to the other spouse for that other spouse's life, remainder at the death of the other spouse to the creator of the trust. In the event that these trusts were of approximately equal value and were established in consideration of each other, each trust will be attributed to the other spouse, on the grounds that the other provided consideration for that trust by establishing an equivalent trust with reciprocal benefits. The husband will be treated as the settlor of the trust established by his wife for his benefit, and vice-versa.

If cross attribution of reciprocal or crossed trusts is done, it then remains simply to determine what the tax consequences will be in view of the property that is deemed to have been transferred, the powers retained or held and the statutory principles of inclusion and valuation in §§ 2035–2038.

Over the years, some cases found that the reciprocal trusts doctrine was not applicable on the facts presented either because there was no concerted action, or because other motives produced the quite simultaneous transfers and the transfers had not really been made directly in consideration of each other. See, *e.g.,* Estate of Ruxton v. Comm., 20 T.C. 487 (1953) (Acq., 1953–2 C.B. 6). It even proved possible for inconsistent decisions to be reached when the doctrine was applied to one spouse but not the other. See Estate of Guenzel v. Comm., 258 F.2d 248 (8th Cir. 1958). The net result was a developing deficiency in the tax law in that trusts could be established by well-to-do spouses who could escape the estate tax even though the spouses granted to each other powers over the trust property that provided each with essentially the same controls as would have resulted from reserving powers, in which event the trust property would have been included in the gross estate of the decedent who reserved such powers.

This problem has been met by the decision of the United States Supreme Court in U. S. v. Estate of Grace, 395 U.S. 316 (1969). There the Supreme Court held that for the reciprocal attribution to be made trusts need not be "in consideration of" each other in the sense of *quid pro quo*. The court ruled that if the trusts were interrelated in the sense that they were simultaneously or nearly simultaneously executed, were substantially identical in their terms and if they left the settlors in approximately the same economic position as if each had named himself or herself as beneficiary, the reciprocal trusts doctrine would be applied and each trust would be attributed to the other transferor. The subjective intent of the parties was deemed not to be crucial. After the *Grace* case, the reciprocal trust doctrine has been and will be more widely applied. By attributing each trust to the opposite spouse and applying I.R.C. §§ 2035–2038, the property viewed as having been transferred by each decedent can, as required, be included in his or her gross estate.

Presumably these same concepts will be used in order to determine the identity of the grantor for purposes of applying the Chapter 13 rules on generation-skipping transfers.

§ 37. Adequate and Full Consideration Under §§ 2035–2038

Each of the Statutory Rules of inclusion in I.R.C. §§ 2035–2038 contains an exception, cast in identical terminology, for a transfer made as a "bona-fide sale for an adequate and full consideration in money or money's worth." What these deceptively simple terms mean turns out to be complicated on further examination.

Some of the most difficult problems of "consideration" have arisen in connection with the surrender or transfer of marital rights in return for a transfer of property otherwise falling within §§ 2035–2038. Some light is shed on this problem by I.R.C. § 2043, examined earlier, which provides that any of the transfers in §§ 2035–2038 (and § 2041) made for a consideration in money or money's worth but in a transaction that is not a bona-fide sale for an *adequate* and *full* consideration in money or money's worth shall result in inclusion in the gross estate of only the excess of the fair market value at the time of death of the property otherwise to be included on account of the transaction over the value of the consideration received therefor by the decedent. See also Regs. § 20.2043–1(a). The Regulations amplify the statutory language slightly by saying that to constitute a bona-fide sale for an adequate and full consideration in money or money's worth, the transfer must have been made in good faith and the price must have been an adequate and full equivalent reducible to a money value. Subsection (b) of § 2043 goes on to provide that a relinquishment or promised relinquishment of dower or curtesy or of a statutory estate created in lieu of dower or curtesy or other marital rights in the decedent's property or estate shall not be considered to any extent a consideration in money or money's worth.

If a transaction constitutes a bona-fide sale for an adequate and full consideration in money or money's worth, there will be no inclusion in the gross estate even though the other conditions of any of §§ 2035–2038 are met. This result is entirely satisfying, since there has been no estate depletion and no evasion of the death tax by any incomplete intervivos gift. If there has not been a sale or if it was not for an adequate and full consideration in money or money's worth, the language of I.R.C. § 2043(a) indicates that if any of §§ 2035–2038 would otherwise apply, there shall be included in the gross estate only the excess of the fair market value of the property or interest otherwise to be included over the value of the consideration received by the decedent. See § 51, *infra*.

If the interest transferred during life is an interest in property which, if retained by the decedent at death, would cause inclusion of some property greater than the interest transferred, the question presented is whether the consideration received for the transfer must equal only the value of the interest transferred or must equal the value that would have been included in the gross estate had that interest been retained by the decedent, in order to fulfill the statutory language "for an adequate and full consideration in money or money's worth"? This is the problem raised in the important case, U. S. v. Allen, 293 F.2d 916 (10th Cir. 1961), involving a transfer in contemplation of death of a § 2036(a)(1) life estate. See § 31, *supra*.

There is no doubt that § 2035 as to gifts within three years of death (the former contemplation-of-death section) is to be read and applied together with §§ 2036–2038. So if a decedent transfers or relinquishes an interest in property within three years of death (without adequate consideration), the decedent's gross estate will include the property subject to the §§ 2036–2038 power to the extent it would be included under §§ 2036–2038 if the decedent has retained the interest or power until death. See Regs. § 20.2035–1(b). (Note that these are just the types of transfer still covered by § 2035 *as amended by E.R.T.A.*) However, if the retained interest was eventually transferred for adequate and full consideration, no inclusion would be required. So the question becomes: What is adequate and full consideration in a case where an estate tax "string" attached to property is finally sold, during life? The *Allen* case took as the measure of adequate and full consideration not the fair market value of the interest actually transferred by a decedent in contemplation of death, but the "estate tax value" of that interest, that is to say the amount of property that would have been included in the decedent's gross estate if she had not made the § 2035 transfer. In that case, in contemplation of death the taxpayer transferred a life estate worth approximately $135,000, the retention of which would have produced inclusion of approximately $900,000 under § 2036(a)(1) if the life estate had been retained. She sold the life estate and received approximately $140,000 in return. The Court held that this was not an adequate and full consideration and, therefore, it included in her gross estate the value of the corpus, less the amount of consideration received.

The approach of the *Allen* case seems sound in cases such as the *Allen* case itself, involving a transfer in contemplation of death. Whether the same approach should be applied in cases that do not involve transfers made in contemplation of death or, now, within three years of death, seems problematical. Much can be said for limiting the *Allen* approach to contemplation-of-death, or within-3-years-of-death, cases or perhaps to cases of real evasion of the estate tax. (Note that post-'81 § 2035 appears to have codified the *Allen* result.) If the *Allen* approach is applied in a pure § 2036(a)(1) case, it would tend to read out of the statute the exception for bona-fide sales for full and adequate consideration. To consider one possibility, suppose that D had placed $1,000,000 worth of Roxer Co. stock in trust, retaining an interest in himself for life with remainder at his death to his heirs. Then, at a later time, he sold his life interest in the trust property to Mr. X for an amount equal to the fair market value of that life interest. If D survived more than three years from the time of this transfer, can or should anything be included in his gross estate by reason of I.R.C. § 2036(a)(1)? The answer would seem to be negative. Thus, one might as a general rule confine the *Allen* approach to those instances where a series of step transactions produce estate tax avoidance unless that theory is applied, and especially to the three-years-of-death or contemplation-of-death situation (where, incidentally, the rules require that the included property be valued at the date of death or alternate valuation date). See § 51, *infra*.

§ 38. The Widow's Election and Adequate and Full Consideration

The widow's election has been a much discussed estate planning device, and one that depends in part on the meaning given to the concept of adequate and full consideration. (It also takes on an altogether different color after the 1981 unlimited marital deduction.) Available both in community property states and in separate property states, the so-called widow's election technique actually can be used by any testator and beneficiary regardless of their relationship and regardless of the kind of property in question. In the typical case, the election is used by a married couple whose assets consist entirely of community property and in which each has a one-half vested property interest, or by a couple in a separate property state if both own separate property.

In the usual community property disposition, the husband (likely to be the first to die) by will purports to transfer both halves of the community property to a trust from which the income is to be paid to the widow for life and the principal distributed on her death to the children. The widow is then put to an election, either to accept a life estate in the entire community property by allowing her one-half interest in all their community property to pass under his will or to insist on taking her full ownership of one-half of the property, in which event her husband's half would pass outright to the children. The husband has a testamentary power over the community property only to the extent of his one-half and therefore the widow's consent is necessary for his disposition to take effect as planned. If she elects to take under the will, she "sells" her remainder to the husband's estate in return for a life estate in his property, which she will have on top of the life interest she retains in her own property. [Alternatively, it can be said, she sells all her property for a life estate in his and in hers. But it will lead to sounder analysis if she is viewed as *retaining* a life estate in her property and *transferring* only the remainder interest.] This does not increase the husband's taxable estate but consists of an inter-vivos transfer by the widow of the remainder interest in her own share of the community property with a receipt back of a life income from her husband's property. In addition to the life estate in her own property that she has thus reserved, the widow also receives under the will a life estate in the husband's share of the community property. (In a separate property state, a parallel transaction is set up if H's will puts his separate property in trust for the wife for life, remainder to their children on condition that W transfers her separate property into the same trust. In a separate property state, the election can be given even if the widow never had any separate property. His will can bequeath her a fixed amount of his property with a choice to accept that bequest or to elect to take an income interest in a larger corpus instead.)

In either situation, the question arises whether the widow has received "consideration" which reduces the taxable amount of the widow's own transfer for gift and for estate tax purposes. If the life estate she receives under the will is wholly or partly not consideration, then her gift will consist of a larger amount and there will also be greater inclusion in her gross estate under § 2036(a)(1) since she has made a transfer of her property under which she retains the income for her life.

At the widow's death, if everything works according to plan, nothing in the trust will be included in her gross estate because she has a terminable interest both in the property contributed by her husband and in the property she transferred, while obtaining a life estate arguably as full and adequate consideration under § 2036(a)(1). Thus the widow's elec-

tion device combines the sale for consideration notion with the fact that I.R.C. § 2033 does not tax an
interest that expires at the decedent's death.

An example will illustrate this technique. For
purposes of comparison, first consider a husband
and wife in a community property state who have
$2,000,000 in wealth, all of which is community
property. If at the husband's death he wills all his
property to the wife and if she dies later she wills
all the property she then owns to their son, the
husband's gross estate will consist of approximately
the $1,000,000 he owned and at the wife's death her
gross estate will consist of approximately the
$2,000,000 the couple had accumulated or otherwise
obtained during their lives. The total gross estates
for tax purposes will be $3,000,000, approximately
$1,000,000 in the husband's estate and $2,000,000
in the wife's. (A parallel result would follow in a
separate property state, under the former, limited
marital deduction.) (The figures used are rough
and assume no depletion for taxes or support and
consumption and also disregard the possibility of
the new unlimited marital deduction.) In fact the
unlimited marital deduction may make the widow's
election an entirely outmoded technique, so long as
the deduction remains unlimited.

Now compare with the foregoing scenario the
following alternative (not yet the widow's election).
If the husband gives his wife a life estate in his
property and remainder to his son, his gross estate
will consist of approximately $1,000,000 at his
death. At the widow's death, her gross estate will

consist of approximately $1,000,000. In other words, estate tax would be based on gross estates totalling approximately $2,000,000 rather than $3,000,000. The husband's $1,000,000 is not taxed in the wife's estate since her interest in that property expired at her death. (A parallel result would be obtained in a separate property state if the husband and wife each had $1,000,000 of separate property.)

Now consider the widow's election technique. In the community property state, for example, if the wife elects to take under the husband's will and surrenders her community property interest, the husband in effect is allowed to put $2,000,000 in trust with the life estate to the wife in return for her surrender of $1,000,000, or, more properly, the remainder interest in $1,000,000 since she has retained, rather than received back, the life interest. The husband's gross estate will consist only of (approximately) $1,000,000, his share of the community property. The wife's gift to the husband's estate will consist only of the excess of the amount she transferred ($1,000,000) over the value of what she received, namely a life estate in $2,000,000, or the excess (if any) of the value of the remainder interest in her $1,000,000 over the life estate in H's $1,000,000. With careful planning the two amounts could be equalized and no gift tax would be payable. For estate tax purposes, she will again be taxed [under § 2036(a)(1) only if the value of her remainder (transferred) exceeded the value of the life estate (obtained) in the husband's share of the community property; if the two are equal, it would seem she sold her property for full and adequate consideration and § 2036(a)(1) would not apply]. If any inclusion in the wife's estate takes place, the amount included would be the value (at her death) of what she transferred minus the value (at the date of her election) of her life estate in the husband's share. There also might be a credit for any gift tax paid earlier on the same transfer. See I.R.C. § 2012(a). As a result, tax will have been based on gross estates totaling less than the $2,000,000 or $3,000,000 of the earlier examples. In a separate property state if the widow has separate property or if she sells back what she has received from her husband to the trust, it may be possible to produce much the same result.

One key problem in the widow's election is the problem of consideration. Some cases have held that, for gift tax purposes, the transfer is for full consideration and hence not taxable as a gift if the value of the life estate she gets in her husband's property equals the value of the remainder interest in her property, which she gives up. (Since she retains or receives a life interest in her own property, she has not "given" that to anyone.) Any excess would be a taxable gift. See *Siegel, infra.* (The other, less useful, way of making the same analysis is to say no gift results if the value of her $1,000,-000 property transferred (including both the life estate and remainder interests in her own property) is equalled by the value of everything she received, namely a life estate in the entire $2,000,000 of trust property.) For estate tax purposes, however, the life estate she retains in her half cannot be regarded as consideration received *by* her. (To do so would read § 2036(a)(1) out of the Code.) Hence some cases suggest she must receive a life interest in her husband's property equal in value to the whole of the property she transferred (comprehending her life estate and remainder interests in her property) to escape at least partial inclusion under § 2036(a)(1). If there is an excess, § 2036(a)(1) will cause inclusion in her gross estate, since, properly viewed, she has *retained* a life estate in property she transferred. See *Vardell* and *Gregory, infra.* However, this carries an "estate depletion" notion of consideration too far. Better analysis would be satisfied if the value of the life interest she received in the one-half equalled the value of the remainder she traded for it. And see Estate of Christ v. CIR, 480 F.2d 171 (9th Cir. 1973).

A shadow has been cast over the widow's election technique by the *Allen* case with its estate-depletion concept of full and adequate consideration. See U. S. v. Allen, 293 F.2d 916 (10th Cir. 1961), *supra* § 37. Possibly that shadow has been lengthened by the decision of the Supreme Court of the United States in U. S. v. Estate of Grace, 395 U.S. 316 (1969) although *Grace* involved a different consideration issue. The *Grace* case suggests that the Supreme Court might view the transfers involved in the widow's election as exemplified in Comm. v. Siegel, 250 F.2d 339 (9th Cir. 1957); Estate of Gregory v. Comm., 39 T.C. 1012 (1963); Zillah Mae Turman, 35 T.C. 1123 (1961); Vardell v. Comm.,

307 F.2d 688 (5th Cir. 1962) and the Supreme
Court's own decision in U. S. v. Stapf, 375 U.S. 118
(1963) as not truly involving a transfer for consideration but rather mutual gifts by the widow and the
decedent to the children. Certainly it is arguable
that in the family context no arm's length, bona-
fide sale for adequate and full consideration is likely
to have taken place. The children are the natural
objects of the bounty of both spouses and there
usually is nothing to suggest a bargaining context.

Conceivably in a family break-up involving divorce or separation, consideration might be found
when parting husband and wife deal with each
other at arm's length and make transfers for the
benefit of one of them and the children. See, *e.g.,*
U. S. v. Past, 347 F.2d 7 (9th Cir. 1965). All in all,
the widow's election must be regarded as a complex
and delicate estate planning instrument not to be
employed without careful study of all the federal
(and state) tax and non-tax issues it involves.

Would it seem to have any utility so long as the
unlimited deduction remains good law?

§ 39. Transfers Incomplete Until Transfer-
or's Death—Gift Tax Consequences

Transfers that prior passages have considered
with respect to the estate tax, that is to say transfers viewed as incomplete until the transferor's
death and hence that produce inclusion in the gross
estate, also must be viewed through the glass of the
gift tax. In fact, many of the transfers that are not
viewed as complete for estate tax purposes until

death are viewed as complete, when first made, in part or as a whole, for gift tax purposes.

At this point, the particular focus is on those transfers that are made during life and which fall under §§ 2036–2038 of the estate tax. Thus the present topic involves the question "what is a completed gift?" or "when is a gift complete for gift tax purposes?". The general problem of what constitutes a completed gift has been addressed earlier, see § 20, *supra*. The present issue is whether a transfer that will produce estate tax consequences under any of §§ 2036–2038, because viewed as not complete until death, will also produce gift tax consequences when made.

The starting point is I.R.C. § 2501. That section imposes a tax "on the transfer of property by gift ... by any individual, resident or non-resident." I.R.C. § 2511 expands this rule somewhat by providing that the tax imposed by § 2501 shall apply whether the transfer is in trust or otherwise, whether the gift is direct or indirect, and whether the property is real or personal, tangible or intangible. I.R.C. § 2512 states that gifts shall be valued at the date thereof and that if the value exceeds consideration received, only the excess shall be taxed as a gift.

These bare statutory provisions do not go far towards determining what transfers are "gifts" or "completed gifts" for purposes of the gift tax. Further elaboration must be found in the Treasury

Regulations, other administrative materials and in reported cases.

As the Regulations make clear, the gift tax is not imposed on the receipt of the property by the donee but is imposed on the donor with respect to the act of transferring the property and is measured by the value of the property passing from the donor; the tax attaches regardless of the fact that the identity of the donee may not then be known or ascertainable. See Regs. § 25.2511–2(a). Thus, the focus is upon the release of dominion and control by the donor, not on the apparent receipt of some benefit by the donee. Furthermore, it should be kept in mind that a gift can be made of a future interest if the gift is complete. Gifts of future interests do not qualify for the annual exclusion, discussed in § 55, *infra*, but this is the result of valuation problems, not problems of completeness. The two concepts should be kept distinct.

Consider the gift tax consequences of a transfer of property, in trust or otherwise, if the transferor retains a power to *revoke* the transfer. Such a transfer will be viewed as incomplete until death under I.R.C. § 2038 for estate tax purposes. Will a gift tax be imposed, only to be somehow relieved if the transfer is revoked and thus the gift ultimately is not made? Or will the gift tax be payable in any event and no adjustment made if the transfer is later revoked? Or, will there be deemed to be a gift back if the power to revoke is exercised?

As one might expect, the law has clearly established that a revocable transfer is not a completed
gift when made and only becomes a completed gift
when the transferor gives up or loses his power to
revoke. See Burnet v. Guggenheim, 288 U.S. 280
(1933). Thus the gift tax consequences coincide
with the estate tax consequences. The result will
be the same whether the gift is revocable because of
a power retained by the donor or revocable because
of a rule of law, such as a rule that a gift made by a
minor person is subject to disaffirmance. See, *e.g.*,
Comm. v. Allen, 108 F.2d 961 (3rd Cir. 1939), cert.
den., 309 U.S. 680 (1940). A revocable transfer will
be regarded as incomplete for gift tax purposes
whether the power to revoke is held by the donor
alone or is exercisable by him only in conjunction
with another person, so long as that other person
does not have a substantial adverse interest in the
exercise of the power or revocation. See Camp v.
Comm., 195 F.2d 999 (1st Cir. 1952). Thus, as the
Regulations put it, a gift is incomplete in every
instance in which a donor reserves the power to
revest the beneficial title to the property in himself.
See Regs. § 25.2511–2(c). If the transfer is not
revoked and as a result annual or other gifts of
income are made from the trust or the property
transferred, these annual transfers will be treated
as annual gifts by the donor, who is deemed to have
made them periodically by refraining from exercising the power to revoke. See Regs. § 25.2511–2(f).

Suppose a person makes a gratuitous § 2036(a)(1)
transfer, that is to say a gift in trust or otherwise

with a reserved life estate. What will be the gift tax consequences of this transfer which, we know, will be regarded as incomplete for estate tax purposes? More specifically, suppose a husband and father transfers property in trust and provides that the income shall be paid to him for his life and at his death the remainder shall be paid to his wife if she is living and if not to their children or their children's heirs. Will a gift tax be imposed at the time the husband makes the transfer? He has retained a life estate but has made a completed transfer of the remainder interest. It is uncertain whether his wife or his children or their heirs will actually come into possession or enjoyment of the remainder interest, but there is no possibility that the donor himself will get it back through a retained interest. By analogy to a gift of one of several pieces of property, the law says that the donor has transferred an interest less than the total of his interest in the property and should be taxed only as having made a completed gift of the interest transferred. However, all the property will be included in the transferor's gross estate at death by virtue of the retained life estate and I.R.C. § 2036(a)(1).

For gift tax purposes, the donor will be deemed to have made a transfer of the remainder interest; the value of the life estate retained, a value determined by actuarial principles, will be subtracted from the value of the property to determine the value of the gift to which the gift tax will apply. If the donor had retained, instead of a plain life estate, a right to a specified annual payment for his life or for a period of years, the retained interest similarly could be valued and the gift reduced by the value of the interest retained. If the property were non-income producing, the retained interest would be worth nothing and thus would not reduce the amount of the taxable gift. If a donor retains a life interest or a term of years in property and later relinquishes that interest, he or she will be deemed to have made a gift of that interest at that later time. Thus, in the above example it is not necessary to compute the separate values of the contingent remainders in the wife and the children, based upon the possibility of the property actually vesting, since it is the husband who is taxed upon the fair-market value of the interest he gave away.

A more complicated disposition involving a life estate, a contingent remainder or executory interest, and a reversion is illustrated by the case of Smith v. Shaughnessy, 318 U.S. 176 (1943). There the taxpayer made an irrevocable transfer of stock in trust with the income payable to his wife for life; upon her death the stock was to be returned to the taxpayer if he were living; if he was not in fact living at that time, the stock was to go to the persons designated by his wife by her will or to her intestate successors. The Court held that the taxpayer had made a completed gift of the life estate and the remainder, but not of the interest and value constituting the reversionary interest retained. In other words, the Court viewed the case as involving three interests, one of which had been retained and two of which had been transferred.

The taxpayer who seeks to reduce gift tax by showing that some interest in property has been retained must bear the burden of valuing that interest, as the companion case, Robinette v. Helvering, 318 U.S. 184 (1943) shows. There a taxpayer also had transferred property with a reserved life estate for herself but had also provided a second life estate for her mother and stepfather if she should predecease them. The remainder was to go to her issue upon reaching the age of 21, or if no issue existed, the property was to go as directed by the will of the last surviving life-tenant. Thus taxpayer retained a contingent reversionary interest. The taxpayer argued that the gifts were not complete because no donee was then in existence to accept the remainder. In any event, she argued, in computing the value of the gift an allowance for the value of her reversionary interest should be made. Since that reversionary interest depended not only on survival but also upon the death of a daughter without issue who should reach the age of 21 years, the Court concluded that there was no recognized method by which to determine the value of the contingent reversionary interest. The burden was on the taxpayer to show that she had retained an interest with an ascertainable value. Since that burden had not been carried, the amount of the gift was not reduced by reason of the retained reversionary interest. Similarly, in Lockard v. Comm., 166 F.2d 409 (1st Cir. 1948), the Court held that there was no method to determine the value of a power of invasion in order to reduce the amount of a gift. If the power of invasion had been limited by a definite standard, the taxpayer might have shown facts and circumstances enabling a valuation to be placed on the likelihood of invasion for purposes of determining the value of the gift. See, *e.g.*, McHugh v. U. S., 142 F.Supp. 927 (Ct.Cl.1956).

Regs. § 25.2511–1(e) deal with the transfer of less than the donor's entire interest in property, including a retention of the remainder interest. They also speak to the problem of a donor's retained interest that is not susceptible of measurement. See also the examples in Regs. § 25.2511–1(h).

If a donor transfers property in trust and gives the trustee power to invade the corpus of the trust for the benefit of the donor, the transfer is likely to be regarded as incomplete, at least if the standard is one that is enforceable against the trustee by the donor. See, *e.g.*, Holtz's Estate v. Comm., 38 T.C. 37 (1962). The Regulations also indicate that if the exercise of the trustee's power in favor of the grantor is limited by a fixed or ascertainable standard as delineated in paragraph (g)(2) of Regs. § 25.2511–1, enforceable by or on behalf of the grantor, then the gift is incomplete to the extent of the ascertainable value of any rights thus retained by the grantor. Regs. § 25.2511–2(b). See also Rev.Rul. 62–13, 1962–1 C.B. 181. In Comm. v. Vander Weele, 254 F.2d 895 (6th Cir. 1958), the settlor of a trust not only retained income rights in the trust but also gave the trustees sweeping powers to invade corpus

for her benefit. The 6th Circuit held that under
these circumstances there would be no taxable gift
inasmuch as there was no assurance that anything
of value would ever pass to the remainderman.
Where property is transferred to a trust under the
terms of which the trustee is given very broad
discretionary powers over the distribution to the
grantor of income and corpus and where there is no
assurance at the time the trust was created that
anything of value will be paid to a beneficiary or a
class of beneficiaries other than the grantor, such
transfer constitutes an incomplete transfer and not
a taxable gift. (Possibly the trust property would
otherwise have escaped inclusion in the grantor's
estate at death, since none of the inclusion rules of
I.R.C. §§ 2036–2038 would seem to apply. Of
course, as property is actually paid out to other
people, the complete gifts would periodically be
made and would be taxable then.)

More difficult gift tax problems are presented if a
person makes a transfer but retains a power to alter
or amend the transfer or otherwise to designate the
beneficiaries who will actually enjoy the property.
For example, suppose that a donor transfers property in trust and provides that the income from the
property shall for 20 years be distributed to his wife
and son in such proportions as he directs, with the
remainder at the expiration of the 20 year period to
his son or heirs. Under a disposition such as this,
the donor has not retained any power of revocation
or any interest that will return the property to him.
Barring the case when the son is a minor or when

the distribution of income to the wife or son would
discharge the donor's obligation of support, there is
no way under the terms of the instrument that the
property will come back to provide its economic
benefits to the donor.   Therefore, one might think
that the gift was complete because, in the language
of the Regulations mentioned earlier, the donor has
not reserved a power to revest the beneficial title to
the property in himself.   However, under the Regulations and the case law this transfer will not be
regarded as a completed gift to the extent of all the
property transferred.   The donor has retained a
§ 2038 or § 2036(a)(2) power, as viewed by the
estate tax, and the property will be included in his
gross estate to some extent at least by virtue of
those statutory rules.   For gift tax purposes, the
transfer also will be regarded as incomplete, to
some extent at least, because of the retained right
or power to alter the distributions to the beneficiaries during the 20 year period.   See Estate of San-
ford v. Comm., 308 U.S. 39 (1939).   Even though
the power to designate new beneficiaries does not
include the donor himself or, for that matter, anyone other than the beneficiaries named in the instrument, the gift will become complete and subject
to the gift tax only at the time the donor relinquishes the power.   The Regulations put it as follows:
"As to any property, or part thereof or interest
therein, of which the donor has so parted with
dominion and control as to leave in him no power to
change its disposition, whether for his own benefit
or for the benefit of another, the gift is complete.

But if upon a transfer of property (whether in trust or otherwise) the donor reserves any power over its disposition, the gift may be wholly incomplete, or may be partially complete and partially incomplete, depending upon all the facts in the particular case." Regs. § 25.2511–2(b).

Thus for gift tax purposes the question is not so much whether the donor has parted with the property and all his title or beneficial interest in the property as an economic matter but rather the question is whether the donor has so parted with dominion and control over the property as to leave no power over it in himself. To put it another way, the power to control the disposition of property that has been transferred is regarded as such an important aspect of ownership as to make the transfer of the property incomplete even for gift tax purposes, until that power disappears. This general principle is slightly curbed by the Regulations. Firstly, a gift is not considered incomplete merely because the donor reserves the power to change the manner or time of enjoyment. See Regs. § 25.2511–2(d). Secondly, if the only power retained is a fiduciary power, the exercise or non-exercise of which is limited by a fixed or ascertainable standard, to change the beneficiaries of the transferred property, the donor will be treated as having made a completed gift and the entire value of the transferred property will be subject to gift tax. See Regs. § 25.2511–2(g).

The relinquishment or termination of a power to change the beneficiaries of transferred property, occurring otherwise than by the death of the donor (the gift tax being confined to transfers by living donors) is regarded as the event which completes the gift and causes the tax to apply. See Regs. § 25.2511–2(f).

Therefore, not only the power to revest the beneficial title to the property in himself but also a power that gives the donor the ability to name new beneficiaries or to change the interests of the beneficiaries as between themselves, unless the power is a fiduciary power limited by fixed or ascertainable standard, will render a gift incomplete. See Regs. § 25.2511–2(c). The donor's power of disposition among beneficiaries will make the gift incomplete if it is exercisable by him alone or in conjunction with any person not having a substantial adverse interest in the disposition of the transferred property or the income from it. A trustee is not as such a person having an adverse interest in the disposition of the trust property or its income. See Regs. § 25.2511–2(e).

Another form of inter-vivos transfer that is viewed by the estate tax as incomplete until death is a conditional or so-called § 2037 transfer. To illustrate, suppose a person transfers property in trust and provides that the income therefrom shall be paid to H, her husband, for his life and remainder at his death to the transferor if she is then living; if she is not living at that time, the property is to be given to specified individuals, X, Y and Z. The transferor has retained a reversionary interest in that she will possess and enjoy the property if she

survives her husband, H. Also, the survivorship
requirement of I.R.C. § 2037 is met because the
remainder-persons X, Y and Z can take possession
or enjoyment of the property through ownership of
the remainder interest only by surviving the decedent. If the decedent's reversionary interest exceeds 5% of the value of the property, § 2037 will
produce inclusion of all or some part of the property
in her gross estate on the ground that the transfer
was incomplete until her death. If at the time of
her death the life estate of the husband is still
outstanding, the interest to be included will be the
property transferred minus the value of the husband's outstanding life estate. See Regs. § 20.-
2037–1(e). If the transferor dies after her husband's death, she will have received the property
back, through her retained reversionary interest,
and the property will be included in her gross estate
under § 2033.

For purposes of the gift tax, the reversion retained by the grantor will serve to reduce the
amount of the gift that is taxable. She will be
deemed to have made a gift of the other interests,
the life-estate and the remainder or executory interest in X, Y and Z, assuming that the transfers to
them were absolute and irrevocable. See Regs.
§ 25.2511–1(e); Smith v. Shaughnessy, 318 U.S.
176 (1943). Even if the reversionary interest retained by the grantor were worth less than 5% of
the property transferred, so there would not be
inclusion under § 2037 in the decedent's gross estate, the small reversionary interest retained would

nevertheless reduce the amount of the gift for gift tax purposes. If the taxpayer cannot attach some value to the reversionary interest she retained, she will be deemed to have made a gift of all the property transferred. See Robinette v. Helvering, 318 U.S. 184 (1943).

Overall, it appears that a retained power or interest, of the kind the estate tax is concerned with in §§ 2036–2038, may render a gift incomplete for gift tax purposes as well, but will not necessarily do so. In other words, the gift tax and the estate tax are not mutually exclusive or perfectly coordinated. Some transfers will be treated as complete when made for gift tax purposes even though they are incomplete until death for estate tax purposes, and vice-versa.

In general, for gift tax purposes one must inquire not only whether the transferor has retained a power to revest beneficial title or enjoyment in himself, but also whether he has parted with dominion and control over the property and its disposition. If he has neither reserved a power to revest the property in himself, alone or with someone who has no substantial adverse interest, nor has retained a power over the disposition of the property either directly for himself or others or by a standard applicable to the trustee, a completed gift of the entire property will be deemed to have been made. Anything less than this will mean that there has not been a completed gift of all interests.

However, a gift will not be considered incomplete just because the grantor retains some administrative or managerial powers. See, *e.g.*, Reinecke v. Northern Trust Co., 278 U.S. 339 (1929).

For purposes of the gift tax, a power exercisable by the donor only in conjunction with someone else must be investigated further to determine whether the other person has a substantial adverse interest. If not, the retention of the power will make the gift incomplete for gift tax purposes. (In contrast, the retention of some such powers, whether or not in conjunction with another person, will produce inclusion in the gross estate under I.R.C. §§ 2036 and 2038.) The substantially adverse interest rule is applied even in the family context where one must recognize that a beneficiary whose interest is apparently adverse to the grantor may in fact consent to a revocation or amendment or designation desired by the grantor because of personal and familial considerations. Some of the outlines of the essentially adverse interests rule are provided by cases such as Camp v. Comm., 195 F.2d 999 (1st Cir. 1952); Latta v. Comm., 212 F.2d 164 (3d Cir. 1954), cert. den. 348 U.S. 825 (1954); Comm. v. Prouty, 115 F.2d 331 (1st Cir. 1940); Cerf v. Comm., 141 F.2d 564 (3rd Cir. 1944); Estate of Gillette, 7 T.C. 219 (1946) (Acq., 1946–2 C.B. 2).

Obviously, if the person whose consent must be obtained for the grantor to exercise a power over the disposition of transferred property has no substantial economic interest in the trust that is adverse to the exercise of the power, the transfer is just as incomplete as if the donor had the power alone. If, in contrast, the donor can exercise his power only with the consent of all persons having an interest in the trust, the reserved power counts for nothing and the gift is complete. If the power to modify beneficial interests in the trust is given to a third party alone, not involving the donor, one would think that such a power would not render the gift incomplete, even if the person possessing the power is just a trustee. See Rev.Rul. 54–538, 1954–2 C.B. 316. However, Rev.Rul. 62–13, 1962–1 C.B. 181 has modified the earlier Revenue Ruling in the event that the powers to invade income and corpus for the benefit of the grantor are so great that under the circumstances there is no assurance that anything of value will be paid to a beneficiary other than the grantor.

Just as the gift and estate taxes are not perfectly correlated, differences in application of the gift tax and the income tax or the estate tax and the income tax can arise. For example, in Comm. v. Hogle, 165 F.2d 352 (10th Cir. 1947) the Court held that a gift had been made earlier for gift tax purposes even though the income currently was to be taxed to the donor because the gift was not complete for income tax purposes. In Lockard v. Comm., 166 F.2d 409 (1st Cir. 1948) the Court held that a taxable gift had been made when a wife set up a short-term trust for her husband, even though for income tax purposes the transfer was regarded as incomplete and the wife was taxed on the trust income during the years that the trust existed.

CHAPTER VI

JOINTLY OWNED PROPERTY AND COMMUNITY PROPERTY

§ 40. Jointly Owned Property and Community Property—Estate and Gift Tax— § 2040, § 2515

Introduction. Property may be jointly owned by two or more people in one of several forms. One of these forms, called joint tenancy (or, in the case of husband and wife as co-tenants, tenancy by the entirety) has the distinctive feature of rights of survivorship. In contrast, tenancy in common is a form of co-ownership of property in which each tenant has a separate, undivided interest in the property, an interest which he or she can transmit at death or during life. The surviving tenant does not become entitled to the decedent tenant's interest. Accordingly, property held by a decedent as a tenant in common will be included in his gross estate under I.R.C. § 2033, which applies to property held at death to the extent of any interest therein. One-half of the property held as a tenancy in common would be included in the gross estate of one of two such tenants who died.

By its nature, joint ownership with rights of survivorship presents special gift and estate tax problems. When one of the co-owners of a joint tenancy or tenancy by the entirety dies, the other tenant becomes the outright owner of the entire property by virtue of the form of ownership in which the property was held. His right of survivorship entitled him to take the property, and the property does not pass by will or intestacy and will not be included in the decedent's probate estate. In other words, the decedent's right in the property terminated at his death. A joint tenancy also can be terminated before death upon agreement of the parties or if one of them severs or partitions his interest or if they convey the property to someone else. If one joint tenant transfers his interests to a third person, the joint tenancy with right of survivorship is destroyed and the result is a tenancy in common between the third person and the other original tenant. A tenancy by the entirety is essentially the same as a joint tenancy except that it can arise only when the co-owners are husband and wife and can last only as long as their marriage endures. Furthermore, neither of the tenants can destroy the tenancy by unilateral act. The tenancy will come to an end if the owners are divorced or if they both agree to end the tenancy or at the death of either spouse.

Each joint tenant is viewed as owning all the property subject to the rights of the other joint tenant or tenants. Income of the tenancy is split between the owners (except in a few jurisdictions where the income of a tenancy by the entirety is attributed to the husband alone).

Joint-and-survivor bank accounts are a form of ownership that very much resembles a plain joint tenancy. Each depositor has a right of survivorship and also has the right during his life to withdraw all the funds in the account, although he may be limited in his freedom to spend or waste those funds for his own benefit after withdrawal.

Still another form of joint ownership is found in the community property systems of a number of states. Community property ownership differs from joint tenancies and tenancies by the entirety, varies somewhat from state to state and has changed from time to time within some states. Community property exists, of course, only among spouses. Under the most prevalent system, each spouse is viewed as having a vested property right to the extent of one-half of the community property. As a result, the interest of each spouse will be includable at death in his or her gross estate for estate tax purposes. For example, in California, where post-1927 community property is held by the wife and husband with each having a vested one-half interest, one-half of their community property will be included in the gross estate of the first spouse to die, under I.R.C. § 2033. In this respect, community property resembles a tenancy in common, for estate tax purposes.

Estate Tax. Property held in joint tenancy and tenancy by-the-entirety provide more difficult federal estate and gift tax problems. Internal Revenue Code § 2040 was enacted to deal with the problem of jointly-owned property. In the absence of

§ 2040, the taxation of property held jointly by the decedent and someone else with a right of survivorship would be difficult to determine. An argument could be made that all, or none, or some portion or other of the jointly-held property should be included in the gross estate of the first joint owner to die.

Whatever the tax consequences in the absence of I.R.C. § 2040, the governing law is now provided by that section. In general, § 2040(a) decrees that a decedent's gross estate includes the value of property held jointly by him and another person or persons with right of survivorship. One exception: if the property was acquired by the decedent and the other joint owner by gift, devise, bequest, or inheritance, only the decedent's fractional share of the property must be included in his gross estate. In all other events, the entire value of the jointly owned property is included in the estate of the first joint owner to die, *except* such part of the entire value as the taxpayer can show was attributable to consideration in money or money's worth furnished by the other joint owner (or owners).

In determining what consideration was furnished by the other joint owners, there is taken into account only that portion of such consideration which is shown not to be attributable to money or other property acquired by such joint owners from the decedent for less than a full and adequate consideration in money or money's worth. Under this general rule, it is obvious that if A gives $10,000 to B, which B turns around and invests as his one-half interest in joint tenancy property with A, there will be inclusion in A's gross estate of the entire value of such property. A major exception, however, is income from property given by the decedent to the future joint tenant. The income from such gift property can be used as valid consideration and will reduce the amount includable in the decedent donor's gross estate. Moreover, the rationale behind this exception applies to income from the joint tenancy itself, which the joint tenants share equally regardless of the fact that one joint tenant provided the entire purchase price. Therefore, all improvements on the joint tenancy property paid for out of income from the property are made with equal consideration from each joint tenant. New joint tenancy property paid for with such income is treated similarly. See Regs. § 20.2040–1(c)(4) and (5) and Rev.Rul. 56–519, 1956–2 C.B. 123.

The treatment of income from gift property, *e.g.*, rent, dividends and interest, must be distinguished from the treatment accorded appreciation in determining adequate consideration. If A gives Blackacre, worth $5,000, to B and B sells it for $10,000 and uses the proceeds as one-half contribution on joint-tenancy property with A, what result? There would seem to be little basis for reaching a different result than if income from Blackacre were used, and the cases agree that B would be treated as having contributed the $5,000 represented by the appreciation in Blackacre. See Harvey v. U. S., 185 F.2d 463 (7th Cir. 1950) and Swartz v. U. S., 182 F.Supp. 540 (D.Mass.1960). This, however, is where the similarity of treatment ends. If instead of selling

Blackacre, B contributed the appreciated property as his share of a joint tenancy with A, the regulations say that A is treated as having contributed the entire consideration for the joint tenancy. See Regs. § 20.2040–1(c)(4). Furthermore, at least one case has held that if one person provided all of the consideration for joint-tenancy property, that property was sold, and the proceeds, including appreciation, were used to buy another property held in joint tenancy by the same parties, none of the appreciation in the first property may be attributed to the non-contributing joint tenant. Endicott Trust Co. v. U. S., 305 F.Supp. 943 (N.D.N.Y.1969). And compare the gift tax treatment of appreciation on sale of a tenancy by-the-entirety in Regs. § 25.-2515–1(c)(2). The court in *Endicott* reasoned that the contributing joint tenant had never relinquished his joint interest in the property. This, along with the difficulties in tracing the precise amount attributable to appreciation, may account for the varying treatments of appreciation and income.

If it is determined that some of the value of the joint property is attributable to consideration furnished by the other joint owner or owners, the part of the entire value that will not be included in the decedent's gross estate is that portion of the value of the property at the decedent's death which the consideration in money or money's worth furnished by the other joint owner or owners bears to the total cost of acquisition and capital additions of the property. Thus, the entire value of the jointly held property will be included in the decedent's gross estate unless his representative submits facts sufficient to show that the property was not acquired entirely with consideration furnished by the decedent or that the property was acquired by the decedent and other joint owner or owners by gift, bequest, devise, or inheritance. See I.R.C. § 2040(a); Regs. § 20.2040–1(a).

To illustrate the application of § 2040(a), one may consider the tax consequences if two people, A and B, *not* husband and wife, purchase real property in joint tenancy and each pays a portion of the purchase price. (The special rules governing spousal joint tenancies will be considered below). The fraction of the purchase price which each unrelated person pays will determine the fraction of the value of the property at the date of death which will be includable in the gross estate of the first to die. If the property were a residence purchased entirely out of A's separate property, at his death the entire property would be included in his gross estate because it could not be shown that any part of the value at his death was attributable to consideration furnished by B, the other joint owner. If A had given B some cash from his separate property so that B joined in the purchase of the property, the entire property would nevertheless be included in A's gross estate at his death because the consideration B furnished in money or money's worth would not be taken into account inasmuch as it would be attributable to money or other property acquired by the surviving joint tenant from the decedent for less than a full and adequate consideration in money or money's worth.

Obviously, difficult problems of proof may face the taxpayer; inadequacies in his records will work only to his disadvantage. Under § 2040(a), it is up to the taxpayer to show the extent to which contributions were made by someone other than the decedent, both as to the original acquisition of jointly-owned property and as to capital additions or improvements. Tracing will be required in instances where there has been a reinvestment. Contributions that have been made out of income from separate property or other jointly-held property will require very precise determination.

Spouses. These tracing problems proved very burdensome, particularly in light of the fact that joint-tenancy is the most common form in which married couples hold title to property. Partly in order to obviate these tracing difficulties and explicitly to recognize a spouse's services toward accumulating joint property (see H.Rep., pp. 19–20, and Estate of Everett Otte, 31 T.C.M. 301 (1972), the '76 Amendments renumbered old § 2040, which is now § 2040(a), added new § 2040(b), a limited exception to § 2040(a) for certain joint tenancies, *between spouses,* created after 1976, and added § 2040(c), with its special rule to apply when a spouse of the decedent materially participated in a farm or other business.

I.R.C. § 2040(b) provided that one-half of any "*qualified*" joint interest is to be included in the estate of the first joint tenant to die, no matter which joint tenant actually furnished the consideration. To qualify, the joint tenancy had to have been created by one or both of the spouses, had to have no other joint tenants besides the two spouses, and had to have been treated as a gift at the time of its creation.

These qualification rules were very complex, due mainly to this interrelation with the gift tax provisions and their associated reporting requirements, which also resulted in a continuing need to monitor and report any subsequent additions in value to the property. Thus the tracing burden remained, albeit to a somewhat lesser extent. Much additional complexity was added by an election mechanism, whereunder spousal joint tenancies created before 1977 could be qualified for post-'76 treatment.

E.R.T.A. significantly simplified the treatment of spousal joint tenancies, for the estates of decedents dying after 1981. This was done by repealing the old post-'76 qualification rules, as well as the associated gift-tax rules and the special § 2040(c) rule of "material participation". (Note, however, that the old pre-'76 rules still apply to all joint tenancies where there are any joint tenants *other than* the decedent and his or her spouse.) New § 2040(b)(2) provides that all joint tenancies solely between the decedent (dying after 1981) and his spouse are "qualified" joint interests, exactly one-half of which will therefore be included in the gross estate of the first to die, under § 2040(b)(1). (Time will reveal more fully the actual ongoing import of this new rule, given the new unlimited marital deduction available under I.R.C. § 2056.)

Pre-E.R.T.A. law (for non-spouses as well as for spouses). Under the wording of I.R.C. § 2040(a), its broad general rule of inclusion applies to the extent of the interest held as joint tenants by the decedent. The time referred to is the time of death. What then will happen if a joint interest that would otherwise fall within the rule of § 2040(a) is disposed of before death? If it is disposed of by transfer for full and adequate consideration, there is no need for § 2040(a) to apply, and it will not apply, since the jointly owned property is not "held" at death and the estate has not been depleted by an inter-vivos, gratuitous transfer. However, suppose the decedent and his wife were to transfer jointly owned property to a member of the family in a gift made within three years of the decedent's pre-'82 death. In that event, no jointly-owned property would be held at death and it would appear that § 2040(a) would not apply. This failure of § 2040(a) might be remedied by old I.R.C. § 2035, which required inclusion in the gross estate of the value of any property transferred within three years of death. However, § 2035 by itself could apparently include only the half interest transferred by the decedent, whereas all of the property would have been included in the gross estate under § 2040(a) if it had been held until death.

By analogy to the *Allen* case, *supra*, § 37, the Commissioner could well argue (and did, at least for a while) that pre-E.R.T.A. § 2035 should be read together with § 2040(a) so that a transfer of an interest in joint property, made within three years of death of a decedent dying before 1982, when the interest transferred would have produced inclusion of more than the transferred interest itself—under § 2040(a)—should not permit the taxpayer to escape the broader inclusion of § 2040(a). In fact, some case-law authority supports the conclusion that only the one-half interest transferred by the decedent would be includable under pre-E.R.T.A. § 2035. See Sullivan's Estate v. Comm., 175 F.2d 657 (9th Cir. 1949); Estate of Brockway, 18 T.C. 488 (1952), affirmed on other issues, 219 F.2d 400 (9th Cir. 1954); Estate of Borner, 25 T.C. 584 (1955). The Revenue Service has now acquiesced in the *Brockway* and *Borner* results. See 1969–2 C.B. xxii–xxiv. (Note that as of 1982, § 2035 no longer applies in the § 2040 context (since § 2040 is not specifically enumerated in § 2035(d)(2)) except as to the inclusion of any gift taxes paid.)

The other side of the coin, however, is that one-half of jointly held property transferred to a third party within three years of the pre-'82 death of *either* spouse, even the spouse who contributed nothing to the original acquisition of the property, will be included in the estate of the decedent. (See Rev.Rul. 76–348, 1976–37 I.R.B. 10.)

A similar problem is involved if a decedent and his wife, holding property jointly so as to require inclusion in the husband's estate under § 2040(a) if the property were retained until his death, transfer the property to a trust and reserve a life estate in the property transferred. Under § 2036(a)(1) alone, the retained life estate should produce inclusion of the interest transferred. But again, that interest would apparently be just the one-half interest of the decedent, not the entire amount that would have been included in his gross estate under § 2040(a) if he had not made the transfer with a retained life estate. The Commissioner has argued that the whole property should be included in the decedent's estate in a situation like this and has explicitly relied on the "estate depletion" theory of the *Allen* case. The courts, however, have refused to apply the Commissioner's theory. See U. S. v. Heasty, 370 F.2d 525 (10th Cir. 1966); Glaser v. U. S., 306 F.2d 57 (7th Cir. 1962); Estate of Brockway, 18 T.C. 488 (1952), affirmed on other issues, 219 F.2d 400 (9th Cir. 1954). The approach of the courts fits the language of §§ 2035 and 2036, but does not fully do justice to the purpose of the estate tax. Nevertheless, the Internal Revenue Service has given in to the *Heasty* result. See Rev.Rul. 69–577, 1969–2 C.B. 173.

Although the authority of the *Heasty* case can be argued against the Commissioner when he tries to deal with a contemplation of death case, the retained life estate fact situation should be distinguished from the contemplation of death situation and the *Allen* theory of estate depletion probably should prevail. Section 2035 and § 2040(a) should be read together to block an otherwise existing loophole. See, *e.g.,* Harris v. U. S., 193 F.Supp. 736

(D.Neb.1961), a contemplation of death case in which the Court did read § 2035 and § 2040(a) together so as to include the total value of the property in the decedent's estate under § 2035.

The constitutionality of the predecessor of I.R.C. § 2040(a) was upheld in U. S. v. Jacobs, 306 U.S. 363 (1939). In that case it was even held constitutional as applied to property transferred before the enactment of the transfer taxes. Justice Black said that the tax did not operate retroactively in an impermissible form merely because some of the facts or conditions upon which the application of the tax depends came into being prior to the enactment of the tax.

The Regulations under I.R.C. § 2040 provide considerable clarification of the convoluted statutory rule and language.

Gift Tax. The gift tax consequences of the formation or termination of a joint tenancy are equally important and have received Congressional attention in the form of the complicated rules of former I.R.C. §§ 2515 and 2515A, which govern the creation of spousal joint tenancies before 1982. [A tenancy by-the-entirety was defined to include "a joint tenancy between husband and wife". See I.R.C. § 2515(d).] These rules are no longer needed, since post-E.R.T.A. spousal gifts are all tax-free because of the new unlimited marital deduction, and because the estate tax inclusion rule of I.R.C. § 2040 no longer depends for its application on former §§ 2515 or 2515A.

If a joint tenancy with right of survivorship is formed with joint owners who are *not* spouses, the results are now, and always have been governed by general gift-tax principles, and not by specific statutory command. In general, if each of the joint tenants contributes a proportionate share of the consideration for the property and if the joint tenancy can be severed so as to defeat the survivorship rights of the other tenants, no gift has been made upon formation and no gift tax consequences will follow at that time. If one of the joint tenants contributes more than his or her proportionate share of the consideration, there is a gift to the extent of the surplus contribution. So, for example, if A and B purchase property for $100,000 and take title as joint owners, and if A contributes the entire purchase price, he will be deemed to have made a gift of $50,000 to B. If A contributed $80,000 and B contributed $20,000, A will be deemed to have made a gift to B of $30,000. The relative ages of the joint tenants do not matter, even though there is a greater possibility that one joint tenant may survive the other than vice-versa. This result follows from the fact that the joint tenancy could be severed by either tenant and thus either could obtain his proportionate share of ownership of the property or the proceeds of selling the property.

CHAPTER VII

LIFE INSURANCE—ESTATE TAX AND GIFT TAX

§ 41. Proceeds of Life Insurance—Estate Tax Treatment—§ 2042

Introduction. I.R.C. § 2042 makes plain two rules for the estate tax treatment of life insurance proceeds paid on a policy on the life of the decedent. The first rule, contained in § 2042(1), requires that the value of the gross estate shall include the value of all property to the extent of the amount receivable by the executor as insurance under policies on the life of the decedent. Therefore if the proceeds of a life insurance policy on the life of the decedent are payable to the executor, the entire proceeds are includable in the decedent's gross estate. More usefully put, the rule is that insurance proceeds receivable *by or for the benefit of the estate* must be included. See Regs. § 20.2042–1(a). Actually, only the proceeds receivable by the estate for administration and distributable as an asset of the estate are deemed receivable by the executor for purposes of this rule. State law will determine whether policies that are in form payable to the decedent's estate actually inure to the benefit of the decedent's widow and children only, for example, and are free of claims of the decedent's creditors. In that event, the proceeds are not includable in the gross estate. But insurance payable to named beneficiaries other than the decedent's estate will be included in the gross estate to the extent that the proceeds are received by such a beneficiary subject to a legally binding obligation to pay taxes, debts or other charges and despite the fact that the decedent possessed no incident of ownership in the policy. See Regs. § 20.2042–1(b). In other words, it makes no difference whether or not the estate is specifically named as the beneficiary under the policy terms. Also, if the insurance had been made payable or assigned as collateral security for a loan to the decedent, it is considered to be receivable for the benefit of the estate. See Regs. § 20.2042–1(b). These results make perfectly good sense because the insurance serves to reduce debts of the estate and thus to increase the net estate that will pass to the heirs just as if the insurance proceeds had been payable directly to the estate.

Under a second rule, set forth in I.R.C. § 2042(2), the gross estate will also include the value of all property to the extent of the amount receivable by all other beneficiaries (other than the executor) as insurance under policies on the life of the decedent with respect to which the decedent possessed at his death any of the incidents of ownership, exercisable "either alone or in conjunction with any other person." To illustrate, one case held that the decedent had an incident of ownership at his death in that his consent was required for his wife to make a change in a trust, part of the corpus of which consisted of the insurance policy on the life of the decedent. See Comm. v. Estate of Karagheusian, 233 F.2d 197 (2d Cir. 1956).

Incidents of Ownership. The term "incidents of ownership" is not employed in a way that limits it to ownership of the policy in a technical sense. It refers more generally to the right of the insured or his estate to the economic benefits of the policy. Accordingly, it includes the power to change the beneficiary, to surrender or cancel the policy, to assign the policy, to revoke an assignment, to pledge the policy for a loan or to obtain from the insurer a loan against the surrender value of the policy.

Until 1974 it also included the power to change the beneficiary reserved to a corporation of which the decedent was sole stockholder. See former Regs. § 20.2042–1(c)(2). The Regulations were then amended, with Regs. § 20.2042–1(c)(6) now controlling this issue. It provides that if such insurance proceeds are payable either to the corporation itself or to a third party for a valid business purpose then the corporation's incidents of ownership will not be attributed to the decedent. On the other hand, if the proceeds are not so payable, the incidents will be attributed to any decedent controlling over 50% of the voting stock. The statute specifies that the term "incident of ownership" includes a reversionary interest only if the value of that interest exceeded 5% of the value of the policy immediately before the death of the decedent. The term "reversionary interest" also includes the pos-

sibility that the policy or its proceeds may return to
the decedent or his estate or may be subject to a
power of disposition by him.   I.R.C. § 2042(2).
However, the terms "reversionary interest" and
"incidents of ownership" do not include the possibility that the decedent might receive the policy or
its proceeds by inheritance through the estate of
another person or as surviving spouse under a statutory right of election or a similar right.   See Regs.
§ 20.2042–1(c)(3).

The decedent will be deemed to possess incidents
of ownership in a policy of life insurance on his life,
at his death, if he has the general, legal power to
exercise ownership without regard to his actual
ability to exercise that power at a particular moment.   See Comm. v. Estate of Noel, 380 U.S. 678
(1965).   In that case, the decedent had purchased
life insurance at the airport and handed the policy
to his wife before he departed; he could not exercise
his power to alter the beneficiary or to assign the
policies while he was in the airplane where he
remained until the time of his death when the
airplane crashed.   Nevertheless, the Supreme Court
held that he did have the incidents of ownership at
his death.

A similar question is whether the formal right to
exercise the incidents of ownership or the practical
power to do so is to be determinative for tax purposes.   In U. S. v. Rhode Island Hospital Trust Co.,
355 F.2d 7 (1st Cir. 1966), the 1st Circuit held that
there would be inclusion of the insurance proceeds
in the gross estate of the decedent-son who held the

incidents of ownership at his death even though the policies had been bought for the son by his father who personally dominated him and was in a position to command or direct his son's behavior, including the exercise of the powers held under the insurance policy. The Court distinguished between so-called "intent facts," those relating to the conduct and understanding of the insured and his father, and "policy facts," those revealed by the insurance contract itself. The court relied on the latter, in construing the statutory rule.

By way of contrast, the 6th Circuit, in Fruehauf v. Comm., 427 F.2d 80 (6th Cir. 1970) declined to hold that the mere possession by a decedent of the incidents of ownership in a *fiduciary capacity* invariably requires inclusion of the proceeds of the policies on the decedent's life and his gross estate. (However, in that particular case the Court upheld the Tax Court's decision that inclusion was required because the decedent had been authorized, both as executor and as trustee, to exercise the fiduciary powers for his own individual benefit.)

With respect to incidents of ownership held by the decedent as a fiduciary and only for the benefit of persons other than the insured, see also Estate of Hector R. Skifter, 468 F.2d 699 (2d Cir. 1972), which, relying on prior judicial interpretations of § 2038, held that such a power not created by the decedent himself but conferred upon him by a third party long after he had divested himself of all interest in the property subject thereto is not an incident of ownership within § 2042. The Fifth

Circuit was in direct conflict on this issue, relying in Rose v. U. S., 511 F.2d 259 (5th Cir. 1975), on the wording of § 2042 itself ("decedent possessed . . . any of the incidents . . ."), and thus giving life insurance harsher treatment than that given to other types of property. The I.R.S. has since announced that it will follow the *Skifter* reading of Regs. § 20.2042–1(c)(4). See Rev.Rul. 84–179, 1984–2 C.B. 195.

A particular problem has arisen with respect to determining whether a decedent has incidents of ownership in group term insurance of the kind provided by an employer for his employees. The question is whether the employee-insured can ever effectively transfer and dispose of all his incidents of ownership in group term life insurance. One incident of ownership is the right to designate and re-designate a beneficiary; another is the right to convert the policy upon termination of employment to an individual policy. By leaving his job, the insured can take away the beneficiary's right to receive the group insurance.

This problem received attention in Revenue Ruling 69–54, 1969–1 C.B. 221. That ruling indicated that the value of the proceeds of the policy would be includable in the gross estate of the insured employee if he had the power to cancel the insurance by terminating his employment or to control the disposition of the insurance through an exercise of a conversion privilege upon termination of his employment. That ruling was subsequently modified, and the power to cancel by terminating the employ-

ment was characterized as a mere "collateral consequence" of leaving one's job, and therefore not an
"incident of ownership," because of its potentially
costly related consequences. See Rev.Rul. 72–307,
1972–1 C.B. 307; Rev.Rul. 84–130, 1984–2 C.B. 194.
This result, though, seems to be in conflict with the
rationale of *Noel, supra,* under which the relevant
factor is the legal power to exercise ownership
rights, and not the actual power to do so, much less
the potential related cost of so doing. However, if
on termination of the insured's employment someone to whom he has irrevocably assigned all ownership of the policy could convert the policy to an
individual policy and if the employee could not have
effected cancellation of the insurance coverage by
terminating his employment, no inclusion will follow at the employee's death. See also Landorf v. U.
S., 408 F.2d 461 (Ct.Cl.1969).

The Circuits are also in conflict on the issue of
whether the right of the insured to elect settlement
option modes relating solely to the timing of future
payments to beneficiaries (*i.e.,* where the beneficiaries themselves cannot be changed by the insured),
is an incident of ownership causing inclusion of the
proceeds in the insured's estate. Estate of Lumpkin v. Comm., 474 F.2d 1092 (5th Cir. 1973), held
that since such a power would cause inclusion under § 2036 and § 2038 (query as to the applicability
of § 2036), it was sufficient also for § 2042 inclusion. The Service then announced that it would
follow *Lumpkin* and not the "economic benefit"
theory of *Skifter, supra.* (See Rev.Rul. 76–261,

1976–2 C.B. 276.) However the same group term policy included in *Lumpkin* was then excluded from the decedent's estate in Connelly v. U. S., 551 F.2d 545 (3d Cir. 1977), on the rationale that the "economic benefit" theory of *Skifter, supra,* made § 2042(2) inapplicable. The Service subsequently revoked Rev.Rul. 76–261 and adopted the *Skifter* reasoning, at least in the event decedent transferred all incidents of ownership, only to reacquire some wholly fiduciary powers in a later transaction "not part of a pre-arranged plan involving the participation of decedent". See Rev.Rul. 84–179, 1984–2 C.B. 195, 196.

This is, in sum, a very difficult area of the law, made all the more complicated by the uncertainties inherent in the application of § 2036 and § 2038 in their own context, which rules are then analogously applied once more in the § 2042 context.

Insurance; Amount Included. The term "insurance" refers to life insurance of every kind and even includes, for example, death benefits paid by fraternal beneficial societies operating under the lodge system. See Regs. § 20.2042–1(a)(1). It includes such things as a New York Stock Exchange Gratuity Fund which provided death benefits comparable to life insurance. See Comm. v. Treganowan, 183 F.2d 288 (2d Cir. 1950), cert. den. 340 U.S. 853 (1950). The term includes proceeds payable under an accidental death insurance policy, including flight insurance. See Comm. v. Estate of Noel, 380 U.S. 678 (1965).

The amount included in the gross estate under either of the two inclusion rules of I.R.C. § 2042 is the full amount receivable under the policy. See Regs. § 20.2042–1(a)(3). If the proceeds are to be paid over a period of years, the amount included in the gross estate is the lump sum which the insured or the beneficiary could have elected to have paid at death or, if no such option was available, the sum used by the insurance company in determining the amount of the annuity. *Ibid.*

Insurance in Community Property Situations. If the proceeds of an insurance policy that is made payable to the decedent's estate are community assets under the applicable community property law and if, as a result, half of the proceeds belongs to the decedent's spouse, only one half of the proceeds will be considered to be receivable by or for the benefit of the decedent's estate. See Regs. § 20.-2042–1(b)(2). So, if the policy is on the husband's life and he dies first, half the proceeds will be included in the husband's estate if the policy is community property and is made payable to the husband's estate. If the wife dies first, one half of the interpolated terminal reserve or replacement cost value of the policy will be included in her estate. See U. S. v. Stewart, 270 F.2d 894 (9th Cir. 1959), cert. den. 361 U.S. 960 (1960). Then, at the husband's death later, if he still holds all the incidents of ownership of the policy on his life, the proceeds of the policy, less the amount includable in her estate earlier, would be includable in the husband's gross estate. If the husband and wife designate their son as the beneficiary of a community property insurance policy and if that designation is revocable, the wife's transfer is not complete until the husband's death since only then does the designation become irrevocable. Therefore at the death of the husband, one half will be included in the decedent husband's estate and the wife will at that point be deemed to have made a gift of her one half interest in the policy. See generally Rev.Rul. 232, 1953–2 C.B. 268.

With respect to community property state decedents and community property funds used to pay premiums on insurance on the life of the husband when the wife pre-deceases him, see also Scott v. Comm., 374 F.2d 154 (9th Cir. 1967). There, the wife bequeathed her interest in the policies on her husband's life to her two sons and the decedent continued to pay the premiums on the policies after his wife died. The Court held, upon the husband's death, that the proceeds of the policies attributable to the premiums paid by him *after* his wife's death were includable in his gross estate. Only one-half of the portion attributable to premiums paid from community funds *prior* to the wife's death was includable in the decedent's gross estate, since the other half was owned by the wife, bequeathed to the sons and constituted more than an interest in one half the cash surrender value. The same principle was used to determine what portion of money borrowed on one of the policies was to be included in the decedent's gross estate.

Some basic rules for taxation of life insurance in community property situations are set forth in the Regulations under § 2042. See Regs. § 20.2042–1(b)(2). If insurance policies are purchased with community funds on the lives of the husband and the wife with the other spouse as beneficiary and owner, one half of the proceeds paid upon the husband's death is included in his gross estate under § 2042 and one half the value of the policy on his wife's life is included in his gross estate under § 2033. See Rev.Rul. 67–228, 1967–2 C.B. 331. This analysis follows from the general rule that the value of a policy on the life of another person, to be included in the estate of the owner-decedent, is to be taxed under I.R.C. § 2033. Some difficult valuation problems can arise. Some guidance for this matter is provided by the Regulations in § 20.2031–8(a)(1) and (2).

Valuation if Simultaneous Death. A special problem is presented if a husband and wife, each owning a life insurance policy on the life of the other, die simultaneously. In Estate of Wien v. Comm., 441 F.2d 32 (5th Cir. 1971), the Court concluded that the wife's estate tax liability for the ownership interest in policies on her husband's life should be valued according to the procedures in Regs. § 20.-2031–8(a)(2). The husband's estate tax liability for his interest in those policies on his wife's life, the Court concluded, should be valued in the same manner.

§ 2042 and Other Inclusion Rules. If the decedent did not possess any of the incidents of owner-

ship at the time of death, or transfer them within three years of death, no part of the proceeds would be includable in his or her gross estate under § 2042. Section 2042 does not apply to the value of rights in an insurance policy on the life of a person other than the decedent (though some other inclusion rule might apply to such property).

If, at the time of his death, the decedent was paying premiums on a policy on his own life but the policy was not payable to or for the benefit of his estate and he did not possess any of the incidents of ownership at the time of death and had not transferred them within 3 years of death, no part of the insurance proceeds would be includable in his gross estate under § 2042. See Regs. § 20.2042–1(c)(1). This rule makes an important change in prior law. Under early Treasury Department Regulations and later under the statute itself, insurance on the life of the decedent was included in his gross estate if the insurance had been purchased with premiums paid directly or indirectly by the decedent, whether or not he held any of the incidents of ownership and regardless of the person to whom the proceeds were payable.

Section 2042, enacted in 1954 as part of the codification that year, eliminated this "premium-payment test." Therefore, a taxpayer now may plan his affairs so as (a) never to hold the incidents of ownership or so as (b) to dispose of them ((if at all) more than 3 years before death) and thus he can avoid an estate tax on insurance proceeds which became payable at his death by reason of his payments of premiums during his life. Along with other tax and non-tax features of insurance, this estate tax rule makes life insurance a frequently used and attractive form of individual estate planning. (But see the analysis, two pages below, of potential inclusion in the gross estate of premiums paid within three years of death, even if the incidents of ownership were transferred earlier, for decedents who died before 1982.)

From time to time it is suggested that the premium payment test of the pre-1954 law should be reinstated so as to require inclusion in the gross estate of the proceeds of life insurance when the premiums have been paid by the decedent, regardless of to whom the proceeds are payable and regardless of who has the incidents of ownership. Some critics view the present state of the law as permitting a transfer that bears quite a similarity to a testamentary disposition of property to be made without estate tax, if the insured decedent divests himself of the incidents of ownership of policies on his life but goes on paying the premiums until his death. Against this testamentary nature of life insurance weighs a contrary policy consisting of a Congressional desire to encourage the purchase of life insurance as a means of providing for a surviving dependent of the decedent, (and thus perhaps relieving the public treasury of some social insurance needs).

Proceeds of life insurance that are not includable in the decedent's gross estate under I.R.C. § 2042 may turn out to be includable under some other section of the estate tax law. For example, death benefits not classified as insurance under § 2042 may nevertheless be taxed as annuities, under I.R.C. § 2039, discussed in § 43 below. For example, see Estate of Lafayette Montgomery, 56 T.C. 489 (1971), affd., 458 F.2d 616 (5th Cir. 1972) involving an insurance-annuity package. In that case, the proceeds of the life insurance were included in the decedent's gross estate under I.R.C. § 2039, because the arrangement involved was considered by the court to consist of a single contract for the investment by the decedent of a total amount of money in return for a fixed monthly payment to the decedent for his life (an annuity) with a provision at his death that a high proportion of the invested sum would go to his beneficiaries. If death benefits are payable to the decedent's estate, they will be included in his gross estate because they amount to property owned by him at death, under § 2033. See Goodman v. Granger, 243 F.2d 264 (3rd Cir. 1957), cert. den. 355 U.S. 835 (1957). (For that matter, in the absence of § 2042, it seems likely that life insurance proceeds receivable by the executor would be held includable in the decedent's gross estate as property owned by him under § 2033.) However, if payments made to the estate of the decedent or to his widow or children were not contractually obligated and amounted to a gift or a "mere expectancy," the payments will not be includable in his gross estate under §§ 2042 or 2033 or under any other Code section. See, *e.g.,*

Estate of Barr, 40 T.C. 227 (1963), Acq. in result, 1978–1 C.B. 1.

Similarly, if the decedent previously had owned a policy on his own life but gratuitously transferred the policy within three years of death, so that neither did he hold any of the incidents of ownership at death nor was the policy payable to his estate, the proceeds will nevertheless be includable under I.R.C. § 2035. This is true even for post-'81 gifts, since new I.R.C. § 2035(d)(2) continues the pre-E.R.T.A. inclusion for transfers of property which would have been included in the gross estate under I.R.C. § 2042 had the property been retained until death. (I.e. § 2035(d)(2) renders the § 2035(d)(1) protection from estate tax inapplicable, leaving the potent combination of § 2035(a) and § 2042 to apply.) Also, although I.R.C. § 2042 does not apply to the value of rights in an insurance policy on the life of a person other than the decedent, some value may be includable in the decedent's gross estate by reason of holding such a policy, under I.R.C. § 2033 or otherwise. And a pre-'82 transfer of such a policy within three years of death would bring § 2035 into play, as with a transfer of any other property. But a post-'81 transfer would not, since § 2033 is not one of the sections enumerated in new I.R.C. § 2035(d)(2).

A particularly difficult problem has arisen in connection with life insurance on his or her life, owned by the insured, transferred by the owner *not* within three years of death and then kept in force by the payment of premiums by the insured after his complete transfer of the insurance policies and until his death. The question, in such event, is whether the premium payments made within three years of death shall produce any inclusion in the gross estate. If it is determined under the usual § 2035 criteria that premiums were paid by the decedent-insured within three years of death, on policies not owned by him at death, one possibility would be to include in his gross estate only the premiums actually paid within three years of death or, after the amendments to § 2035, to include nothing because the payments amounted merely to gifts of cash. Another possibility, at the other extreme, would be to require inclusion of the entire proceeds of the life insurance policies on the ground that they were kept in force by the premium payments; the payment of premiums thus accomplished a transfer of the entire insurance proceeds within three years of death. A less extreme position would be to insist that the value of the amount receivable as insurance which is attributable to those premiums paid within three years of death would be includable in the decedent's gross estate. This amount would be determined by comparing the proportion of the premiums paid within three years of death to the total amount of premiums paid.

The Internal Revenue Service at one time insisted that at least the proportion of the proceeds of the life insurance policy attributable to the premiums paid within three years of death must be included in the decedent's gross estate. See Rev.Rul. 67–463, 1967–2 C.B. 327. The Commissioner was largely unsuccessful in asserting this position in the courts, however. A number of courts held Rev.Rul. 67–463 to be invalid. See *e.g.,* Gorman v. U. S., 288 F.Supp. 225 (E.D.Mich.1968); Estate of Coleman, 52 T.C. 921 (1969); First National Bank of Midland, Texas v. U. S., 423 F.2d 1286 (5th Cir. 1970). As a result, the Commissioner has now revoked Rev.Rul. 67–463 and will follow the decision in the *First National Bank Co.* case, *supra*. See Rev.Rul. 71–497, 1971–2 C.B. 329. The rule now asserted by the Commissioner is that no part of the proceeds of whole life insurance policies transferred by the decedent more than three years prior to his death are includable in his gross estate, but the amount of premiums paid by the decedent within three years of death are includable. But there is no inclusion for such premium payments made by a decedent dying *after 1981,* because § 2042 does not itself apply, and therefore neither does new § 2035. (Similarly the proceeds of life insurance policies themselves transferred within three years of death are includable, with a pro-rata exclusion for any premiums paid by the donee after transfer, by analogy to improvements or additions to property made by the donee.) See § 28, *supra*.

An insurance policy on the life of the decedent or, for that matter, on the life of someone else, can be the subject of an inter-vivos disposition that is incomplete until the death of the decedent and hence will produce inclusion in his gross estate under I.R.C. §§ 2036–2038. For example, if a life insurance policy were transferred in a revocable transfer or in one in which the transferor retained a life estate, §§ 2036–2038 would come into play.

In one illustrative case, a § 2036 question arose with respect to insurance proceeds paid on the death of the decedent-insured. In that case, Fidelity-Philadelphia Trust Co. v. Smith, 356 U.S. 274 (1958), the decedent had purchased three single premium life insurance policies. As a condition to selling the decedent those policies, the company required the decedent also to purchase a separate, single premium, non-refundable life annuity policy. The size of each annuity was calculated so that, in the event the annuitant-insured died prematurely, the annuity premium, less the amount allocated to annuity payments already made, would combine with the companion life insurance, plus interest, to equal the amount of insurance policies to be paid. Each annuity policy could have been purchased without the insurance policy for the same premium charged for it under the annuity-life insurance combination. The Commissioner argued that this entire transaction consisted of a transfer of property by the decedent with a retained income interest (in the form of the annuity payments). Therefore, the Commissioner argued, the life insurance proceeds which were paid to the decedent's children after her death should be included in the decedent's gross estate under § 2036(a)(1). However, the executor of the estate argued that the annuity payments were income from the annuity policies which were separate from the insurance policies. Since decedent had assigned the life insurance policies before her death, she had retained no interest at death so as to produce inclusion in the gross estate. The Court agreed and held that the Commissioner could not aggregate the two types of policies into one investment and conclude that by receiving annuities the decedent had retained income from the life insurance contracts. Had the facts shown that the transactions were indivisible, the result in the case might well have been contrary.

Since the provisions of § 2042 are not exclusive, other Code sections might in principle be applied if they would bring into the gross estate something more than the inclusion that would result under § 2042. I.R.C. § 2037 might be such an alternative, but even if a transaction involving life insurance satisfied the requirements of § 2037, it appears that § 2042 would produce a similar or more inclusive result with less uncertainty. Similarly, § 2042 is likely to pre-empt § 2036 and § 2038 in most instances. A transaction that meets the requirements of those sections will, if it involves life insurance, probably satisfy the requirements of § 2042. Section 2039 is expressly made inapplicable to insurance as such and § 2040 only applies if the decedent had an ownership interest with others in the property at his death. Under § 2041, a power of appointment that would produce inclusion would also constitute an incident of ownership under § 2042. Therefore, it seems that pre-E.R.T.A. § 2035 is the principal code section other than § 2042 that is likely to include amounts in the decedent's gross estate that would not otherwise be includable. (As an exercise in comprehension of the statute, it may be interesting to speculate about the taxability of life insurance proceeds on the life of the decedent if § 2042 were removed from the Code.)

Life insurance is often used in a business context, for example in order to provide funds for business purchase agreements. Great care must be used in planning such life insurance arrangements in order to minimize taxes and also to maximize the non-tax utility of insurance. One pitfall to watch for is the danger that not only the business interest owned by the decedent will be included in his gross estate, but also the insurance carried on his life in order to enable the surviving partner to purchase the decedent's business interest.

§ 42. Life Insurance—Gift Tax Consequences

The abolition of the premium-payments test in the estate tax has created a strong incentive for inter-vivos transfers of life insurance policies which, if not transferred, would produce inclusion in the gross estate of the insured-decedent under the "incidents of ownership" test of I.R.C. § 2042. A taxpayer can remove the proceeds of the insurance from his gross estate by a transfer of the incidents of ownership before his death, unless some section other than I.R.C. § 2042 will call for inclusion. To avoid such other estate tax rules of inclusion, the donor must be careful not to make the transfer within three years of death (see § 2035) and must not retain any reversionary interest or any power to revest the economic benefits in himself or his estate or any power to change beneficiaries or any right to income from the transferred property (see §§ 2036–2038).

The price of making an inter-vivos gift of life insurance, to minimize estate taxes or for any other purpose, is susceptibility to federal gift taxation. Just like any other item of property, a policy of life insurance can be the subject of a gift transfer, potentially taxable as such under the gift tax, whether the policy given away is one on the life of the donor or on the life of some other person. Also, a gift may take place if one person (donor) pays premiums on a policy of life insurance owned by another person (donee), whether or not the policy itself was ever the subject of a transfer. The payment of premiums itself amounts to a gift when the policy is owned by someone other than the person paying the premiums.

As the Regulations elaborately state, if the insured purchases a life insurance policy or pays a premium on a previously issued policy, the proceeds of which are payable to a beneficiary or beneficiaries other than his estate, and with respect to which the insured retains no reversionary interest in himself or his estate and no power to revest the economic benefits in himself or his estate or to change the beneficiaries or their proportionate benefits (or if the insured relinquishes by assignment, by designation of new beneficiary or otherwise, every such power that was retained in a previously issued policy), the insured has made a gift of the value of the policy, or to the extent of the premium paid, even though the right of the assignee or beneficiary to receive the benefits is conditioned upon surviving the insured. See Regs. § 25.2511–1(h)(8). Although this portion of the Regulations refers to a gift by a person who is the insured under the policy transferred, it is equally clear that a donor may make a gift for purposes of the gift tax by transferring property rights in a policy or by making premium payments on a policy insuring some third person or even the donee.

As indicated by the Regulations, the time when a transfer of a life insurance policy is complete for gift tax purposes is when the donor has divested himself or herself of all incidents of ownership, all dominion and control, over the policy. See Regs. § 25.2511–2; § 25.2511–1(h)(8). However, if the donor transferred all incidents of ownership except the power to name the beneficiary of the life insurance proceeds at the death of the insured, gift tax would not be imposed at the time of transfer. If the donee were to surrender the policy for its cash surrender value, however, a completed gift would be deemed to have taken place at that time. (If the donee did not surrender the policy and the donor retained the power to designate a beneficiary until his death and if he is also the insured, § 2042 would include the proceeds of the policy in the donor's gross estate at that time. In this way, the Regulations seek to coordinate the gift and estate tax treatments of transfers of the incidents of ownership of life insurance policies.)

When a gift of a life insurance policy is made, valuation of the insurance policy for purposes of the gift tax is determined under the principles set forth in the Regulations at § 25.2512–6(a). In general, the valuation of a policy is determined by its cost or by the price of comparable contracts by the same company. If valuation through that method is not readily ascertainable, the value is to be approximated by adding to the interpolated terminal reserve value of the policy at the date of the gift the proportionate part of the gross premium last paid before the date of the gift which covers the period extending beyond that date. [The formula for determining the value of an insurance policy transferred inter-vivos for purposes of the gift tax is essentially the same as the formula for determining the value of a policy owned by the decedent on the life of someone else if that policy is includable in the decedent's gross estate under §§ 2031 and 2033 of the estate tax. See Regs. § 20.2031–8(a).]

When life insurance is the subject of, or vehicle for, a gift transfer, the question arises whether one or more annual per-donee exclusions will be available to the donor under I.R.C. § 2503(b). If the gift qualifies for an annual per-donee exclusion, the first $10,000 will not be taxed. Since § 2503(b) allows an exclusion in the case of gifts *other than gifts of future interests* in property made to any person by the donor, the law requires a determination whether the gift of insurance is the gift of a present interest or of a future interest. This question arises whether the gift consists of a transfer of a policy or the payment of premiums on a policy of insurance on the life of the donor.

In general, a gift of an insurance policy, even one having no immediate cash value, will be treated as a gift of a present interest for purposes of determining the gift tax exclusion authorized by § 2503(b) of the Code. See Regs. § 25.2503–3(a); Rev.Rul. 55–408, 1955–1 C.B. 113. Of course, to be a gift of a present interest, the transfer must give to the donee all present rights and interests in the insurance policy, including the right to turn it in for its cash surrender value (if any), the right to borrow against it, the right to designate a beneficiary and so on. If the rights or interests of the donee are restricted in some fashion, the gift will be deemed to be a transfer of a future interest and will not qualify for the annual exclusion. See Regs. § 25.2503–3(b); and see, *e.g.,* Nashville Trust Co. v. Comm., 136 F.2d 148 (6th Cir.1943) (terms of settlement options, assignments and policies themselves made the transfer a gift of future interest.)

Community property law, if applicable, complicates the gift tax treatment of a transfer of a life insurance policy or the payment of premiums on a policy owned by another. The Regulations provide some guidance. For example, if property held by husband and wife as community property is used to purchase insurance upon the husband's life and a third person is revocably designated as beneficiary and if under state law the death of the husband is considered to make absolute the transfer by the wife, there is a gift by the wife at the time of the husband's death of half the amount of the proceeds of such insurance, but only if the surviving spouse receives less than his or her community share of the estate or there is some evidence of donative intent. See Kaufman v. U. S., 462 F.2d 439 (5th Cir. 1972).

More generally, the husband and the wife are each deemed to be an owner of one-half of a life insurance policy on the life of one spouse under many community property law systems. This principle applies broadly to a transfer of the policy to a third person by the spouses during their lives. If such a transfer is complete at the time made, the gift will be taxable at that time. However, if the transfer is made in such a form as to be revocable by both spouses, or by one spouse because the transfer violates his or her rights under community property law and exceeds the authority of the donor-spouse, the taxable gift will not be deemed made until the transfer is complete and no longer revocable. Thus, if the husband makes a gift of community property life insurance in fraud of the wife's rights and without her knowledge, and if under state law she is entitled to recall the transfer within a reasonable period after discovering it, the gift will not be complete until she has consented to the gift or until the reasonable period of recall has elapsed. If the wife has not given her consent and if as a result she can call back the entire transfer during the husband's life but can recall only half the transfer after his death, there is no assurance that the beneficiary will receive anything until the time of the death of the husband or the wife's consent and, therefore, no gift has been made at the time of the initial transfer. In other words, to analyze the tax consequences of a gift of insurance by a single spouse under community property law, the courts look to the spouse's powers under state law.

CHAPTER VIII

ANNUITIES AND EMPLOYEE DEATH BENEFITS—ESTATE TAX AND GIFT TAX

§ 43. Estate Taxation of Annuities—§ 2039

Section 2039 of the Internal Revenue Code sets forth the basic estate tax rules for the taxation of annuities. Section 2039 is not exclusive, however, and the possibility remains that some other estate tax section will apply. (That possibility will be discussed briefly after an examination of § 2039.)

In order to understand § 2039 and the problem to which it is addressed, one must understand something about the nature of an annuity and how it can present matters of interest to an estate tax system. An annuity is a payment or the right to a payment or payments, for a period of time, such as for life or for a term of years or for any other period. Sometimes an annuity is purchased by the one entitled to receive payments under it, sometimes the annuity is given to him or her as a gift and sometimes it is provided by an employer as a form of compensation. The purchased annuity provides the best illustration for estate tax purposes. Thus, if a taxpayer transfers property to an annuity company (or any other person) in return for a promise on the part of the transferee company to pay $8,000 a year to the taxpayer, called the annuitant, the taxpayer has purchased an annuity and each payment each year is a payment of the annuity. If the taxpayer transferred property in return for the transferee's promise to pay $8,000 a year to the taxpayer for as long as the taxpayer might live, without any additional promises, the arrangement would be called a single-life, non-refund annuity.

A single-life, non-refund annuity does not present an estate tax problem and is not taxable upon the death of the annuitant. See Fidelity-Philadelphia Trust Co. v. Smith, 356 U.S. 274 (1958). It resembles a life estate which expires upon the death of the person who purchased it. Nothing passes to any other person at that time and no taxable transfer has been made. So to speak, the decedent "used up" his property during life.

Other annuity arrangements, however, do amount to transactions to which the estate tax should, and will, apply. For example, some annuity contracts provide that if the annuity period comes to an end before a certain minimum number of dollars have been paid out, the company will pay a refund to the estate of the annuitant. Such a refund feature often accompanies a single life annuity contract. At the death of the annuitant, a refund will (or may) be payable to the annuitant's estate or to named persons.

Other contracts provide that upon the death of the primary annuitant the annual payment he has been receiving will be paid to another person for the life of the other person. This is a so-called self-and-survivor annuity or a survivorship-or-longer-life annuity. Another kind of annuity contracts, called a joint-and-survivor annuity, provides that a specified sum is to be paid each year to two annuitants jointly during their joint lives and then the same amount, or a smaller amount, is to be paid to the survivor for his or her life.

Unlike the single-life, non-refund contract, an annuity that provides for something to be paid to someone other than the primary annuitant after his death will produce estate tax consequences, either under I.R.C. § 2039, I.R.C. § 2033 or possibly under some other section of the Code. This follows because such an annuity consists, at least in part, of an arrangement to dispose of wealth at death. It provides for a transfer of property at death and thus substitutes for an ordinary testamentary disposition. Enacted in 1954, I.R.C. § 2039 is designed to impose an appropriate estate tax burden on such annuity transfers.

The basic rule of I.R.C. § 2039 is as follows. The gross estate shall include the value of an annuity or other payment receivable by any beneficiary by reason of surviving the decedent, under any form of contract or agreement entered into after March 3, 1931 (other than as insurance under policies on the life of the decedent) if, under that contract or agreement, an annuity or other payment was payable to the decedent, or the decedent possessed the right to receive such annuity or payment, either alone or in conjunction with some other person for his life or for any period not ascertainable without reference to his death or for any period which does not in fact end before his death.

The term "annuity or other payment" as used with respect both to the decedent and the beneficiary refers to one or more payments extending over any period of time whether they are equal or unequal in amount, conditional or unconditional, periodic or sporadic. The term "contract or agreement" includes any arrangement, understanding or plan. An annuity or other payment "was payable" to the decedent if at the time of his death he was in fact receiving an annuity or other payment, whether or not he had an enforceable right to have the payments continued. Also, the decedent "possessed the right to receive" an annuity or other payment if, immediately before his death, he had an enforceable right to receive payments at some time in the future, whether or not at the time of his death he had a present right to receive payments. See Regs. § 20.2039–1(b). (That section of the Regulations contains some helpful examples.)

The general rule, stated in subsection I.R.C. § 2039(a), clearly means that nothing will be included in the gross estate of a decedent who, before his or her death, was receiving annual payments under a single life annuity without a refund. Thus, if Mary Taxpayer, having reached retirement age, wishing to provide for her support and maintenance during her remaining years, transfers $100,000 in cash to an annuity company in return for the annuity company's agreement to pay her $8,000 a year for as long as she might live, there would be no inclusion in Mary's estate under § 2039 at her death. Since nothing will be receivable by any beneficiary by reason of surviving Mary, § 2039(a) does not apply. This result accords with that obtained under § 2033 or § 2036(a)(1) when an interest that has not been transferred by the decedent expires at his or her death. For example, if Mary's father had transferred property in trust and provided that the income would be paid to Mary during her life, the remainder at her death to go to someone else, there would be no inclusion in Mary's estate at the time of her death by reason of the life-estate granted by her father. (Also, § 2036(a)(1) would not apply because Mary was not the grantor or settlor of the trust.) Thus, the result is just as if Mary had spent her entire $100,000 during her life (as in fact she did) and held nothing at her death that would pass to some other person.

Similarly, if during her life Mary had purchased an annuity contract that was to go into effect only upon Mary's death and at that time begin to pay annual amounts to her surviving spouse or child or some other person Mary wished to see supported during the other person's life and after Mary's death, there would be no estate tax inclusion under § 2039 since Mary did not have any interest in the annuity and was not receiving or entitled to receive any payments at the time of her death. See Regs. § 20.2039–1(b); see also Kramer v. U. S., 406 F.2d 1363 (Ct.Cl.1969); compare Wadewitz's Estate, 339

F.2d 980 (7th Cir. 1964). (Gift tax would apply, however, at the time of purchase.)

In other words, § 2039 confines its rule of estate tax inclusion to survivor annuities, whereby some beneficiary receives something by surviving the decedent, and it only applies to such arrangements if the annuitant had a right to or was in fact receiving annuity payments at his death. Thus it is refund or survivorship annuities that § 2039 comprehends and it taxes only the value of payments to be made to the estate or the survivor. In fact, the simple refund-to-the-estate annuity is covered by I.R.C. § 2033.

Before the enactment of § 2039 in 1954, annuities had to be taxed under other transfer sections, such as I.R.C. §§ 2033, 2035, 2036(a)(1), 2037, and 2038. The enactment of § 2039 provided a central, focused rule for such annuities which removed some uncertainties and also dealt specifically, in subsection 2039(b), with the problem of annuities purchased in part by contributions of the decedent and in part by contributions of others.

The general rule of § 2039(b) is that the rule of inclusion contained in subsection (a) of § 2039 can apply only to such part of the value of the annuity or other payment receivable under the contract or agreement as is proportionate to that part of the purchase price contributed by the decedent. Therefore, if Mary's husband had contributed part of the purchase price of the annuity for the survivor's benefit, not everything the survivor received would be includable in Mary's gross estate at her death.

Section 2039 also deals with the important problem of how to tax a refund or survivor annuity that has been purchased by an employer for an employee. Prior to 1954, employee annuities established by the employer, with contributions made only by the employer, were not included in the gross estate of the employee at death even if the annuity payments would shift then from the employee to the surviving beneficiary. In 1954 Congress became convinced that such employee annuities should be taxed just as if the employee annuitant had made all the contributions himself, since they were rooted in the employee's work and constituted compensation for it. As a consequence, § 2039(b) specifically provides that any contribution by the decedent's employer or former employer to the purchase price of an annuity contract or agreement is to be considered as contributed by the decedent if made by reason of his or her employment. Accordingly, if the other tests of § 2039 are met, inclusion in the employee's gross estate will follow even if the employee has not directly or personally contributed a penny to the purchase of the annuity. Of course, if an employer pays an annuity to beneficiaries selected entirely by the employer and does not make any payments to the employee and if the employee had no right to any payments before death, § 2039 will not include the value of payments to the survivors in the employee's estate. See Kramer v. U. S., 406 F.2d 1363 (Ct.Cl.1969). (However, if the employee had the power to designate the beneficiaries, a § 2041 power of appointment might be found to exist, even if § 2039 did not apply because nothing was payable to the employee before his death. As to I.R.C. § 2041, see Ch. IX, *infra*.)

Section 2039 requires a "contract or agreement." Therefore payments made to an employee or his survivors under a social security system involving "contributions" in the form of taxes will not be treated as a § 2039 annuity. See Rev.Rul. 60–70, 1960–1 C.B. 372. Similarly, an informal or gratuitous plan or an occasional transfer to employees or their surviving dependents will not amount to a "contract or agreement" with resulting inclusion under § 2039. See Estate of Barr, 40 T.C. 227 (1963), where the court held against inclusion of voluntary and gratuitous death benefits either under § 2033 or § 2039. In contrast, in Estate of Bahen v. U. S., 305 F.2d 827 (Ct.Cl.1962), the Court of Claims held that § 2039 required inclusion of contingent deferred compensation paid to an employee's widow, along with other death benefits under a death benefit plan and deferred compensation plan which the Court read together as an integrated package of benefits.

In applying § 2039 to an employee benefits situation, it is customary for a court to read various employee benefit plans together. For example, in Gray v. U. S., 410 F.2d 1094 (3rd Cir. 1969), the court held that an employee's vested right in a retirement annuity under a retirement plan together with payments to the employee's designated beneficiary under a survivorship plan when the employee failed to live to retirement age, rendered the beneficiary's benefits includable in the employee's gross estate under § 2039 since the retirement plan and survivorship plan viewed together constituted a contract or agreement within the meaning of the statute.

If the right to payments is forfeitable at the time of the employee-decedent's death, and forfeitable as a result of events not entirely within his control, there will not be any inclusion—because he did not at death have an enforceable right to the payments in the future. On the other hand, if the right to the payments was not forfeitable or was forfeitable only by acts within the control of the decedent, he will be deemed to have had an enforceable right to the payments even if they were to be made only in the future. See, *e.g.,* Estate of Wadewitz, 39 T.C. 925 (1963), aff'd 339 F.2d 980 (7th Cir. 1964). (It is possible, of course, that the death of the employee itself ends any possibility of forfeiture or other conditions, including the unilateral revocation by the employer, in which event the vesting of the benefits in the spouse or other beneficiary would become taxable under § 2039.)

Under the general rule of § 2039(a), the amount included in the gross estate of the decedent is the amount receivable by the surviving beneficiary, as valued at the date of death (and pro-rated for the decedent's contribution). So, if Mary transferred $100,000 to an annuity company to pay her $8,000 a year for her life and at her death to pay $8,000 per year (or) annually to for as long as he might live and if Mary is survived by her husband, the value (at the date of her death) of her husband's right to receive $8,000 a year, given his life expectancy, is the value of the interest to be included in Mary's gross estate. The amount of payments received by Mary before her death is not at all the measure of the transfer subject to estate tax. See Regs. § 20.-2039–1(c). The tax applies to the amount of wealth transferred by the decedent or passing from her at death.

The general rules of § 2039(a) and (b) have no application to an amount which constitutes the proceeds of insurance under a policy on the decedent's life. See Regs. § 20.2039–1(a). This exemption leaves, in some instances, the difficult problem of drawing a line between insurance and annuity payments. See, *e.g.*, All v. McCobb, 321 F.2d 633 (2d Cir. 1963) [held: a § 2039 annuity, not insurance, because no mortality risk shifting or distribution or other indicia of life insurance under the standards of Helvering v. Le Gierse, 312 U.S. 531 (1941).] Payments exempted from § 2039 by the "insurance" clause will then be tested under I.R.C. § 2042, applicable to life insurance. However, § 2039 can apply to a certain portion of an annuity-life insurance package, or to an insurance arrangement that has been recharacterized as an annuity. See, *e.g.*, Montgomery's Estate, 56 T.C. 489 (1971), aff'd 458 F.2d 616 (5th Cir. 1972). Also, the fact that an annuity or other payment is not includable in the decedent's gross estate under § 2039(a) and (b) does not mean that it is not includable under some other section of the estate tax.

Annuities or other payment under certain "qualified plans" were exempted under § 2039(c), a subsection whose intricacies must be placed beyond the scope of this discussion. The estate tax exclusion for qualified retirement plan benefits was repealed, in 1984, for decedents dying after 1984, with limited "grandfather" exceptions. The repeal took place in the context of enlarging the unified credit (exemption-equivalent) and removing the ceiling on the marital deduction.

To illustrate possible application of other estate tax inclusion rules: if the estate of the primary annuitant is entitled to a refund at his death, whether or not there might be inclusion by applying the language of § 2039, § 2033 will bring the refund into the gross estate for estate tax purposes. Cf. Goodman v. Granger, 243 F.2d 264 (3d Cir. 1957). See also Estate of Albright, 356 F.2d 319 (2d Cir. 1966) (holding that § 2033 required inclusion of a lump sum refund of the decedent's contribution which was paid to his widow when the decedent died before the annuity payments began). And see Porter v. Comm., 442 F.2d 915 (1st Cir. 1971) (held: § 2035 may include value of employee death benefits where requirements of § 2039 not met), but note that post-E.R.T.A. estates are not subject to this rule unless §§ 2036–2038, 2041 or 2042 are also involved. See new I.R.C. § 2035(d). Again under other sections of the Code, the question has sometimes arisen whether the exercise by a taxpayer of an option to take a lower joint and survivor annuity, for example, instead of a larger

single annuity, amounted to a transfer with a retained life estate or a transfer otherwise includable
under § 2036 or 2037. In Comm. v. Estate of
Twogood, 194 F.2d 627 (2d Cir. 1952), the court
held that no transfer taxable under the forerunner
of § 2036(a)(1) was involved.

Altogether, § 2039 cannot be regarded as exclusive. See Regs. § 20.2039–1(a). Employee annuity
arrangements have sometimes proved to be taxable
under § 2036, § 2037 or some other section. See,
for example, Rev.Rul. 260, 1953–2 C.B. 262; Rev.
Rul. 158, 1953–2 C.B. 259. However, if the employee's rights have not vested at the time of an election
to take a reduced annuity, some courts have held
there was no "property" transferred, for purposes
of §§ 2035–2038. See, *e.g.*, Estate of Miller v.
Comm., 14 T.C. 657 (1950) (Non-Acq., 1950–2 C.B.
6).

In community property states, the application of
inclusion rules other than § 2039 to an annuity,
particularly in an employee benefit context, becomes more difficult. For example, in Rev.Rul. 67–
278, 1967–2 C.B. 323, the Service declared that if
the vested interest of a surviving spouse in a qualified employee's plan was community property, the
value of the pre-deceased non-employee wife's community interest in the arrangement was includable
in her gross estate under § 2033 and that interest
then would not qualify for exclusion under the
special rules of § 2039(c). Then in 1972 a special
rule, § 2039(d), was introduced, which allowed a
proportionate exclusion to the non-employee spouse

whose interest in the benefits arose because of community property rights, analogous to the § 2039(c) exclusion for the employee-spouse. Finally in 1976, § 2517(c) was added to the Code, allowing similar treatment for the non-employee spouse in the gift context. Since then, however, §§ 2039(c) and (d) and § 2517 have been repealed. See P.L. 99–514, § 1852(e)(1)(A) and (e)(2)(A); P.L. 98–369, § 525(a).

A private annuity, that is to say a transfer of property by the decedent to someone other than a commercial annuity company, often a family member or associate, for a promise of payments in return is subject to testing under I.R.C. § 2039. If not includable there, or in any event, such a transfer must also be tested under § 2036 and the other grantor sections, inasmuch as it involves a transfer of property which must be examined for "strings attached." If the transaction amounts to a transfer of property with a retained life estate, either because the transferred property is security for the promised annuity payments to the transferor or because the amount of the payments is directly geared to the income from the property, § 2036 will require the inclusion of all the transferred property (not just the value of a survivor's annuity, the amount that would be includable under § 2039 alone).

§ 44. Annuities—Gift Tax

All that need be said about application of the gift tax to annuities is that such application is possible in principle and must be analyzed under general gift tax rules. This need to resort to general principles has been heightened by the repeal of some special statutory rules that had been constructed in I.R.C. § 2517 applicable to certain annuities under qualified plans, an election of survivor benefits under which will not invoke a gift tax, with an exception to the subsection (a) rule in § 2517(b) for certain transfers attributable to employee contributions and the § 2517(c) exemption for some community property created annuity interests as mentioned above.

Under general gift tax principles, a taxable gift may be involved if one person purchases an annuity solely for the benefit of another. (Of course, it is possible that such a transaction involves compensation for services or the purchase of property with potential income tax, but not gift tax, consequences to follow.) Also, if one person purchases an annuity that will benefit both himself and someone else, at once or later, a gift may be involved, since the purchaser is making a transfer in part to or for the benefit of the other person. Further information must be obtained to ascertain when the transfer is complete, what off-setting consideration, if any, has been received, whether the transfer is at arm's length and in the ordinary course of business and, altogether, what amount must be included in the gift tax base. Also, a problem may arise with respect to a gift of a future interest in an annuity setting.

CHAPTER IX

POWERS OF APPOINTMENT—
ESTATE AND GIFT TAX
CONSEQUENCES

§ 45. Powers of Appointment—Estate Tax Consequences—§ 2041

Under § 2041, a decedent's gross estate includes the value of property with respect to which the decedent possessed, exercised or released certain powers of appointment. The rules for inclusion vary with the nature of the power, the time it was created and whether or how it was exercised, released or held.

A power of appointment is a power over property held in trust or otherwise, a power exercisable either during life or at death by will (or both), to determine who shall become the owner of property or the recipient of income. For estate tax purposes, moreover, the term "power of appointment" includes all powers which are in substance and effect powers of appointment regardless of the nomenclature used in creating the power and regardless of local property law connotations. Regs. § 20.2041–1(b). Therefore, a power to appropriate or consume the principal of a trust is a power of appointment. A power to affect the beneficial enjoyment of trust property or its income by altering, amending, or revoking the trust instrument or terminating the trust is a power of appointment. For example, a decedent's power, as one of four co-trustees under a trust set up by his father, to terminate the trust, and thereby accelerate his own remainder interest, if all four agreed that "it was in the interest of the beneficiary" to do so, constitutes a general power of appointment sufficient to include the trust corpus in his estate under § 2041. (See Maytag v. U. S., 493 F.2d 995 (10th Cir.1974)). If community property law confers upon a wife a power of testamentary disposition over property in which she does not have a vested interest, she is considered to have a power of appointment.

In discussion, powers of appointment are classified in two categories according to the appointees who may be designated as the takers of the property. A so-called *general power* of appointment is one exercisable in favor of an unrestricted selection of beneficiaries. A so-called *special power* is one that, by its terms, can be exercised in favor only of a restricted or specified group of beneficiaries. The term "general power of appointment" takes on an even more specialized meaning in the estate tax, as will be elaborated below. See I.R.C. § 2041(b)(1); Regs. § 20.2041–1(c).]

In general, the holder of a taxable power of appointment need not ever have owned the property subject to his power (though he may have) and need not have any other interest in the property, such as a life estate or a remainder interest (though he may have), to be taxable on the power. Unlike §§ 2036–2038, § 2041 is not a "grantor" section. It is enough that he or she has the described power over the property or income to be deemed, in general, the holder or exerciser of a taxable power of appointment.

From the nature of a power of appointment, one can easily infer that estate tax consequences may and should be involved. For example, the actual testamentary exercise of a power, particularly a power over property earlier transferred by the holder in trust or property which he or she could obtain by exercising the power in his own favor, amounts to a testamentary gift of property. Even the mere ownership of such a power (without actual exercise) could be viewed as owning the property or income that could have been obtained or disposed of by exercising the power.

Originally, the estate tax statute did not contain a provision specifically aimed at taxing property subject to a power of appointment. Under property law concepts, the holder of the power of appointment (without any ownership interest) was viewed merely as exercising a kind of fiduciary authority over the property such that the property actually was being transferred from the original owner to the ultimate beneficiary. Accordingly, the holder of a power of appointment who had no other ownership interest in the property or income was not viewed as himself transferring property at death or upon inter-vivos exercise of the power, much less by holding a power and not exercising it, in which

event the property passes by default. Consequently, in an early case, the United States Supreme
Court held that property subject to a power of
appointment held by the decedent at his death was
not includable in his gross estate. See U. S. v.
Field, 255 U.S. 257 (1921). In the *Field* case, the
power of appointment actually had been exercised
by the decedent's will and thus the situation looked
very much like a transfer of property at and by
reason of decedent's death, notwithstanding which
the Court held against inclusion. Later, the Commissioner also attempted to use the predecessor of
§ 2033 to include property subject to a power of
appointment and in which the holder also held a life
interest on the ground that the holder of the power
was the constructive or substantial owner of the
property. However, the Supreme Court refused to
apply the constructive ownership doctrine in this
estate tax situation. See Helvering v. Safe Deposit
and Trust Co., 316 U.S. 56 (1942).

When the courts failed to include in the gross
estate property subject to a power of appointment,
exercised or not, Congress took action. By statutory law until 1942, property was included in the
gross estate of the holder of the power of appointment but only if the power was a "*general* power of
appointment," was actually *exercised*, either by will
or by inter-vivos transfer, under circumstances
which would have brought the property into the
gross estate if the exercise had actually been a
transfer of property, and only if the property actually *passed under the exercise* of the power. Under

these statutory requirements, the United States Supreme Court held, in Helvering v. Grinnell, 294 U.S. 153 (1935), that the mere exercise of a general power of appointment was not sufficient to require inclusion, if the property did not actually pass under the exercise of the power. (In that case the appointees had renounced the shares appointed to them under the power.)

In 1942, Congress expanded the coverage of the statute dealing with powers of appointment to include property subject to a power that was *held but not actually exercised*, on the ground that the possession of the power resembled ownership and that non-exercise of the power also constituted dominion and control over the property and its disposition. The 1942 legislation was applicable to pre-1942 powers held by decedents who died after the new law was enacted in 1942. Some provisions of the 1942 legislation generated much controversy and dissatisfaction. As a consequence, the law was changed in 1951 when the predecessor of § 2041 was enacted, later to be codified in 1954 as § 2041. Section 2041 still distinguishes between pre- and post-1942 powers and restores much of the pre-1942 law with regard to earlier powers. Therefore, the non-exercise of such a power results in no estate tax and the release is permitted without imposition of tax. Under the Regulations, the date of the creation of a power is controlled by the date the instrument creating the power takes effect. See Regs. § 20.2041–1(e).]

Section 2041 of the Internal Revenue Code provides, in general, that the value of the gross estate shall include the value of all property to the extent of any property with respect to which the decedent at the time of his death *has* a *general* power of appointment (created after October 21, 1942). It also includes all property with respect to which the decedent has at any time *exercised* or *released* a general power of appointment by a disposition which is of such a nature that if it were a transfer of property owned by the decedent, such property would be includable in the decedent's gross estate under §§ 2035–2038. See I.R.C. § 2041(a)(2). As to general powers of appointment created *before* October 21, 1942, the gross estate includes the value of all property to the extent of any property with respect to which a general power of appointment is actually *exercised* by the decedent either by will or by a disposition that if it were a transfer of property owned by the decedent would be includable in the decedent's gross estate under §§ 2035–2038. See § 2041(a)(1). The different rules for powers created before and after the crucial date reflect the change in the law made on that date, a change not to be given retroactive application. The difference between the pre- and post-1942 rules is very great—the difference between holding and actually exercising a power of appointment. The following discussion will concentrate on the post-1942 rule, as it now has become preeminent in importance.

Putting aside for the moment some technicalities and the differences between the rules applicable to pre-1942 powers of appointment, one may observe generally that § 2041 will require inclusion in the decedent's gross estate of property which he may never have owned during his life and which he may never have personally possessed or enjoyed and whose ownership or receipt he has never actually determined by the exercise of a power of appointment.   In other words, the mere possession of a general power of appointment, as defined in the statute, is treated as the possession of such an important component of ownership that the decedent should be subject to a transfer tax.   He is treated just as if he had owned the property and transferred it at his death or otherwise had determined who would take "his" property at his death. Unlike §§ 2035–2038, § 2041 is not a "grantor section" and, therefore, an inter-vivos transfer of an interest in the property is not a prerequisite to the application of § 2041.   A power held by Tom over property put in trust by Alice can cause inclusion in Tom's estate at his death.

The mere ownership or even the exercise of a power of appointment that is *not* a "general power of appointment" (as defined in the statute) will not produce inclusion in the decedent's gross estate of the property that is subject to the power or that passes by virtue of the exercise of the power. Hence, it becomes crucial to differentiate between a "general power of appointment" and a so-called "special power of appointment."

I.R.C. § 2041(b)(1) defines a *general power* of appointment, for purposes of the inclusion rules in sub-section (a), as a power which is exercisable in favor of the decedent, his estate, his creditors or the creditors of the estate, with certain exceptions specified in the statute. The language of the statute is cast in the alternative and it is clear that the power to appoint any of the specified appointees is sufficient to make the power a general power. A power is *not* a general power if it is (a) exercisable only in favor of one or more designated persons or classes of persons other than the decedent or his creditors or the decedent's estate or creditors of his estate or (b) expressly not exercisable in favor of the decedent or his creditors, or the decedent's estate or the creditors of his estate. See Regs. § 20.2041–1(c)(1)(a) & (b). In general, then, a "general power of appointment" for statutory purposes is a power of appointment (broadly construed), that is exercisable in favor of the decedent directly, or indirectly by appointment to his creditors or to his estate. Statutory exceptions are made for a power to consume, invade or appropriate property for the benefit of the decedent when that power is limited by an ascertainable standard relating to the health, education, support, or maintenance of the decedent, and another exception is provided for powers held jointly by the decedent and another person, such as the creator of the power or someone having a substantial, adverse interest. See I.R.C. § 2041(b)(1); Regs. § 20.2041–1(c)(2) and –3(c).

Thus the 1954 Code uses the term "general power" to describe something that might be labeled a "beneficial power," that is to say a power which can be exercised with a resulting financial benefit to the holder of the power. By so doing, the law requires the gross estate to include property which the decedent might have obtained for his own personal benefit by exercising an inter-vivos power of appointment in his own favor, or which he might have "sold" by exercising an inter-vivos power of appointment in favor of someone else in return for a payment or other favors to him. Section 2041 also requires inclusion of property which the decedent could not have personally enjoyed during life because his power was exercisable only through his will but which he could appoint to beneficiaries he himself selected, by exercise of the testamentary power. By also requiring the inclusion of property subject to a general power exercisable by will even though that power was not in fact exercised, the statute requires inclusion of property whose receipt or ownership at and after the decedent's death evidently was satisfactory to him (because he could have changed the result by an exercise of the power which he in fact chose not to do).

As to post-1942 powers, the first question is whether the decedent had a *general* power of appointment at the time of his death. If he held a general power, it is taxable to him whether or not actually *exercised*. The decedent will be deemed to have such a general power at the time of his death even if the exercise of the power will not be effec-

tive until a stated time after the exercise or even if
the holder cannot exercise the power except after
giving some notice and allowing a stated period to
elapse before exercising the power and even if the
notice has not been given before his death. See
§ 2041(a)(2). (The Regulations also make clear
that a disclaimer or renunciation of a general power
of appointment is not to be deemed a release of
such power.) However, if the power is exercisable
only after some event has happened and if that
event has not occurred and is not within the control
of the decedent, the decedent will not be deemed to
have the power at his death. See Regs. § 20.2041–
3(b).

Still as to post-1942 powers, if the decedent's
power is one that is *not* a general power as defined
in the law, no inclusion will follow even if he
exercises the power—with one exception. Section
2041(a)(3) provides that property will be included in
the gross estate if the decedent by his will, or by a
disposition of such a nature that if it were a transfer of property owned by the decedent would be
includable under § 2035, § 2037 or § 2038, exercises a post-1942 power of appointment (whether general or special) by creating another power. Even
then, the property will be included in the gross
estate only if the power created by exercise of the
first power can be validly exercised as a matter of
state law so as to postpone the vesting of any estate
or interest in the property or to suspend the absolute ownership or power of alienation of such property for a period without regard to the date the first

power was created. For example, if the decedent were the life beneficiary of a trust with a $100,000 corpus, and had the power to appoint the property only to his children, the entire $100,000 would be included in his gross estate if by will he appointed one of his children as life beneficiary and gave him or her a power to appoint the remainder and the creation of this second power postponed the vesting of the estate under state law. See Regs. § 20.2041–3(e).

The purpose of this somewhat arcane rule is to prevent an indefinite succession of untaxed powers with an indefinite suspension of the absolute ownership of property, even if local law were to permit. But for this rule, a special power (*i.e.*, a non-general power) could be created, exercised by the creation of another special power and so on and on without tax. Property could thus be transferred from one generation to another without imposition of an estate tax. Section 2041(a)(3) blocks this possibility.

The second question under § 2041 is whether a general power of appointment, though not *held* at death, may nevertheless result in inclusion by reason of its exercise. Section 2041 not only requires inclusion if a post-1942 general power is held or exercised at death, but also calls for an estate tax if a general power is exercised or released, under certain circumstances. Those circumstances parallel the incomplete-until-death circumstances of I.R.C. §§ 2035–2038, and those statutes are incorporated by reference in § 2041(a)(2). Under this statute, property must be included in the decedent's gross estate if it is property with respect to which the decedent at any time (*i.e.,* even during life) exercised or released a general power of appointment by a disposition equivalent to a §§ 2035–2038 transfer of property owned by him. For instance, a power used to appoint a remainder to someone while retaining a life interest fits the model § 2036(a)(1) transfer, while an appointment of a remainder and retention of the right to revoke it fits § 2038. See also Regs. § 20.2041–3(d); § 20.-2041–2(c) (examples 1–4).

A release of a post-1942 general power is treated as the equivalent of an exercise of the power. Moreover, the lapse of a power created after 1942 is treated as the equivalent of a release and hence equal to an exercise of the power. See § 2041(b)(2). Therefore, property will be included in the gross estate of the holder of a power if he releases that power in such a way that had he transferred the property it would have been included in his gross estate under §§ 2035–2038. A special exclusion is granted in the case of a power that is permitted to lapse; the estate tax will not apply to the extent that the property subject to the lapsed power did not exceed $5,000 or 5% of the trust property, whichever is greater. See I.R.C. § 2041(b)(2).

The typical lapse or release situation occurs when the life beneficiary of a trust has the power to invade the corpus up to a certain amount of money every year. If the beneficiary does not exercise that power during the year, then the amount, if any, that exceeds the greater of $5,000 or 5% will be considered the release of a power coming within § 2041(a)(2) and § 2036(a)(1), since the beneficiary has, in effect, transferred the amount of property subject to the unused power to the remainderman while retaining his or her life interest. See Regs. § 20.2041–3(d)(3).

Section 2041(a)(2) will *not* require inclusion in the gross estate if a post-1942 general power of appointment is irrevocably exercised, released or allowed to lapse *during life* if the exercise or release was not made within three years of death (as in § 2035) and if after the exercise or release the former holder of the power retains no interest in or control over the property which would cause the property to be included in his or her gross estate under §§ 2036–2038 if the property had been transferred by the holder.

The amount of property to be included when § 2041 applies to a power of appointment depends on which portion of § 2041 is called into effect. If a pre-1942 power is involved, § 2041 will cause only the property with respect to which the power was exercised to be included in the gross estate. If a post-1942 power is involved, the gross estate will include all the property subject to the power of the decedent held at his death or with respect to which he had exercised or released the power in a way covered by § 2041. (A special allowance is made for lapsed powers, as noted above.) If a power of appointment exists only over a limited interest in property or only as to part of an entire group of assets, § 2041 applies only to such interest or part. See Regs. 20.2041–1(b)(3).

By virtue of the broad definition of "general power of appointment" in the statute and the regulations, an overlap between §§ 2041 and 2036–2038 becomes possible. In the event of such an overlap, § 2041 will *not* be allowed to have the effect of reducing the amount of the inclusion in the gross estate determined under other sections of the Code. The Regulations take the position that the term "power of appointment" does not include powers reserved by the decedent to himself within the concept of §§ 2036–2038. See Regs. § 20.2041–1(b)(2). Therefore, the other sections will apply exclusively in the case of a reserved or retained power. Similarly, § 2033 might apply if the decedent actually owned an interest in the property.

By way of a last word, it should be mentioned that a tax advisor has at his or her disposal a very useful estate planning tool in the form of the nontaxable power of appointment. By steering clear of the rules of inclusion in § 2041, an individual can pass important powers over the disposition of property to a succeeding beneficiary or generation while keeping the property in trust or otherwise within restrictions that would be lost if outright ownership were conferred and without the tax bill that outright ownership would impose, subject only to tax on generation-skipping transfers.

§ 46. Powers of Appointment—Gift Tax— § 2514(b)

In many respects, the rules of the gift tax with respect to powers of appointment complement the rules of the estate tax. The general rule of the gift tax, embodied in § 2514(b), is that the *exercise* or *release* of a post-1942 general power of appointment shall be deemed a transfer of property by the individual possessing the power. A *disclaimer* or *renunciation* of such power shall not be deemed a release of the power. A *lapse* of the power is treated as a release of the power by § 2514(e), but only to the extent that the property that could have been appointed by the exercise of the lapsed power exceeds the greater of $5,000 or 5% of the assets out of which, or the proceeds of which, the exercise of the lapsed powers could be satisfied. A statutory definition of what is a "general power of appointment" for gift tax purposes can be found in § 2514(c); it is almost identical to the estate tax definition in § 2041(b). See also Regs. § 25.2514–1.

Since the mere possession of a post-1942 general power of appointment causes estate tax consequences, some incentive is created to exercise or release such a power during life. By treating lifetime exercise or release as a taxable event, the gift tax rule of § 2514 backstops the estate tax and prevents easy, tax-free avoidance of § 2041.

Slightly different rules are applicable with respect to pre-October 21, 1942 powers. Under I.R.C. § 2514(a), the exercise of a pre-1942 general power is taxable as a transfer of property by the person possessing the power. However, failure to exercise a pre-1942 general power or the complete release of such a power is not deemed to be an exercise of the power and hence is not a taxable transfer. Furthermore, a pre-1951 partial release of a pre-1942 general power, the effect of which is to cut down the general power to a special power, is not treated as a taxable gift at the time of the release and the exercise of the reduced power at a later time will not give rise to gift or estate tax. See § 2514(a). In other instances, a partial release and subsequent exercise or release will be telescoped and treated as an exercise or release of a general power.

Finally, paralleling the special rule in the estate tax, § 2514(d) declares that the inter-vivos exercise of a post-1942 power by creating another power that under applicable state law can be exercised in such a way as to postpone vesting of any interest or estate in the property, or to suspend the absolute ownership or power of alienation of such property, for a period ascertainable without regard to the date of the creation of the first power will be treated as a transfer of property by the holder of the power, to the extent of the property subject to the second power.

The regulations under § 2514 provide substantial explanatory material. See Regs. §§ 25.2514–1 through –3. Many of the definitions and other rules in the gift tax sections coincide with or parallel the estate tax regulations on the same points. For example, as with the estate tax regulations, the

Commissioner states that the term "power of appointment" in the gift tax law does not include powers reserved by a donor to himself. See Regs. § 25.2514–1(b)(2). Nor is any provision of § 2514 or of the regulations under that section to be construed to limit the application of any other section of the Code or the Regulations. Specifically, the power of an owner of property to dispose of his interest is not a power of appointment and the interest is includable in the amount of his gifts to the extent that they would be includable under § 2511, without regard to § 2514. So, if a trust created by H provides for payment of the income to W for life with power in W to appoint the entire trust property by deed during her lifetime to a class consisting of her children, and a further power to dispose of the entire corpus by will to anyone, including her estate, and if W exercises the inter-vivos power in favor of her children, she has made a transfer of her income interest which constitutes a taxable gift under § 2511(a), without regard to § 2514. See Regs. § 25.2514–3(e). (This transfer also results in a relinquishment of her general power to appoint by will, which constitutes a transfer under § 2514 if the power was created after October 1, 1942.)

If the power of appointment applies only to part of an entire group of assets or only to a limited interest in property, § 2514 applies only to that part or interest. Regs. § 25.2514–1(b)(3).

To sum it up, the gift tax treats someone who exercises a post-1942 general power of appointment in favor of someone else, even in the favor of the taker in default, much as it treats an owner of property who transfers the property to another. (The same approach is taken to the exercise of a pre-1942 power, but failure to exercise or a complete release of a pre-1942 power are treated differently.) The exercise of such a power will be taxable as a gift even though the property never belonged to the possessor of the power; by exercising a general power in favor of someone else he is deemed to be transferring property he could have taken for himself, but did not, and gave to the appointee instead. In contrast, the exercise or release of a non-general power of appointment is not treated as a transfer of property for gift tax purposes (except in particular circumstances when it is used unduly to suspend vesting or alienation, as defined in § 2514(d)). In the case of the non-general power, no gift transfer from the holder of the power to the appointee is deemed to occur. The exercise of the power merely effects the transfer from the original owner and donor of the power to the appointee.

Although § 2514 attempts to spell out when dealings with a power of appointment constitute a transfer, whether such transfer constitutes a taxable gift can only be determined in the light of other gift tax principles as to completion, consideration, renunciations, and the amount and value of the gift, if any.

CHAPTER X

INCLUSION AND VALUATION

§ 47. Inclusion and Valuation—Introduction

The question of what interest or property must be *included* in the gross estate of a decedent is a question separate from the *valuation* to be placed on the included property or interest. When applying an estate tax inclusion rule, the first question is whether any interest will have to be included in the decedent's gross estate as a result of the rule in question. Once it has been determined that an interest is to be included, the valuation of that interest must then be ascertained by determining the fair market value of the property in which the interest is held and then by determining the value of the interest that is to be included in the gross estate, if that interest is less than all of the property.

Preceding chapters of this book have dealt with the extent of inclusion or with the determination of which interest is to be included under the various rules of the estate tax. Similarly in gift tax topics, the question has been what property or interest has been the subject matter of the gift and thus will provide the base for the gift tax. This chapter of the book turns first to the question of how (admittedly includable) interests shall be valued for estate tax purposes and, later, how property or an interest in property that admittedly is the subject of a taxable gift shall be valued for gift tax purposes. From time to time, dimensions of the inclusion question will crop up again, but the prime focus will be upon the separate issue of valuation.

§ 48. Valuation—Estate Tax—§ 2031

If property is included in the gross estate of the decedent under I.R.C. § 2033, to the extent of the interest therein held by decedent at his death, the value used shall be the value at the date of death, unless the executor elects the alternate valuation date (as to which, see § 50, *infra*). The date of death rule is established by I.R.C. § 2031(a) which states that the value of the gross estate of the decedent shall include, to the extent provided for in the inclusion sections of the estate tax, the value at the time of his death of all property, wherever situated.

The Regulations under § 2031 provide elaborate guidance about the manner of valuation to be used for property included in the gross estate and valued at the time of death. (Regulations under § 2032 supplement the rules under § 2031 in order to cope with those special problems that arise as a result of the election of the alternate valuation date.)

In general, property included in the gross estate is valued at its fair market value at the time of the decedent's death (or on the alternate valuation date or other date applicable under I.R.C. § 2032). The

fair market value is defined as the price at which
the property would change hands between a willing
buyer and a willing seller, neither being under any
compulsion to buy or sell and both having reasonable knowledge of relevant facts. See Regs. § 20.-
2031–1(b). The fair market value is not to be
determined by a forced sale price and is not to be
determined by the sales price of an item in a market
other than that in which the item is most commonly
sold to the public. Therefore, if an item of property
includable in the decedent's gross estate is generally
obtained by the public in the retail market, the fair
market value of that item is the price at which it or
a comparable piece would be sold at retail. In the
case of an automobile, for example, it is the price
for which an automobile of the same or similar
description could be purchased by a member of the
general public and not the price for which the
automobile would be purchased by a dealer in used
automobiles. The Regulations go on to say that all
relevant facts and elements of value as of the applicable valuation date shall be considered in every
case.

The Regulations provide specific rules for the
valuation of property, such as stocks and bonds,
that consists of units. See Regs. § 20.2031–1(b)
and § 20.2031–2. Specifically, stocks and bonds are
valued at their fair market value per share or bond
on the applicable valuation date. Fair market value
is based upon selling prices where possible and
otherwise on bid and asked prices, as described in
Regs. § 20.2031–2(b)–(d). See also Federal Rules of

Evidence, Rule No. 803(17), which makes market reports admissible as an exception to the hearsay rule.] If such prices do not reflect fair market value, other factors may be considered. Regs. § 20.2031–2(e). If selling prices or bid and asked prices are completely unavailable, then the fair market value of the stock or bonds is to be determined by taking into account the soundness of the security, the interest yield, the date of maturity and other relevant factors in the case of bonds, and in the case of stock, the company's net worth, prospective earning power and dividend paying capacity, as well as other factors. See Regs. § 20.2031–2(f). The statute itself provides that stock and securities whose value cannot be determined with reference to bid and asked prices or with reference to sale prices because they are not listed on an exchange, shall be valued by taking into consideration, in addition to all other factors, the value of stock or securities of corporations engaged in the same or similar line of business which are listed on an exchange. I.R.C. § 2031(b). The Regulations go on to provide additional rules to govern securities that have been pledged, or that are subject to an option or contract to purchase, or stock that is selling "ex dividend" on the date of the decedent's death. See Regs. § 20.2031–2(g)–(i). [See I.R.C. § 2703 and the Regulations at § 25.2703 for special rules involving options and agreements (including contracts to purchase) entered into or substantially modified after October 8, 1990.]

An interest in a business, whether a partnership or proprietorship, is also valued at the net amount which a willing purchaser would pay a willing seller. The net value is determined on the basis of all relevant factors including a fair appraisal of the assets and earning capacity of the business and other factors. See Regs. § 20.2031–3. (For special rules for valuing the transfer of an interest in a corporation and for the treatment of unpaid qualified payments at the death of the transferor or an applicable family member, see I.R.C. § 2701 and the discussion at § 48A *infra.*)

Promissory notes are valued at the amount of unpaid principal and accrued interest, unless the executor can establish that the value is lower or that the notes are actually worthless. See Regs. § 20.2031–4. Cash at hand or on deposit is, of course, to be valued at its face value. See Regs. § 20.2031–5.

Household and personal effects similarly are to be valued at the price a willing buyer would pay a willing seller. Special rules are provided for small and miscellaneous items, items of substantial value and household effects disposed or prior to investigation. See Regs. § 20.2031–6.

Somewhat more complex rules are necessary to determine the valuation of annuities, life estates, terms for years, remainders and reversions. Such rules are set forth in the Regulations. See Regs. § 20.2031–7 and § 20.2031–10. In valuing life estates, remainders and reversionary interests, as well as in valuing annuities, the longevity of a person who is alive on the valuation date often becomes central. Usually such an interest is valued on the assumption that the particular measuring life will turn out to be just exactly as long as the mortality statistics suggest the life of a person of that age and sex would be on the average. Mortality tables are contained in the Regulations. See Regs. § 20.2031–7. Complications that cannot be solved by the simpler use of these tables can be determined under other tables or with the assistance of the Internal Revenue Service.

The valuation of certain life insurance and annuity contracts and the valuation of shares in an open-end investment company (a mutual fund) are guided by the regulations in § 20.2031–8. The old requirement in the Regulations that mutual fund shares be valued at the public offering price of a share, which amounts to replacement cost, rather than at the price for which those shares could be resold to the mutual fund itself, the redemption value, was held to be invalid by the Supreme Court. See U. S. v. Cartwright, 411 U.S. 546 (1973). As a result, mutual fund shares will be valued at the (lower) redemption price, rather than the fund's asking price. The Regulations were thereafter amended to comply, in both the estate tax [see § 20.2031–8(b)] and gift tax [see § 25.2512–6(b)] valuation contexts.

The fair market value rule, the general rule of valuation for property held at death, whether valued on the date of death or at the alternate valuation date, is simpler to state than to apply. Even expert appraisers can often differ on the value of a particular piece of tangible property, and the variation among appraisals of an intangible ownership right or an interest in a going business is likely to be very substantial. Special rules attempt to take into account some particular market problems. For example, the "blockage rule" discounts the value of shares of stock for the large number of shares held by the estate and the effect on the market price that could be expected were those shares suddenly to be released for sale. See Helvering v. Maytag, 125 F.2d 55 (8th Cir. 1942); Regs. § 20.2031–2(e). On the other hand, a block of stock representing control of a corporation may well be valued at more than just the per share value times the number of shares held. See, *e.g.*, Estate of Salsbury, 34 T.C.M. 1441 (1975), where the per share value of the block was surcharged an additional 38%, representing the value of the control element. Similarly, the valuation of good-will in a partnership is often a difficult stumbling block, one of the problems being whether the pre-death good-will survives the death of the decedent. Another problem involves restrictive agreements and agreements for the purchase or sale of business interests and their impact on valuation for estate tax purposes. See *e.g.*, May v. McGowan, 194 F.2d 396 (2d Cir. 1952).

§ 48A. Special Valuation Rules—§§ 2701–2704

In 1988, the Omnibus Budget Reconciliation Act of 1990 (P.L. 101–508, 104 Stat. 1388) added new

I.R.C. Chapter 14 (§§ 2701–2704) to provide elaborate valuation rules for transfers, between family members, of interests in corporations, partnerships, and trusts, to get at the problem of special intra-family gifts, such as "estate freezes", made for estate planning and tax avoidance purposes. These sections generally apply to transfers taking place after October 8, 1990. Section 2701 places a value of zero on a distribution, liquidation, put, call, or conversion right that is attributable to an applicable retained interest in a corporation or partnership held by the transferor or a member of the transferor's family immediately after the transfer. Consequently, the entire amount of the transfer is valued, and thus taxed, as a gift. An exception to the zero valuation exists if the retained interest consists of a qualified payment (a dividend payable on a periodic basis under cumulative preferred stock to the extent that the dividend is determined at a fixed rate) and there are one or more liquidation, put, call, or conversion rights with respect to such interests. See § 2701(a)–(c). Section 2701 does *not* apply if (1) market quotations are readily available on an established securities market for the transferred or retained interest, (2) the interest is of the same class as the transferred interest, or (3) the interest is proportionally the same as the transferred interest, without regard to nonlapsing differences in voting power (or, for a partnership, nonlapsing differences with respect to management and limitations on liability). See § 2701(a)(2). Consult the statute and the regulations at § 25.2701 for further detail on the operation of § 2701.

Section 2702 applies a similar zero-value rule for retained interests in transfers of interests in trusts to, or for the benefit of, a member of the transferor's family. Section 2702 does not apply to "incomplete transfers"—those that would not be treated as a gift whether or not consideration was received for such transfer. See § 2702(a)(3)(B). Section 2702 has several other exceptions that are beyond the scope of this discussion; consult the statute and the regulations at § 25.2702 for more detail. New § 2702 has the effect of making obsolete many forms of "G.R.I.T.s" (Grantor Retained Income Trusts).

Section 2703 provides that the value of property shall be determined without regard to "any option, agreement, or other right to acquire or use the property at a price less than the fair market value of the property (without regard to such option, agreement, or right)," or any restriction on the right to sell or use such property. Section 2703 does *not* apply if the option, agreement, right, or restriction meets the following requirements: (1) It is a *bona fide* business arrangement; (2) It is not a device to transfer such property to members of the decedent's family for less than full and adequate consideration; and (3) Its terms are comparable to similar arrangements entered into by persons in an arm's length transaction. Consult the Regulations at § 25.2703 for more detail.

Under § 2704, if (1) there is a lapse of voting or liquidation rights in a corporation or partnership, and (2) the individual holding this right immediately before the lapse and members of his or her family hold control of the entity both before and after the lapse, the lapse is treated as a transfer by gift or a transfer that is includable in the gross estate of the decedent. The value of the transfer is the excess of the value of the interests held before the lapse over the value held after the lapse. Consult the statute and the regulations at § 25.2704 for further detail.

The following are useful discussions of new Chapter 14 and the planning opportunities that exist therein: Cass & Campbell, New Internal Revenue Code Chapter Fourteen Replaces Section 2036(c), 79 Ill.B.J. 508, Oct. 1991; Alexander & Spector, Code Section 2036(c) And The Revenue Reconciliation Act of 1990, 49 Tax Notes 913 (Nov. 19, 1990); Solomon, New Estate Freeze Rules For Strategic Tax Planning, 50 Tax Notes 871 (Feb. 25, 1991); and Reverse Recapitalizations And Other Planning Techniques Available Under The Chapter 14 Regulations, 45 Major Tax Planning, p. 11–1 (1993).

§ 49. Special Use Valuation—§ 2032A

There is one exception to the general rule that the transfer tax value of given property is its fair market value on the applicable date. This is the "special use valuation", permitted only for estate tax purposes under § 2032A, a new section introduced into the Code in 1976, and significantly liberalized by E.R.T.A. (1981). This section permits an election with respect to qualifying farm and small business real property, under which the qualifying property can be valued at less than its fair market value. See, generally, Regs. § 20.2032A.

This special relief was needed because the normal concept of fair market value presupposes that property will be valued at its potential "highest and best use". Therefore the fair market value of a particular piece of property, a farm for example, may well greatly exceed its income potential as a farm, because of the possibilities of developing the land for other, more lucrative uses. In other words, what might be called "speculative value" is part of fair market value. If the heirs of the property wish to keep it in use as a farm, they may have great liquidity problems that result from an estate tax value that is not commensurate with the earning capacity of the land. The purpose of the special use valuation is to minimize these liquidity problems and thus to encourage the continued existence of the family farm or small business, by relieving the need to sell the property in order to pay the estate tax.

To qualify for the election, the property itself must have been used as a farm or in a small business and must be family owned and operated. It must pass to a "qualified heir", that is, to a member of the decedent's family. If the facts satisfy many complex conditions, *e.g.*, that the property in question constitutes a significant portion of the estate, then the "speculative value", any part of the value attributable to a potentially different use of the property, may be excluded from its estate value, up to a maximum of $750,000. One of two separate evaluation methods may be elected to determine the special use valuation, *i.e.*, the value of the property for the use under which it qualifies. There are also recapture provisions, which will impose "additional estate tax" on the property in the event that the special use ceases, that the property is transferred to a non-family member, or that the "qualified heir" discontinues his "substantial participation" in the business. This "additional estate tax" is the personal liability of the "qualified heir", and the potential recapture period lasts for 10 years (15 years for pre-E.R.T.A. decedents) or until his or her death, whichever is earliest.

The provisions of § 2032A are very complex. In addition to the complexity of the section itself, there are many unresolved questions relating to its inter-action with other aspects of the transfer tax system, for example, the marital deduction. Other trouble spots are its application in a corporate or partner-ship context, and the transfer tax or income tax consequences in cases of a subsequent transfer within the recapture period. In the proper situa-tion, substantial estate tax savings are possible (at the cost of increased administrative expenses).

§ 50. Alternate Valuation Date—§ 2032

As an alternative to the date of death rule, the executor may elect to value all of the property included in the gross estate according to the alter-nate valuation rules set forth in I.R.C. § 2032. If

elected, these rules provide that property included
in the gross estate which has not been distributed,
disposed of, sold or exchanged as of the alternate
valuation date—which is a date six months after the
decedent's death—shall be valued as of that date.
I.R.C. § 2032(a)(2). If property has been distributed, sold, exchanged or otherwise disposed of between death and the alternate valuation date, the
property shall be valued as of the date of distribution, sale, exchange or other disposition. I.R.C.
§ 2032(a)(1). Finally, any interest or estate that is
affected by mere lapse of time shall be included at
its value as of the time of death (rather than as of
the alternate valuation date) with adjustment for
any difference in its value as of the alternate valuation date that is not due to a mere lapse of time.
I.R.C. § 2032(a)(3). This includes property rights
such as a patent, or a life estate *per autre vie* (for
the life of another), the value of which normally
decreases with the passage of time.

Whenever any section of the estate tax law refers
to the value of property at the date of the decedent's death, such reference shall be taken to refer
to the value of that property used in determining
the value of the gross estate, which would mean the
alternate valuation date if elected by the executor.
I.R.C. § 2032(b). The election of the alternate valuation date must be made by the executor on his
estate tax return if filed within the time prescribed
by law (currently nine months, § 6075), or before
the expiration of any extension of time properly

granted for the filing of the return. I.R.C. § 2032(c). See generally Regs. § 20.2032–1.

The original purpose of an alternate valuation date was to soften the impact of the estate tax when property held by the decedent at his death plummeted in value shortly thereafter and before the estate tax was payable. In particular, the stock market crash and the drop in property values after 1929 were responsible for the relief provision.

Although it is the purpose of § 2032 to permit a reduction in the amount of tax payable if the gross estate has shrunk in aggregate value during the period after decedent's death, the alternate valuation date is not automatically employed in all such cases but must be elected. If the executor elects the alternate valuation date, the alternate valuation method applies to all the property included in the gross estate; it cannot be applied to a portion of the property only.

I.R.C. § 2032(c) limits the opportunities to elect the alternate valuation date; it prohibits such an election unless electing it will decrease (1) the value of the gross estate, *and* (2) the sum of the estate tax and the Chapter 13 generation-skipping tax with respect to property includable in the gross estate (reduced by credits allowable against such taxes).

Election of the alternate valuation date creates uncertainties about whether property earned or accrued or changed after death but before the alternate valuation date is to be included in the values taxed in the gross estate. At one time, the Treasury took the position that when the alternate valuation date was used, the gross estate would have to include income earned by the estate up to the valuation date. However, the Supreme Court of the United States held that this Regulation improperly interpreted the statute. See Maass v. Higgins, 312 U.S. 443 (1941). The Regulations were then changed to exclude that income from the gross estate. However, income realized after death but accrued prior to death is includable. See Regs. § 20.2032–1(d). Unfortunately, it is not always clear just what constitutes "income" for these purposes. See, *e.g.*, Rev.Rul. 58–576, 1958–2 C.B. 625 (involving stock dividends). For example, some cases insist on differentiating between pre- and post-death earnings of a corporation which pays dividends after death and others do not. Similar problems can arise involving contributions to a joint tenancy under I.R.C. § 2040. See, *e.g.*, Tuck v. U. S., 282 F.2d 405 (9th Cir. 1960). A comparable issue also was involved in Rev.Rul. 63–52, 1963–1 C.B. 173, where the decedent's estate was a beneficiary under insurance policies on the life of another person who died during the period between death and the alternate valuation date. The Internal Revenue Service ruled that the "appreciation" in the value of the policies by reason of the insured's death was includable.

In explaining use of the alternate valuation method when property has been received or changed after death but before the valuation date, the Regulations use the concepts of "included property" and "excluded property." Property interests existing at the date of death and included in his or her gross estate by §§ 2033–2044 but valued in accordance with the provisions of § 2032 are referred to as "included property." Furthermore, they remain "included property" for valuation purposes even though they change in form during the alternate valuation period by being actually received or disposed of in whole or in part by the estate. See Regs. § 20.2032–1(d). In contrast, property earned or accrued after the date of the decedent's death and during the alternate valuation period with respect to any property interest existing at the date of the decedent's death which does not represent a form of "included property" itself or the receipt of "included property" is excluded in valuing the gross estate under the alternate valuation method. Such property is referred to in the Regulations as "excluded property." See Regs. § 20.2032–1(d). Several examples are given. An interest-bearing obligation, such as a bond or a note, includes two elements of "included property" at the date of the decedent's death, namely the principal amount of the obligation itself and interest accrued to the date of death. Interest accrued after the date of death and before the subsequent valuation date constitutes "excluded property." Regs. § 20.2032–1(d)(1). As to leased property, the realty or personalty itself and the rents accrued to the date of death constitute "included property," but any rent accrued after the date of death and before the subsequent valuation date is "excluded property." Regs. § 20.2032–1(d)(2).

Any interest or estate that is affected by a mere lapse of time, such as a patent, an estate for the life of a person other than the decedent, a remainder or a reversion, is valued under the alternate valuation method at its value as of the date of the decedent's death, but with adjustment for any difference in its value as of the subsequent valuation date which is not due to a mere lapse of time. See Regs. § 20.-2032–1(f).

§ 51. Estate Tax Inclusion and Valuation of Property Transferred During Life

The preceding sections dealing with valuation problems have focused on the valuation of property includable in the gross estate because it was held by the decedent at death. It is also possible, under inclusion sections of the estate tax law other than § 2033, however, that some interest in property will be includable in the gross estate of the decedent even though he or she did not hold that property at death. More specifically, inclusion may be required of an interest in property transferred by the decedent some time during his life and before his death. See, *e.g.*, I.R.C. §§ 2035–2038. When property transferred inter-vivos is to be included in the gross estate, one question is whether the value at which it is to be included should be its value at the date of the transfer or the value of the same property at the date of death (or the alternate valuation date) if the property has risen or fallen in value in the interim. If income has been earned after transfer but before the applicable valuation date, is the income to be included in valuing the property? Will it be included only if accumulated or reinvested, or even if spent? Another question arises if, before the decedent's death or before the alternate valuation date, the donee has squandered, disposed of or conserved and enlarged the property transferred by the decedent. If the donee exchanged the property or sold it and reinvested the proceeds, is the value to be included in the decedent's gross estate the value of the gift property at the date of death or at the date the donee disposed of it? Is it to be the value of the property received by the donee in exchange for the gift property or the value at death of the property in which he has invested the proceeds from sale of the gift property? The answers to some of these questions are uncertain, but answers to some others can be given with confidence.

The valuation question throughout §§ 2035–2038 is, in a sense, whether the language of the statute is to be taken literally or not. The terms of I.R.C. § 2031 broadly imply that when an inter-vivos transfer gives rise to estate tax liability, the value to be included is the value of the gift at the decedent's death (or the alternate valuation date), not the value at the earlier time of transfer. The language in each of the inter-vivos transfer sections, §§ 2035–2038, says that the gross estate shall include the value of all property to the extent of any interest in the property of which the decedent has at any time made a transfer, by trust or otherwise.

Literally interpreted and applied, the language of both § 2031 and §§ 2035–2038 would seem to lead to the result that the specific property that was the subject of an includable inter-vivos gift (and only that specific property) must be valued at death. If, however, the specific property has been disposed of, must it be traced and valued in the hands of someone else? Might the result turn on whether property was includable because transferred within three years of death or, in contrast, because of a retained power over corpus or income? Should the rule be different for sale and reinvestment as distinguished from squandering and as differentiated from accumulating income or nurturing capital?

Transfers Within Three Years of Death. * When inclusion occurs by virtue of § 2035, reference is made to the value at death of the property or interest actually transferred. See Regs. § 20.2035–1(e). This general approach has been interpreted to mean that if the gift was made in the form of cash, the value to be included in the decedent's gross estate is the amount of the cash gift, even if the recipient of the cash spent it or invested it improvidently with the result that the property into which the cash was converted was worth much less at the valuation date. See Humphrey v. Comm., 162 F.2d 1 (5th Cir. 1947), cert. den. 332 U.S. 817 (1947). Or, if taxpayer were to give 100 shares of stock, worth $16,000, to his son within three years

* (Note that while the following discussion of *valuation* under § 2035 remains valid, gifts of the actual interests valued in the cases cited might no longer be subject to § 2035 at all, because of E.R.T.A. 1981 amendments.)

of death, and if those same shares, whether still held by the son or not (see Rev.Rul. 72–282, 1972–1 C.B. 306), were worth $23,000 at the date of the donor's death (or alternate valuation date if elected), the valuation for tax purposes would be $23,-000. The post-transfer appreciation would be covered by the valuation rule. Post transfer diminution in value likewise would be taken into account; if the stock were only worth $14,000 at the valuation date, that value would enter the gross estate, not $16,000.

However, the Regulations under § 2035 state that neither income received subsequent to the transfer nor property purchased with such income is considered in valuing the interest to be included. See Regs. § 20.2035–1(e). Accordingly, in Estate of McGehee v. Comm., 260 F.2d 818 (5th Cir. 1958), the Court held that stock dividends representing earnings accrued after the time of an inter-vivos transfer made in contemplation of death would not be includable in the gross estate of the decedent. Income earned by the property after transfer but before death will not be included even if it is added to the corpus of a trust created in contemplation of death. See Burns v. Comm., 177 F.2d 739 (5th Cir. 1949). See also Comm. v. Gidwitz' Estate, 196 F.2d 813 (7th Cir. 1952). (It might make a difference, of course, whether post-transfer income consisted of stock or property dividends that capitalized earnings from the period before the transfer rather than after the transfer; *McGehee* left open the pre-transfer capitalized earnings situation.) If the donee makes improvements that increase the value of the property after the gift, that increase will not be taxed in the estate.   See Regs. § 20.2035–1(e).

Transfers With Retained Powers.   However much the approach taken in contemplation of death cases may seem agreeable, both in terms of the language of the statute and in view of the purpose and philosophy of the contemplation of death rule, a different result might and perhaps should follow in at least some of the §§ 2036–2038 areas.

Where the taxpayer has retained an interest in or a power over the transferred property, whether it be a power to revoke the transfer or a power to designate the beneficiaries or an interest in the income of the transferred property, it can be argued that the decedent has not sufficiently parted with the property to entail the valuation of exactly the property transferred during life and nothing more in the decedent's gross estate.   To illustrate, if the decedent has transferred property but retained a power of revocation, his gross estate should include whatever he could have gotten back until the moment before his death, even if that is larger in value than the property he transferred during life.   Similarly, if the decedent has retained a power to designate the beneficiaries of property, even though he cannot get the property back directly for himself, § 2036(a)(2) arguably should require inclusion of the value of whatever property was subject to his power of designation at the time of his death, even if that is not the same as the value of property which he had earlier transferred.

Some authority for a more reaching approach to valuation of lifetime gifts includable under §§ 2036–2038 has been forthcoming. In one case involving a transfer with a power of revocation such that inclusion was called for by § 2038, the estate was required to include the value, on the applicable valuation date, of investments that had been purchased by the recipient of a cash gift even though this value of the investments was greater than the amount of the lifetime gift. See Howard v. U. S., 125 F.2d 986 (5th Cir. 1942). Conceivably, the fact that the *Howard* case arose under § 2038 may differentiate it from the *Humphrey* decision (above) under § 2035. The power of revocation genuinely gave the decedent the power to recapture for himself the larger value, consisting of the purchased investments, up until the time of his death. In contrast, the gift within three years of death is not a gift that is *incomplete* until death. Rather, it was made includable in the gross estate simply to prevent evasion of the (then) higher estate tax rates by gifts, admittedly taxable under the (then) lower gift tax rates, made on "the eve" of death and in order to escape the death tax. (And, in 1981 Congress drastically cut back the reach of § 2035, particularly as to outright gifts within 3 years of death.)

To generalize, a power to revoke a transfer or otherwise, by altering or amending it, to recapture property transferred and income or appreciation will cause the full value of what the transferor could have gotten back to be included in the gross estate. In such a case, the transferor at death finally relinquished a power to get back whatever the power covered and will be taxed accordingly. If the power held at death pertained only to some interests in the transferred property, or only to income from it, then § 2038 would require the inclusion only of the value of that particular interest. See, *e.g.*, Industrial Trust Co. v. Comm., 165 F.2d 142 (1st Cir. 1947); Walter v. U. S., 341 F.2d 182 (6th Cir. 1965); Rev.Rul. 70–513, 1970–2 C.B. 194.

More difficult to determine is what valuation must be made when a decedent dies possessed of a power to alter or designate the interests of beneficiaries other than himself, under § 2036(a)(2) or § 2038, when an irrevocable transfer has been made. One prominent authority on the valuation-inclusion question under retained power rules is the *O'Malley* case, in the U.S. Supreme Court, involving § 2036(a)(2). See U. S. v. O'Malley, 383 U.S. 627 (1966). In that case the settlor had established irrevocable trusts to which he transferred property, a major aspect of which consisted of its income. He relinquished all rights to the income except a power to distribute that income to the income beneficiaries or to cause it to be accumulated and held for the remaindermen of the trusts. In point of fact, he exercised his retained power by choosing to accumulate the income and adding it to the principal of the trusts. The Court held that each addition to trust principal from accumulated income constituted a "transfer" by the settlor within the statutory terms so as to require inclusion in his gross estate of all the trust principal at death *including those portions which resulted from accumulations of income.*

O'Malley settles the question of actually accumulated trust income under § 2036(a)(2) but leaves other questions unanswered. What if the income had not actually been accumulated, although decedent had power to compel accumulation? Or, what if the income had in fact been accumulated but not by virtue of a power exercised by the decedent, notwithstanding which inclusion of some interest was required because of a power to alter or amend or to designate who should enjoy the property? Some judicial language suggests that a retained § 2036 or § 2038 power makes the transfer incomplete until death and hence the valuation of the property is made at death and the measure of the tax is the value of that property brought into enjoyment at and by reason of death. See, *e.g.*, Round v. Comm., 332 F.2d 590 (1st Cir. 1964); U. S. v. O'Malley, 383 U.S. 627 (1966). Although this language was addressed to the accumulated income question, it suggests a still broader effect—everything and whatever is subject to a retained § 2036 or § 2038 power at death is to be included in the valuation of the includable interest.

The *O'Malley* case might be thought not only to support a very comprehensive rule of inclusion and valuation under the grantor or retained powers sections but also to cast a cloud over *McGehee* to suggest a different result even in the § 2035 (transfers within 3 years of death) area. However, it is also possible to differentiate the cases in the two areas because of the different rules of inclusion and policy problems involved.

As a general rule, if property is transferred during life and the transferor retains such a power over the property that it must be included in his gross estate under I.R.C. §§ 2036–2038 the value of the property at the applicable valuation date should include accumulated or investment income, since the transfer was not complete until his death. The technical argument that the decedent has not *transferred* the income has been put to rest by *O'Malley*. The § 2035 cases should not control in the §§ 2036–2038 area. However, the general principle advocated above does not serve to answer all the possible questions and variations that may arise with property that has been traded, sold, consumed or wasted.

In summary, the answers to many of the questions posed earlier remain uncertain; it cannot simply be stated whether in all instances the statute will be read literally to include only the value of that physical property actually transferred by the decedent or whether there will also be inclusion of accumulated income, investment income, stock dividends, property into which the transferred property is converted, or other improvements. Current rulings and cases should be consulted in pursuing these issues further. And see Lowndes and Stephens, Identification of Property Subject to the Federal Estate Tax, 65 Mich.L.Rev. 105 (1966).

Estate Tax Valuation of Consideration Received for an Incomplete Inter-vivos Transfer. If decedent makes an inter-vivos transfer with a §§ 2035–2038 string attached and receives in return something that qualifies as consideration for estate tax purposes, shall the consideration received be valued at the time of the transfer or at death (or the alternate valuation date if chosen)? If valuation of the consideration is to be made at the later date, it would retrospectively affect the proportion of the original transfer that was to be deemed a gift because the transfer exceeded the value of consideration received. See generally I.R.C. § 2043.

This issue arose in one case in which a woman transferred stock with a retained life estate such that § 2036(a)(1) compelled inclusion in her gross estate. She received, in exchange, a life interest in shares transferred by her nephews. The case boiled down to a question whether the value of the consideration received should be deemed to be the amount of income decedent actually received under her life interest in the nephew's stock or the value of her life interest as mortality tables would have predicted it at the date of the transfer. (Because she lived longer than average, she actually collected $229,890 rather than the $35,773.16 that the tables set as of the time of the gift-exchange in 1950. The value of the shares she had transferred, as of the optional valuation date, was $379,200.) The district court concluded that the includable transfer was to be reduced by the total amount the decedent actually received. Under this rule, the longer a decedent lives, the greater would be the consideration and the smaller the net addition to the gross estate. The Eighth Circuit reversed and held that the statute means consideration received by the transferor-decedent at the date the transfer for insufficient consideration is made, not as of the subsequent date of the decedent's death. Her lifetime dollar receipts from the consideration property are not the governing measure of value. See U. S. v. Righter, 400 F.2d 344 (8th Cir. 1968). Cf. U. S. v. Heasty, 370 F.2d 525 (10th Cir. 1966); Rev.Rul. 69–577, 1969–2 C.B. 173 revoking Rev.Rul. 57–448, 1957–2 C.B. 618.

Thus far, the answer seems clear: the value of the consideration received shall be determined at the time of the exchange; it is not to be based on subsequent facts, even though the property transferred is to be valued for estate tax purposes at a later date—the date of death or alternate valuation date. See Regs. § 20.2043–1(a).

§ 52. Valuation for Gift Tax Purposes

Valuation for purposes of the gift tax is solved by principles largely resembling the general principles applicable in the more complex estate tax realm. Under I.R.C. § 2512, a gift made in property is to be valued at the date of the gift. If property is transferred for less than an adequate and full consideration in money or money's worth, then the amount by which the value of the property exceeded the value of the consideration is deemed a gift. The value of offsetting consideration evidently is to be established as of the date of the gift. See § 2512(b) and Regs. § 25.2512–8. Cf. U. S. v. Righter, 400 F.2d 344 (8th Cir. 1968). The Regulations under I.R.C. § 2512 provide quite elaborate guidance to valuation problems under the gift tax (and parallel, in substantial measure, the principles enunciated in the Regulations under § 2031). Value is determined as of the date of the gift and it is the price at which the property would change hands between a willing buyer and a willing seller, neither being under any compulsion to buy or sell and both having reasonable knowledge of the relevant facts. Similar rules about the appropriate markets in which to make comparisons are given and special guidance is set forth for the valuation of stocks and bonds, interests in businesses, promissory notes, annuities, life-estates, terms-for-years, remainders and reversions, life insurance and annuity contracts and mutual fund shares. See generally Regs. § 25.-2512. See also Rev.Rul. 93–12, holding that the factor of corporate control in the family is not considered in valuing each interest in shares transferred from a donor to his children. Regulations have been published to deal with the valuation of life estates, terms for years, remainders and reversions in certain depreciable property. See Regs. § 25.2512–9. See § 2701 and regulations, as well as the discussion at § 48A *supra,* for valuation of transfers of interests in corporations and partnerships to family members, and § 2702 for valuation of transfers of interests in trusts to family members.

There is no alternate valuation date for gift tax purposes. Since the date of valuation is the date of the gift, the problems and uncertainties involved in concluding when a gift is complete for gift tax purposes affect the valuation question as well as other issues. In actual application, determining the value when the timing of a gift is questionable can turn out to be a difficult matter.

The special valuation procedures of § 2032A for certain small farms and businesses are available only for estate tax purposes, and have no counterpart in the context of gift tax valuations.

CHAPTER XI

EXEMPTIONS AND EXCLUSIONS—GIFT TAX (GIFTS OF FUTURE INTERESTS AND GIFTS TO MINORS)

§ 53. Exemptions

No longer are exemptions to be found in the Estate Tax or the Gift Tax. The former exemptions ($30,000 lifetime exemption in the gift tax; $60,000 per decedent exemption in the estate tax) have been consolidated and converted into a unified credit that is set at levels corresponding to desired exemption levels, but with a tax benefit that remains constant no matter how the size of the estate varies (so long as there is tax liability equal to the applicable credit). The credit is not refundable; it can only be used to offset tax otherwise due.

§ 54. Gift Tax Exclusions—§ 2503

In computing taxable gifts, an annual, per-donee *exclusion* of $10,000 ($3,000 for pre-'82 gifts) is afforded by I.R.C. § 2503 to every donor. The annual per-donee exclusion is authorized in I.R.C. § 2503(b). That section states that in computing taxable gifts for the calendar year, in the case of all gifts (other than gifts of future interests in property) made to any person by the donor, $10,000 of such gifts to such person shall not be included in the total amount of gifts made during that year, for purposes of subsection (a) of § 2503. Subsection (a) of § 2503 defines "taxable gifts" (in the case of gifts made after December 31, 1970) as the total amount of gifts made during the calendar year, less the deductions provided in I.R.C. §§ 2522–2524. Since a gift of a future interest does not qualify for the annual exclusion, the entire value of a future interest in property must be included in the total amount of gifts for the calendar year in which the gift is made. In other words, a total of $10,000 in the form of a present interest given by a donor to a particular donee during a calendar year is simply excludable in determining gift tax liability. In the event of a gift in trust, the beneficiary of the trust is the donee. See Regs. § 25.2503–1, –2. (As to the definition of present and future interests, see § 55 below.)

At least one court has applied "substance-over-form" analysis in the gift-tax context. Heyen v. U.S., 945 F.2d 359 (10th Cir.1991). In *Heyen,* decedent transferred stock to over twenty-five intermediate recipients, who simply received the stock certificates and signed them in blank so that the stock could be reissued to a member of the decedent's family. Each intermediate recipient received shares valued at less than $10,000, in an attempt to take advantage of the § 2503(b) exclusion. The court held that "decedent merely used those recipients to create gift tax exclusions to avoid paying gift tax on indirect gifts to the actual family member beneficiaries," and since indirect gifts are subject to gift tax by virtue of § 2511(a), decedent was, in fact, liable for gift tax. *Heyen,* 945 F.2d at 363.

The purpose of the annual exclusion was, so to speak, to keep the tax Commissioner from having to sit beneath the Christmas tree or at the side of the birthday cake. The exclusion removes the necessity for keeping records of and reporting small incidental gifts or most ordinary family or holiday transfers. (A more cynical way of stating much the same idea is to say that the per-donee annual exclusion prevents the law from making liars of us all, since many small intra-family gifts would probably go unreported, if they were not exempted from tax.)

The per-donee annual exclusion not only exempts many gifts from tax but also relieves taxpayers of a heavy burden of reporting all gifts by filing tax returns. Under I.R.C. § 6019, gift tax returns must be filed for any year if transfers during that period cannot be excluded by virtue of the annual exclusion, the new tuition and medical care deduction, or the marital deduction. See § 6075. The tax is to be paid when the return is filed. See I.R.C. § 6151(a). Since the per-donee exclusion under § 2503(b) is available on an annual basis, the liability for gift tax can grow during the year as the annual exclusion is consumed by periodic gifts. Another annual exclusion becomes available only after the turn of the calendar year; an unused exclusion expires at year end and cannot be carried over or accumulated.

The size of the annual exclusion has been changed from time to time. These changes remain relevant in later years by reason of the way the gift tax is calculated. Although the gift tax is payable yearly, its rates and other application are cumulative over the lifetime of a donor. To determine the tax payable for a given tax period, the total taxable gifts made since enactment of the gift tax on June 6, 1932 to the end of the current period must be aggregated and the tax on such gifts must be computed at present rates. From that tax liability must then be deducted the tax, again determined at present rates, on the total taxable gifts made up to the beginning of the current taxable period. The amount so calculated is the gift tax for the current period. See I.R.C. §§ 2501–2504. For purposes of determining the aggregate amount of taxable gifts in past years, the annual exclusions may be taken as they were allowed in the year that those gifts were made. See I.R.C. § 2504. Consequently, the dimensions of the exclusion allowed in past years remain important in determining the present tax liability. In some years, the annual exclusion amounted to $5,000 and in some years to $4,000. For gifts made after December 31, 1942, the annual exclusion remained $3,000 until the passage of E.R.T.A, which increased it to $10,000, effective for gifts made after 1981. Against the gift tax so computed may be offset any unused portion of the unified credit.

Although there is no statute or regulation directly on point, it has always been assumed that transfers in satisfaction of a support obligation are not gifts subject to transfer taxes. This proposition is supported by inference from numerous judicial sources. Education and medical care are marginal "gift-support" items which are now excluded from taxable gifts by new § 2503(e), enacted as part of E.R.T.A. effective for "gifts" made after 1981.

New § 2503(e) excludes amounts paid on behalf of an individual as tuition to an educational organization described in § 170(b)(1)(A)(ii) for the education or training of such individual, or to any person who provides medical care for such individual as payment for such care. Note that the beneficiary need not be a dependent of the donor, nor need the educational institution be tax exempt. It would appear that the exclusion does not apply where the donor gives cash to the beneficiary who then himself pays the school or doctor, or to the beneficiary to reimburse him for amounts previously paid to the school or doctor. (See House Committee Report on H.R. 4242, 7/24/81.)

§ 55. Gifts of Future Interests—§ 2503(b)

The per-donee annual exclusion is limited in one exceedingly significant way; the exclusion is available only for gifts of "present interests" in property. No exclusion is available for a gift of a "future interest" in property. This limitation, contained in I.R.C. § 2503(b), has produced reams of interpretation, litigation and comment.

The rule that no gift tax exclusion will be available in the case of a gift of a future interest apparently has its roots in the idea that an exclusion should be available only if the donee or donees are known with certainty and only if the values of the interests to be received by each donee can definitely be ascertained. With some gifts of a future interest, it is not possible at the time of gift definitely to ascertain the identity of the ultimate recipient of the gift or the exact value of the interest eventually to be received by each recipient. As if in an exaggerated fear that too many annual exclusions might be allowed, Congress has blocked the availability of *any* exclusion in the case of a gift of a future interest and has done so even when the gift of the particular future interest involved *is* susceptible of valuation and determination of the identity of the ultimate recipient is possible.

As the Regulations put it, no part of the value of the gift of a future interest may be excluded in determining the total amount of gifts made during the taxable year. The Regulations go on to say that "future interests" is a term that includes reversions, remainders, and other interests or estates, whether vested or contingent, and whether or not supported by a particular interest or estate, which are limited to commence in use, possession, or enjoyment at some future date or time. See Regs. § 25.2503–3(a). Thus the prohibition against an annual exclusion for a gift of a future interest will apply even in the case of a vested remainder where there is no possibility of the interest shifting by some contingency or condition and where the identity of the ultimate taker, or at least the person who himself or whose estate will enjoy the interest, can be determined at the time of the gift. Also, the exclusion will be disallowed when a future interest is involved even though it can be said with certainty that at least some *one* person will take and enjoy the property, although admittedly the extent of his interest and his actual identity cannot be known at the time of the transfer.

The broad language of the Regulations would seem to suggest that any gift whose economic value or enjoyment will be available in part or as a whole at a later time would be treated as a future interest with the result that no annual exclusion would be available. However, the term "future interest" does not refer to the contractual rights that exist in a bond, promissory note (even when it does not bear interest until maturity), or in a policy of life insurance the obligations of which are to be discharged by payments in the future. See Regs. § 25.2503–3(a). (Of course, a future interest or interests in such contractual obligations can be created by limitations contained in a trust or other instrument of transfer used in effecting a gift of such obligations.)

In attempting to help describe what *does* constitute a present interest in property, the Regulations say that an unrestricted right to the immediate use, possession or enjoyment of property or the income from property (such as a life-estate or term-certain) is a present interest in property. Therefore, an exclusion is allowable with respect to a gift of such an interest, but not in excess of the value of that interest. See Regs. § 25.2503–3(b).

I.R.C. § 2503(b), also paraphrased by the Regulations, states that where there has been a transfer to any person of a present interest in property, the possibility that such interest may be diminished by the exercise of a power shall be disregarded in applying the future interest rule, if no part of such interest will at any time pass to any other person. Therefore, for example, if the terms of a trust provide that the net income from property in trust is to be paid to X for his life with the remainder payable to Y on X's death, and if the trustee has the uncontrolled power to pay the corpus over to X anytime, X's present right to receive the income may be terminated but no other person has the right to such income interest. Therefore, an annual exclusion will be available under I.R.C. § 2503(b).

In the case of a transfer in trust, the United States Supreme Court held that it is the individual beneficiary, not the trustee, who is the donee for purposes of determining the annual exclusion. See Helvering v. Hutchings, 312 U.S. 393 (1941). Therefore, even though the donor of a gift in trust completely divests himself of ownership, dominion and control over the property, he will not be entitled to the annual exclusion unless he can show that a beneficiary can receive some present enjoyment from the property that has been transferred. As the Supreme Court put it in the leading case of Fondren v. Commissioner, 324 U.S. 18 (1945), the term present interest connotes the right to substantial present economic benefit. The question is of time: the time not when title vests, but when enjoyment begins. If anything puts a barrier of a substantial period before the power of the beneficiary or donee now to enjoy what has been given him, the gift is one of a future interest. See 324 U.S. 18 at 20–21.

The determination of what is a future interest for purposes of the statutory rule in § 2503(b) can turn out to be very troublesome, particularly in the case of gifts made in trust. Although the underlying origins of the future interest rule, having to do with the apprehended difficulty in many instances of determining the number of eventual donees and the values of their respective gifts, cannot serve as a perfect guide to the interpretation of the statute, they nevertheless must be kept in mind as providing some guidance to the law. The taxpayer must carry a burden of showing that a present interest that is ascertainable in value has been transferred. If the admittedly present interest cannot be valued because a power or succeeding future interest may affect it in ways not susceptible of reliable prediction, the taxpayer will not be able to show that he is entitled to any annual exclusion. See, *e.g.*, Funkhouser v. Comm., 275 F.2d 245 (4th Cir. 1960).

A mandatory accumulation trust will not qualify for annual exclusion, since even the right to income is limited to commence in use, possession or enjoyment at a future date or time. See U. S. v. Pelzer, 312 U.S. 399 (1941). A discretionary accumulation trust is more problematical. Probably the beneficiary's income interest is a future interest and would not qualify for the annual exclusion. See Comm. v. Herr, 303 F.2d 780 (3d Cir. 1962).

If the trustee has power to invade corpus for the benefit of the remaindermen, but that power is limited to a certain fractional share of the corpus, the income interest of the income beneficiary would probably be taken to be a gift of the present interest to the extent of the fractional share of the corpus that could not be touched by the power of invasion. See Kniep v. Commissioner of Internal Revenue, 172 F.2d 755 (8th Cir. 1949).

A gift in trust in which the trustee has the absolute discretion to allocate income among several life beneficiaries is also a gift of a future interest since the amount of income to be received by each beneficiary cannot be ascertained at the time of the gift. See Regs. § 25.2503–3(c), Example 3.

If beneficiaries of a trust have a power to compel the payment to them of principal or income or both upon demand, such a power makes the gift a gift of a present interest. See Crummey v. Commissioner, 397 F.2d 82 (9th Cir.1968) Gilmore v. Commissioner, 213 F.2d 520 (6th Cir. 1954). Also, while the addition of a spendthrift clause to a trust instrument, with the effect of prohibiting the income beneficiary from alienating, assigning or otherwise anticipating the income, might threaten to cause a gift of the present right to income to be considered a future interest, the Commissioner takes a contrary position.   See Rev.Rul. 54–344, 1954–2 C.B. 319.

A gift to a corporation, which is treated as a gift to the shareholders of the corporation, is a gift of future interests.   See Heringer v. Commissioner, 235 F.2d 149 (9th Cir. 1956), cert. den. 352 U.S. 927 (1956).

As these cases and regulations make clear, the focus is upon the certainty of receiving and the amount or value of what is to be received.   If either receipt or value is problematic, the gift is of a future interest.   Additionally, it is helpful to keep separate the requirements for a taxable gift—a complete transfer of property—from the future interest rule. A gift that is incomplete because the donor retained too much power over its enjoyment, see § 39, *supra*, will not be taxable at all.   On the other hand, a gift may be made with the very same powers given to an independent trustee and the gift will be taxable, though ineligible for the $10,000 per year exclusion because it is a future interest.   Therefore, first determine whether a taxable gift has been made, then apply the future interest rule.

The future interest rule is especially troublesome in case of gifts made to or for the benefit of minor beneficiaries.   This problem has been addressed in part by the statute in I.R.C. § 2503(c), to be discussed next.   Since § 2503(c) is not exclusive, however, some of the general principles discussed in this section can apply also in the case of a gift to a minor.

§ 56. Gifts to Minors, *Crummey* Trusts and Section 2503(c)

The future interest rule becomes especially troublesome and complex when a gift to a minor is involved. Because of legal disabilities imposed by state law, minors cannot presently enjoy ownership in property in the same way that adult donees can.

Because of such disabilities, there was, for a time, concern that even an outright gift to a minor would have to be treated as a gift of a future interest, without a donee exclusion available, because of the minor's legal disability to deal fully with his property. This concern was dispelled by the Treasury in Rev.Rul. 54–400, 1954–2 C.B. 319. (Of course, if the gift is in trust and so limited as to grant a future interest, the exclusion will be unavailable as dictated by the general principles set forth in § 55 above.)

Often, however, a gift to or for the benefit of a minor is necessarily or most prudently made to a custodian or trustee for the benefit of the minor, rather than as a direct gift. Before the enactment of § 2503(c) (see next paragraph), and since that enactment in areas that fall outside the statutory rule, there was some controversy and uncertainty about whether a gift of property to a guardian or trustee for a minor could be regarded as a gift of a present interest. The courts in some circuits held that the gift is a transfer of a present interest if the trustee did not have any discretion to withhold payment or if a guardian could demand payment of the income or property on behalf of the minor. See

Crummey v. Commissioner, 397 F.2d 82 (9th Cir. 1968); Gilmore v. Comm., 213 F.2d 520 (6th Cir. 1954); Kieckhefer v. Comm., 189 F.2d 118 (7th Cir. 1951). In contrast, another circuit would not hold that there had been a gift of a present interest unless a guardian was appointed and authorized to act for the minor at the time of the gift. See Stifel v. Comm., 197 F.2d 107 (2d Cir. 1952).

The I.R.S. has adopted the "*Crummey* approach". A *Crummey* withdrawal power given to a minor will qualify a transfer in trust as a present interest so long as there is no impediment to the appointment of a guardian who could exercise the withdrawal power on the minor's behalf. The withdrawal power must be exercisable for a reasonable period. Thirty days is a sufficient time, but two days is not. See Rev.Rul. 73–405, 1973–2 C.B. 321; Rev.Rul. 81–7, 1981–1 C.B. 474. See P.L.R. 8004172, Nov. 5, 1979 for I.R.S. guidance about an assured *Crummey* Trust present interest exclusion.

The uncertainty of the case law led to the enactment in 1954 of I.R.C. § 2503(c). The statute provides another way in which a gift that is not outright and does not require immediate expenditure for the benefit of the minor may nevertheless qualify for the annual exclusion.

Section 2503(c) says that no part of a gift to an individual who has not attained the age of twenty-one years on the date of the transfer shall be considered to be a gift of a future interest in property for purposes of subsection (b) of § 2503 (the future interest rule) if the property and the income from it may be expended by or for the benefit of the donee before he attains the age of twenty-one years and, to the extent not so expended, will pass to the donee when he attains the age of twenty-one years or, if he dies before that age, will be payable to the estate of the donee or as he may appoint under a general power of appointment as defined in I.R.C. § 2514(c). More detailed rules and elaborations on this theme can be found in the Regulations. See Regs. § 25.2503–4. (Note that a properly designed *Crummey* trust need not meet these requirements.)

If the requirements of I.R.C. § 2503(c) are fully satisfied, both the income interest and the gift of corpus will qualify for the annual exclusion. Otherwise, possibly some, but not all, of the interests will qualify. If, for example, a trust for a minor is to continue, with corpus going to the donee upon reaching a later age, such as age 25, then (only) the income interest until age 21 will qualify as a present interest. "Property" in § 2503(c) means not *corpus*, but any property interest (See *Herr, supra*).] The income interest for the years between ages 21 and 25 will be treated as a future interest, even though the interest immediately preceding it is a present interest by virtue of § 2503(c). (See CIR v. Estate of Levine, 526 F.2d 717 (2d Cir. 1975)). This may seem contrary to the spirit of § 2503(c), which is not to penalize the donor merely because his donee is a minor under certain legal disabilities. To highlight the point: Of a gift in trust to A, aged 22, with all income yearly to A, corpus to B upon

A's reaching age 25, A's income interest qualifies entirely as a gift of a present interest. If A is aged 20 at the time of the gift, however, then under *Levine*, only the income interest for the first year qualifies as a present interest, and the following four years' income cannot be "tacked on". See also Rev.Rul. 76–179, 1976–1 C.B. 290 (extension of income interest of trust, made one year after creation of trust that provided an income interest in an adult donee for a 5 year period, is the gift of a separate, future interest not eligible for the § 2503(b) annual exclusion).

If neither the statutory requirements nor the *Crummey* tests are satisfied, a gift may nevertheless be eligible for the exclusion if the gift can satisfy another non-statutory test of what is a future interest. See Regs. § 25.2503–4(c). The Regulations give as an example of a gift that qualifies for the exclusion without meeting the requirements of the statute a transfer of property in trust with income required to be paid annually to the minor beneficiary and corpus to be distributed upon attaining the age of twenty-five, which the Regulations say would be a gift of a present interest with respect to the right to income although it would be a gift of future interest with respect to the right to corpus. So, if a donor is reluctant to comply with the rules of I.R.C. § 2503(c), for example because he is unwilling to trust the property to the donee's complete ownership at the tender age of twenty-one, and does not want to grant a *Crummey* power, it may be possible for at least some of the gift that does not satisfy the requirements of § 2503(c) to qualify for the annual exclusion.

All of the States have enacted laws designed to facilitate gifts of stocks and bonds to minors. These statutes are in the form either of the Uniform Gifts to Minors Act or the Model Gift of Securities to Minors Act. Rev.Rul. 59–357, 1959–2 C.B. 212 expresses the position that gifts under either Act will qualify for the annual exclusion.

CHAPTER XII

DEDUCTIONS—ESTATE AND GIFT TAX

§ 57. Estate Tax Deductions for Expenses, Debts, Taxes, Losses—§§ 2053–2055

Section 2051 of the Internal Revenue Code decrees that the value of the *taxable estate* shall be determined by deducting from the value of the *gross estate* the *deductions* provided for in the statute. The taxable estate, thus determined, is the base against which the tax rates of I.R.C. § 2001 are applied. (The rates themselves are, of course, a function of all the post-1976 gratuitous transfers of the decedent, including inter-vivos gifts. See § 13, supra.)

I.R.C. § 2053(a) grants a *deduction* in determining the taxable estate from the gross estate for several items, including funeral expenses, administration expenses, claims against the estate and for unpaid mortgages on, or indebtedness in respect of, property whose value had been included in the decedent's gross estate undiminished by such mortgage or indebtedness. These deductions are allowed for such expenses or claims only to the extent that they "are allowable by the laws of the jurisdiction" under which the estate is being administered.

See generally the Regulations under § 2053, Regs. § 20.2053, for additional information about the scope and terms of the deductions allowed under § 2053.

Bear in mind, however, that the Regulations, in general, are subordinate to the Code itself in cases of conflict. This is true even when the Regulation in question is of very long standing. For example, Regs. §§ 20.2053–3(a) and –3(d)(2), substantially the same and unchallenged since 1919, declare that administrative expenses will be allowed as deductions only if they are "necessary" for the administration of the estate, as opposed to, for example, for the benefit of the beneficiary. Estate of Park v. CIR, 475 F.2d 673 (6th Cir. 1973) refused to give effect to these Regulations, in a case where the expenses had been allowed in state probate proceedings, because § 2053(a) declares that deductibility is governed by state law alone. But see Estate of Smith, 510 F.2d 479 (2d Cir. 1975), where the "necessity" of the expenses was re-examined in the federal court, under the aegis of Comm. v. Estate of Bosch, 387 U.S. 456 (1967).

I.R.C. § 2053(b) allows, in addition, a *deduction* for amounts representing expenses incurred in administering property not subject to claims, (i.e., not included in the decedent's probate estate), which is included in the gross estate, to the same extent such amounts would be allowable as a deduction under § 2053(a) if such property were subject to claims, but only if such amounts are paid before the expiration of the period of limitation for assessment provided in § 6501. Under this provision, for example, a deduction has been allowed for expenses involved in defending a lawsuit brought by a residual legatee under the will to contest the validity of a revocable inter-vivos trust created by the decedent. See Central Trust Co. of Cincinnati v. Welch, 304 F.2d 923 (6th Cir. 1962).

Section 2053(c) imposes important limitations on the deductions available under sub-sections (a) and (b). One of the most important is the following: the deduction allowed in the case of claims against the estate, unpaid mortgages or any indebtedness shall, when founded on a promise or agreement, be limited to the extent that they were contracted bona-fide and for an adequate and full consideration in money or money's worth. In addition, agreements between family members must have been bargained for at arm's length. See Bank of New York v. U. S., 526 F.2d 1012 (3d Cir. 1975).

Thus a taxpayer cannot convert a nondeductible bequest into a deductible payment of a claim merely by making an enforceable promise which then becomes a claim against his estate. In the event of a promise of a gift to charity, the limitation for consideration in money or money's worth will not apply, but the deduction will be allowed only to the extent provided in I.R.C. § 2055. See § 2053(c)(1)(A). In any event, amounts that may be deducted as claims against the estate are limited to personal obligations of the decedent existing at his death, plus interest accrued to death. Liabilities imposed by law or arising out of torts are deductible. See Regs. § 20.2053–4.

Any income taxes on income received after the death of the decedent, or property taxes not accrued before his death, or any estate, succession, legacy or inheritance tax, shall not be deductible under § 2053. See I.R.C. § 2053(c)(1)(B). On the deductibility of taxes in general, see Regs. § 20.2053–6.

Items deductible under the general rule of § 2053(a) will be disallowed to the extent they exceed the value of property subject to claims, except to the extent the amounts actually have been paid before the date for filing estate tax returns. Under this rule, amounts paid by someone other than the estate can sometimes be deductible. I.R.C. § 2053(c)(2).

Under I.R.C. § 2053(d), the executor is given an option to elect to deduct certain state and foreign death taxes, in which event he will be deemed to have waived the right to claim a credit against the federal estate tax for any tax paid to a foreign country. See § 2053(d)(3). (I.R.C. § 2011(e) describes the effect of a deduction taken under § 2053 on the credit for state death taxes and § 2014(f) describes the effect of a deduction taken under § 2053 on the credit for foreign death taxes.) See § 70 below, on the credit for foreign taxes.

In a community property state, the claims and expenses that can be deducted under § 2053 are only those which were the obligation of the decedent or of his or her estate. Therefore, an obligation which is allocable to the community property, of which only one-half is included in the decedent's gross estate, can be deducted only to the extent of one-half its total amount. Similarly, expenses of administration incurred in connection with the entire community property, all of which probably will come into the jurisdiction of the executor or administrator for purposes of administration, even though only half is included in the decedent's gross estate for tax purposes, can be deducted only to the extent of one-half. However, some expenses can be shown to be attributable to the decedent's estate itself and will be fully deductible. If funeral expenses are attributable to the estate, the entire amount will be deductible. However, if state law treats such costs as those of the community property, only half the amount can be deducted. Claims against the estate in a community property state can be deductible in full if they represent personal debts of the decedent, but if they are debts of the community only one-half of the amount can be deducted. Accordingly, a mortgage indebtedness on community property can be deducted only to the extent of one-half. In general, state law bears heavily upon these questions.

These principles and the complexities that community property law introduces are illustrated by U. S. v. Stapf, 375 U.S. 118 (1963). In that case, the will of a decedent in a community property state directed his executors to pay all the debts and administration expenses attributable to community property if his wife elected to take under the will and forego her interest in the community property.

(State law provided that the husband's community property interest was liable for only one-half of the community debts but that he was personally liable for all the community debts, with a right to proceed against the wife's interest.) She so elected, but the court nevertheless held that the estate was entitled to deduct only the amounts attributable to the decedent's interest in the property, because the "basic rule" of state law provided that the husband's interest alone was liable for half the community debts and in view of the Congressional purpose to equalize the incidence of taxation in community property and separate property states. Therefore, the court characterized the payment by the estate of more than one-half of the debts and expenses as a bequest to the surviving spouse, rather than the payment of a deductible expense or claim.

Section 2054 allows a deduction for losses incurred during the settlement of an estate if the loss arises from fire, storm, shipwreck or other casualty or from theft, when the loss is not compensated for by insurance or otherwise. If the loss is partly compensated, the excess over the compensation may be deducted. See generally Regs. § 20.2054–1.

In general, the deductions allowed by § 2053 and § 2054 are employed by the law to reduce the tax concept of the gross estate to a figure called the "taxable estate," which corresponds to what a layman might call the "net estate." In other words, there is an effort to determine the amount of property transferred by the decedent at his death to beneficiaries. That net amount transferred is the proper base to determine the amount of tax on an "ability to pay" theory. The correct determination of the taxable base is essential to horizontal equity and vertical equity in the tax law.

Under the graduated tax rates, deductions (and exemptions or exclusions, but not credits) serve to reduce the *marginal* rate of tax and thus they have a "wealth-variant" quality. For example, a funeral expense deduction of $1,000 will have a different tax effect in the case of a decedent with a very large gross estate than it will in the case of a decedent with a very low gross estate. By reducing the large gross estate to a taxable estate that is $1,000 smaller, the $1,000 deduction for funeral expenses will reduce the tax payable by the estate by an amount determined by multiplying $1,000 by the marginal rate of tax payable "at the top" by the estate. The top marginal rate in 1993 was 55%, for a taxable estate in excess of $3,000,000. Consequently a $1,000 deduction from an estate in this bracket would save $550 in tax. In contrast, a $1,000 deduction for funeral expenses in the estate of a decedent whose taxable estate is thereby reduced from $700,000 to $699,000 will save an amount equal to $1,000 multiplied by the applicable marginal rate, 37%, or $370. This "wealth-variant," or more properly, "estate-size-variant" effect of the deduction is perfectly proper, given a graduated rate structure as in § 2001. A smaller net estate pays tax at a lower rate and hence should be relieved of less tax than a large net estate, and vice-versa.

I.R.C. § 642(g) provides that an estate may not take the deductions permitted by §§ 2053 and 2054 both on its estate tax return and on its income tax return; the double deduction possibility is precluded. Similarly, deductions allowable under § 2621(a)(2) and § 2622(b) of the generation-skipping tax may not be claimed on two returns.

Since the 1977 amendment of § 642(g) the same has been true of the expenses of selling property. Before 1977, this type of "double-deduction" was available, since technically the expenses of sale are not a "deduction" for income tax purposes, but are rather an "offset" to the sale price. As a result, an executor or administrator often has a choice to take the deduction, for example a deduction for losses under § 2054, against either the gross estate or the income of the estate, whichever will produce the greatest tax saving, but not against both.

No longer is there a deduction for amounts expended by the estate for the support of dependents of the decedent during the period of administration. This deduction was removed from the Code in 1950. Therefore, even though state law permits an estate to spend the money to support a surviving spouse or other dependent, such expenditures cannot be deducted from the gross estate in arriving at the taxable estate.

§ 58.   Estate Tax Charitable Contribution Deduction—§ 2055

Section 2055 of the Code allows a deduction, in determining the taxable estate, for the amount of all bequests, legacies, devises, or transfers to a unit of government or to a charitable corporation or to a trust, order or association organized for religious, charitable, scientific, or educational purposes as described in the statute, or to a veterans' organization. The purpose of this estate tax allowance is to encourage such contributions and to serve as an incentive for such socially desirable activity. To the extent the activity supported by deduction-induced contributions provides benefits and services that otherwise would have to be financed by government, the deduction serves to reduce the cost of government at the same time that government foregoes some revenue from the estate tax.

The Regulations under § 2055 detail the kind of association or organization qualified for deductible bequests. In general, the recipient must be organized and operated exclusively for charitable purposes, no part of its earnings may inure to or benefit private stockholders or individuals (other than as a legitimate object of its charitable purposes) and no substantial part of its activities may consist of carrying on propaganda or otherwise attempting to influence legislation.

If a decedent possessed a power of appointment as a result of which the property subject to the power was included in his gross estate, he is entitled to a charitable deduction for amounts actually received by charity as a result of the exercise or failure to exercise, release, or lapse of the power. See Regs. § 20.2055–1(b)(1). Under the Regulations a special charitable deduction is allowed in the case of a bequest in trust to a surviving spouse who is over 80 years old at the time of the decedent's death, who is entitled for life to all the income from the property, who has a testamentary power of appointment exercisable in favor of charities that qualify under § 2055(a)(2) and who actually exercises the power in favor of such organizations, as well as meeting some other conditions. See Regs. § 20.-2055–1(b)(2).

If, before 1970, a trust was created to pay the income to someone for life and at his or her death to pay the remainder to a charity, the present value of the remainder could be deducted to the extent it was presently ascertainable and receipt by the charitable recipient could definitely be determined. However, a charitable deduction was not allowed for a contingent remainder to charity, for example, if there was a more than negligible chance that the charity would not receive anything at all. See, *e.g.*, Comm. v. Estate of Sternberger, 348 U.S. 187 (1955). Or, if the trustee held a power to invade trust corpus for a non-charitable beneficiary, whether according to an ascertainable standard or not, no charitable deduction was allowed for the charitable remainder. In other words, the courts took an all or nothing approach; if it could not reliably be predicted that some ascertainable interest would be taken by the beneficiary, no deduction was allowed at all. However, if despite some uncertainties it could reliably be ascertained that a determinable value would be taken by the charity, the deduction was allowed. See Estate of Schildkraut

v. Comm., 368 F.2d 40 (2d Cir. 1966). Now, however, see § 2055(e), discussed in § 60, below.

As government finds itself more and more in need of additional revenues, the efficiency of the charitable contribution deduction as a way of providing support to private charities or as a way of relieving government of some cost of providing social benefits should be reanalyzed. In particular, the "wealth-variant" operation of the charitable contribution allowance when structured in the Code as a deduction should be reevaluated. A deduction for a contribution of, say, $1,000 to charity will have a very different impact in the estate of a very wealthy taxpayer from the impact it will have in the estate of a very poor taxpayer. The after-tax cost for a very wealthy decedent to make a gift of $1,000 to his favorite charity can be as little as $450 ($1,000 contribution minus $550 saved in taxes by the deduction for an estate in the 55% bracket yields a net cost of $450 to the taxpayer). For a taxpayer who, as a result of other deductions, credits or exemptions, would have no taxable estate, the charitable contribution deduction afforded by § 2055 provides no benefit at all. The after-tax cost of his gift is equal to the amount of the gift—$1,000 in the example. This wealth-variant effect may appear unjust, but it must be remembered that in the case of the high bracket estate the deduction merely relieves the estate of the relatively high tax it would have had to pay if the gift to charity had gone elsewhere. Moreover, as an incentive, the tax allowance may stimulate more charitable giving by giving a greater per-dollar (of contribution) tax benefit to larger estates.

It would be possible to construct an allowance for contributions to charity that would not be "wealth-variant." For example, each taxpayer might be given a *credit* against his tax of some percentage of the amount he contributed to charity. Then, the dollar-for-dollar benefit of a charitable contribution would be the same for a decedent with a large gross estate and the decedent with a small one. Or, the deduction might be geared to a percentage formula so as to provide a tax benefit that did not vary with the size of the estate. More radically, the tax benefit could be made to vary *inversely* or to phase-out with the size of the estate, so that a greater tax saving per dollar of contribution would be afforded to a poorer taxpayer than to a richer one. All in all, whether the deduction should remain in the Code or should be repealed or should be converted to some other form of tax allowance should not be taken for granted but should be reviewed. Similar re-analysis led to conversion of the former "personal" and "lifetime" exemptions to a credit, in 1976.

Racial and Other Discrimination. Whether an educational or other charitable institution is eligible to receive tax deductible contributions (and tax-exempt income) even though it practices racial discrimination became a prominent issue in the 1970s and 1980s. In 1967 and 1971, the U.S. Treasury ruled that racial discrimination would disqualify an educational or nonprofit recreational institution as a tax-exempt charity which could receive tax deductible gifts or bequests. See Rev.Rul. 67–325, 1967–2 C.B. 113; Rev.Rul. 71–447, 1971–2 C.B. 230. Eventually, the Supreme Court upheld the constitutionality of a Regulation to the same effect vis-a-vis the income tax and concluded that revocation of a discriminatory school's tax-exempt status was proper, in a case that surely stands for the same principle for estate and gift tax purposes. See Bob Jones University, 461 U.S. 574 (1983).

§ 59. Gift Tax Charitable Contribution Deduction—§ 2522

I.R.C. § 2522 allows a deduction for transfers to charities quite parallel to the deduction in the estate tax. As a result, contributions to charities are not treated as taxable gifts, largely in order to encourage or avoid erecting a tax bar to such donations. See generally Regs. § 25.2522. Especially see Regs. § 25.2522(a)–2 as to transfers not exclusively for charitable purposes and § 25.2522(c)–1 as to disallowance of charitable deductions because of prohibited transactions by the recipient organization. This deduction, like the charitable deduction in the estate tax, has a "wealth-variant" or "gift-variant" quality. That is to say, a taxpayer who has considerable wealth and who has made substantial gifts in the past will save more in gift taxes by making a deductible gift to a charity in lieu of a taxable gift to some other recipient than will a poorer taxpayer. The basis for this effect is revealed by a glance at the graduated gift tax rates set forth in I.R.C. § 2502. A "limiting case" of the wealth-variant effect of the charitable gift deduction is that of the taxpayer who has not sufficiently used up his or her annual exclusions to have to pay any tax on a non-charitable contribution. For him or her, no tax is saved by making a charitable rather than a non-deductible gift. As a result, no incentive is provided to make a deductible charitable contribution rather than a non-deductible gift.

§ 60. Disallowance of Charitable Deductions—Estate Tax and Gift Tax— § 2055(e) and § 2522(c)

The 1969 Tax Reform Act inserted new rules that disallow a gift tax or estate tax deduction for some gifts of future interests to a charitable beneficiary. These rules were added to prevent abuses by taxpayers who took deductions for the present value of a future interest to charity that was estimated lawfully but often exceeded the value or proportion that eventually found its way to the charity. This could happen for any number of reasons, such as a depreciation in the value of the corpus during the interim income period, or trustee investment policy favoring the income interest with a concomitant (risk of) depletion of the principal.

The new rules apply to remainder interests in trust and also to remainder interests on legal life estates or estates for years. Deduction is still allowed for the remainder, but the income portion must be clearly defined and the deductible amount is reduced by raising the discount or interest rate used to determine present value from 3½% to 6%.

Section 2055(e) disallows a deduction for a bequest of (most) remainder interests to charity unless a charitable remainder annuity trust or unitrust (described in § 664) or a pooled income fund [§ 642(c)(5)] is used, while § 2522(c) does the same in the gift tax context.

The charitable remainder annuity trust is one under which the non-charitable income beneficiary must receive a fixed dollar annuity but not less than 5% of the value of the trust corpus at the time it first is placed in the trust. The unitrust is one under which the non-charitable beneficiary is to receive income of a fixed percentage not less than 5% of the trust assets valued annually. A pooled income fund is one that is maintained by the donee charity, receives funds from a number of contributors and pays income to the contributors or their nominees for life with the remainder to the charity.

A special rule which treats a work of art and the copyright thereon as two separate properties was introduced by E.R.T.A. The transfer of *either* to a § 501(c)(3) organization (which is not a private non-operating foundation), if the donee's use is related to its exempt purpose, will now qualify for a charitable deduction. See I.R.C. §§ 2055(e)(4) and 2522(c)(3).

§ 61. Deductions in the Generation-Skipping Tax

Deductions found in the tax on generation-skipping transfers were described in the Chapter outlining the Federal transfer taxes, and will not be repeated here. See §§ 6 & 15, *supra*.

CHAPTER XIII

THE MARITAL DEDUCTIONS AND SPLIT GIFTS

§ 62. Introduction to the Marital Deduction and Split Gifts

Section 2056 of the I.R.C. provides a marital deduction in the estate tax for a decedent's transfer to his or her surviving spouse. I.R.C. § 2523 grants a similar marital deduction in the gift tax for an inter-vivos gift to the spouse of the donor. I.R.C. § 2513 permits a gift by a husband or wife to a third party to be considered as if made one half by each of the spouses. These statutory rules, to be explored in much greater detail in following sections, first entered the Internal Revenue Code in 1948 and presently serve as very important opportunities and obstacles for the estate planner.

Until the Tax Reform Act of 1976, the purpose of the marital deduction had been to allow a spouse to pass non-community property to his or her surviving spouse with the same tax consequences that would have obtained if the spouses had lived and saved and transferred property in a community-property system, so long as the separate-property taxpayers were in fact in the same economic position as community-property taxpayers. Thus, the marital deduction rules have their roots in community-property laws, whose tax advantage the marital deduction is designed to neutralize.

Early in the development of federal taxation, the Supreme Court held that income earned by a married spouse in a community-property state was taxable only half to him and the other half to his or her spouse, since the non-earning spouse was entitled to half the income as a matter of state law. By the same token, half the income from property owned as community property was taxable to each spouse. Similarly, at the death of one spouse, only half the family's community property was regarded as owned by him or her and therefore includable in the decedent's gross estate, even if all the property had originated with his or her efforts or other sources. Under a parallel rule, if one spouse made a gift of community property, the gift was considered to be made one-half by each spouse. These income, estate and gift tax rules, which mirrored state property law, provided very substantial tax savings for spouses to whom community-property law was applicable, compared to spouses living in separate-property states or transferring separate property though living in community-property states.

To remove the difference in tax consequences between community-property and separate-property systems, Congress first attempted to eliminate the estate and gift tax advantages formerly enjoyed by spouses living in community-property states. Legislation in 1941 and 1942 was directed toward this end. The income tax advantages of community-property law, however, remained unabated, and some states that historically had operated under the common-law, separate-property system changed or attempted to change to community-property law, solely because of its federal tax advantages.

In 1948, Congress enacted the income tax joint return and split-income rules in order to give essentially the same income tax treatment to separate-property spouses as was available to community-property spouses. At the same time, amendments were made in the estate and gift tax laws in order to remove the discrepancies in treatment between separate-property and community-property states. The marital deduction and split-gift provisions originally were enacted in order to grant to separate property spouses the transfer-tax advantages that only the community-property spouses had enjoyed before the 1942 legislation. The starting point for understanding the marital deduction and split-gift provisions is the marital deduction section of the estate tax, I.R.C. § 2056.

§ 63. The Estate Tax Marital Deduction— I.R.C. § 2056

Until 1977, Section 2056 allowed a deduction from the gross estate, in determining the taxable estate, of an amount equal to the value of property passing to the surviving spouse to the extent that the property transferred did not exceed *one half* of the decedent's "*adjusted gross estate*," and so long as other conditions were met.

In the years immediately preceding the Reform Act of 1976, numerous proposals (*e.g.*, 1969 Treasury Proposals), had suggested that inter-spousal transfers should not be subject to the transfer taxes at all. The theory was that, as between husband and wife, such transfers should be regarded as merely non-taxable arrangements for the technical title holding of shared marital wealth; in other words, for transfer tax purposes, the couple should be treated as a unit, with transfer tax consequences to follow only upon the transfer of property to outside parties or younger generations. This idea—a complete inter-spousal exemption or "unlimited marital deduction"—was not accepted in its entirety by Congress in 1976, but was adopted by E.R.T.A. in 1981.

The 1976 Reform Act did introduce what can be characterized as "a limited 100% marital deduction" in both the estate and gift tax contexts. This was accomplished by providing for a marital deduction in the estate tax of the greater of a fixed dollar sum ($250,000) or the old 50% limits, thus providing a 100% deduction for transfers of amounts up to the minimum figure. For smaller estates, this indeed did amount to a 100% deduction and it sometimes was referred to as the small estate marital deduction. (The gift-tax minimum marital deduction is described in § 66, *infra*.) The dollar minimum amounts differed for the two taxes, as do the old substantive rules for the allowance of the deductions, which were not changed by the Reform Act. These marital deduction rules are applicable to the estates of decedents dying after 1976 and before 1982, with some exceptions, to prevent unfair surprise for unamended, formula-clause wills.

E.R.T.A. removed all quantitative limits on the marital deduction, for the estates of decedents dying after 1981, once again subject to a phase-in period in order to prevent surprise in the case of certain pre-existing, unamended wills in which the marital deduction clause was drafted in terms of "the maximum allowable marital deduction". See P.L. 97–34, § 403(e)(3) for the E.R.T.A. 1981 transition rules.

Section 2056, in allowing a marital deduction for death transfers to the surviving spouse, requires that the transfer be one of "*any* interest in property" that has been *included* in the decedent's gross estate and which *passes* from the decedent to the surviving spouse. In addition, the statute requires that the interest received by the surviving spouse not be a "*terminable interest*" as defined in the statute. Also, if the interest is to be paid out of assets some of which would not qualify for the marital deduction, the value of the otherwise eligible interest must be reduced by the value of ineligible assets. (Prior to E.R.T.A., the marital deduction could in no event exceed in amount the greater of $250,000 or 50% of the decedent's "adjusted gross estate", as defined in the statute to consist of the decedent's gross estate minus the deductions allowed under I.R.C. §§ 2053 and 2054.)

Prior to E.R.T.A., community property did not give rise to any marital deduction—with one exception involving the small estate marital deduction and former § 2056(c)(1)(C), to be described later. Consequently, a husband who left his interest in community property to his wife (usually) could not take a marital deduction with respect to this interest which passed to her at his death. Nor is any deduction allowed, even after E.R.T.A., with respect to the wife's own interest which was vested before her husband's death and which does not pass to her at his death but remains hers. This follows under the Code because the wife's already vested ½ interest is not part of the decedent's gross estate under § 2033. In determining the adjusted gross estate, under former § 2056(c), for purposes of computing the ceiling on the marital deduction, the gross estate had to be reduced by community property held by the decedent at death, community property transferred by the decedent during life, insurance proceeds to the extent purchased with premiums paid with community property, and an amount bearing the same ratio to the deductions allowed under §§ 2053 and 2054 as the value of property included in the gross estate diminished by the community property interests just described bears to the gross estate. See former § 2056(c)(2)(B) and Regs. § 20.2056(c)–2. The marital deduction, therefore, generally was not available if the decedent's gross estate consisted entirely of community property. Regs. § 20.2056(a)–1(a).

Before E.R.T.A., the marital deduction was generally denied with respect to community property because even without that deduction one-half of the community property held by the decedent and his wife at death was received by her without any inclusion in the husband's gross estate. If a marital deduction had been allowed with respect to the one-half of the family community property that was included in the husband's gross estate, the net result would have been to allow the husband to pass to the surviving wife three-quarters rather than just one-half the property acquired or saved during his life, without imposition of any transfer tax. Since the purpose of the marital deduction and the principle of horizontal equity would be violated if the marital deduction did not give approximately the same tax treatment to separate property interest as that given to community property interests, the marital deduction had to be denied with respect to any community property, whether in an estate in which all the property was community property or in which part of the family wealth was community property, except when the post-'76 small estate minimum marital deduction was involved.

Although it was said that the decedent's ownership of community property did not give rise to a marital deduction, nonetheless, even prior to E.R.T.A., particular assets that were community property could be transferred to the surviving spouse tax-free in satisfaction of a marital deduction generated by the existence of separate property

or by the small estate marital deduction of $250,-
000.

It was even true that an estate of a person who
owned no assets other than community property
assets could have and use a marital deduction.
This was true because of the post-'76 $250,000
minimum marital deduction. In separate property
states, that could exceed one-half the marital property (in small estates). Since this treatment was
more generous than that inherently given by community property rules, fairness seemed to require
that some similar minimum deduction be extended
to holders of community property. However, to give
them a full minimum marital deduction of $250,000
in addition to the built-in advantages of community
property, would have .been over-compensatory.
Therefore the minimum marital deduction of former § 2056(a) was subject to a complex reduction in
the event that there was any community property
in the decedent's estate. See former § 2056(c).

There was one more adjustment which had to be
made to the allowable marital deduction, which had
no counterpart under pre-'77 law. Although both
the gift and estate tax marital deductions prior to
E.R.T.A. were cast in the amount of a fixed sum *or*
one-half of either the adjusted gross estate (for the
estate tax deduction) or one-half of the value of the
gift [for the gift tax deduction (see § 66, infra)],
there was a *cumulative* unified maximum of $250,-
000 or one-half of the adjusted gross estate or gift
value set on the marital deductions taken together.
This meant that the estate tax marital deduction

amount had to be reduced by the excess of the gift tax marital deductions allowed the decedent over 50% of the value of the taxable gifts on which those deductions were allowed. See I.R.C. § 2056(c)(1)(B). This had the effect of neutralizing the $100,000 gift tax minimum marital deduction and replacing it, upon death, with the estate tax minimum marital deduction.

The statutory terms "interest in property" and "passes or has passed from the decedent to his surviving spouse" are given further meaning by the statute, the Regulations, rulings and litigated cases. In particular, the Regulations under I.R.C. § 2056 prove very helpful in explaining the meaning and operation of the marital deduction. See Regs. § 20.2056. Some of these statutory terms and rules will be further discussed in subsequent passages. And see § 2056(d) (definition of "interest passing").

To accomplish the basic purpose of the marital deduction, it was necessary to design a number of sub-rules qualifying the deduction. These sub-rules attempted to make sure that the deduction will be allowed only when the surviving spouse received the same kind of economic values in a separate property situation as his or her counterpart in the community property situation. This accounts for the statutory terms "interest in property," "passing" to the wife from the husband, and the requirement that the property be included in the husband's gross estate. It also was necessary to insure that the wife would be taxable at her death on what she received from her husband tax-free because of the marital deduction. The sub-rules for this purpose are the terminable interest rule and the exceptions to the terminable interest rule which apply when the wife will in fact be taxed on the interest she receives from her husband even though that interest is in general a terminable interest. See generally I.R.C. § 2056(b), discussed in § 64 below. And see the rules on power of appointment trusts under § 2056(b)(5), on life insurance in § 2056(b)(6), on qualified terminable interest property under new § 2056(b)(7) and on charitable remainder trusts under new § 2056(b)(8). Another sub-rule was necessary to make sure that the deduction was limited to the interests actually received by the wife from the husband.

In order to explore the actual operation of the marital deduction (before and after E.R.T.A.), it is useful to give a specific example and to assign dollar values to the interests involved, for ease of reference. The important thing is to understand the structure of the marital deduction and how it operates in terms of concepts. (The I.R.S. issued a large set of final regulations on the estate and gift tax marital deduction in Spring 1994. Generally they adopt regulations proposed in 1984, with amendments to reflect subsequent law changes. They are extensive and helpful. See Regs. under I.R.C. §§ 2056, 2523 etc.)

Consider, by way of illustration, the estate tax situation of a husband and wife who live in California, a community property state, and have family wealth in the amount of $1,300,000. Of that amount, assume that $600,000 consists of post-1927 community property, that is property in which the wife under California law is deemed to have a present, vested interest during her life. For ease of reference, assume that the community property consists of their family residence and surrounding ranch and vineyard land. Suppose also that the other $700,000 of the family's wealth is the separate property of the husband, inherited by him from his parents. Assume also that the husband dies first and in his will leaves everything to his wife. Therefore, the wife will receive the husband's half of community property plus all the husband's separate property and will own that in addition to the half of the family community property in which she had a vested ownership interest during her life. (In point of fact, in a community property system, *all* of the community property, including the surviving spouse's half, is likely to come under the jurisdiction of the executor or administrator for purposes of administration.) Assume also in the example that expenses and losses of the kinds described in I.R.C. §§ 2053 and 2054 amount to $130,000. Also assume that of the total of such expenses and losses, $30,000 is attributable to the wife's half of the family's community property. As such, those $30,000 expenses will not be allowed as deductions from the husband's gross estate. Therefore the amount allowable under §§ 2053 and 2054 in computing the husband's taxable estate will be $100,000.

The Estate Tax Marital Deduction Before E.R.T.A.—The Limited Marital Deduction.

[For the estates of decedents dying after 1981, the marital deduction is *unlimited*. The next long paragraph is pertinent only for calculations as to those who died before 1982. It can be skipped or skimmed by most readers for most purposes.]

If the husband died before 1982, the effective date of E.R.T.A., then in order to determine the marital deduction available in computing the husband's taxable estate, it is necessary to compute the husband's *adjusted gross estate*, because of the 50% rule in former I.R.C. § 2056(c)(1)(A). To compute the adjusted gross estate, one may start informally with the family's net worth or *wealth* as a beginning concept. That amount was $1,300,000 in this example. Of that amount, $300,000 is the wife's half of post-1927 community property and hence will not be included in the husband's *gross estate* because it is not property owned by him at death under I.R.C. § 2033. Nor is it includable under any other section of the Code. Consequently, the husband's *gross estate* amounts to $1,000,000 ($1,300,000 minus $300,000). To compute the husband's *adjusted gross estate*, the gross estate of $1,000,000 must be reduced by another $300,000, the husband's half of community property. This follows from former I.R.C. § 2056(c)(2)(B)(i) and from the fact that the husband's half of the community property should not give rise to any marital deduction, if that deduction is to equalize community property and separate property states. So the husband's gross estate is reduced from $1,000,000 to $700,000 by subtracting his half of community property. A further reduction of $70,000 must be made because that is the proportion of the aggregate expenses, taxes, and debts described under § 2053 and § 2054, which is attributable to the husband's separate property. The amount of $70,000 is computed under the rule of former § 2056(c)(2)(B)(iv). The logic of this rule is to not reduce the husband's *adjusted gross estate* for that proportion of the expenses (all of which in fact will be allowable and deductible under §§ 2053 and 2054 in computing the *taxable estate*) that are attributable to the husband's one-half of the family's community property, since that portion is not included in his *adjusted* gross estate, and so does not give rise to any marital deduction. Since the husband's separate property consisted of 70% of his gross estate ($700,000 compared to $1,000,000), only 70% of the $100,000 expenses deductible under §§ 2053 and 2054 must be deducted in computing the *adjusted gross estate*. Thus, in conclusion, the husband's adjusted gross estate is $630,000 ($700,-000 minus $70,000). Since all of the husband's property has been willed to his wife, the maximum amount of the marital deduction is determined by the rule of former I.R.C. § 2056(c)(1)(A). 50% of the adjusted gross estate of $630,000 equals $315,-000. The small estate or minimum fixed dollar marital deduction amount is in this case $250,000 see former § 2056(c)(1)(A)(ii)] less the value of the decedent's share of the community property, $300,-000, plus the deductible expenses of $30,000 attributable thereto, *i.e.*, $250,000 less the net community property in the estate. See former

§ 2056(c)(1)(C), which convolutedly mandates this treatment. Since 50% of the adjusted gross estate ($315,000) exceeds this fixed-dollar amount, the amount of the maximum marital deduction available in this estate would be $315,000.

The Estate Tax Marital Deduction After E.R.T.A. Of course, if the husband died after 1981, none of the foregoing calculations is necessary because his estate would be entitled to an unlimited marital deduction, equal to the value of all qualified property passing to his wife. The entire concept of the "adjusted gross estate" is itself superfluous for post-E.R.T.A. decedents.

The Taxable Estate. Having determined the maximum marital deduction available, the tax counselor must now turn to the determination of the actual *taxable estate* and thus the computation of the estate tax. To do this, even for a pre-E.R.T.A. decedent, one puts aside for the moment the computations just completed, the computations of the *adjusted gross estate* and of the maximum marital deduction.

The *taxable estate* is determined under I.R.C. § 2001 and § 2051. Under those sections, the amount of the *taxable estate* is derived directly from the *gross estate* without the intervention of the concept of an *adjusted gross estate*, even for *pre-*E.R.T.A. decedents. To determine the taxable estate under § 2051, in the example under discussion, the *gross estate*, consisting of $1,000,000, must be reduced by all available *deductions*. These available deductions include the aggregate expenses, debts, and taxes deductible under §§ 2053 and 2054. By hypothesis, these allowable deductions are $100,000 in amount. (Notice that the total expenses, debts, taxes and losses were said to be $130,000, but $30,000 of that amount was allocable to the wife's half of the community property and hence would not be allowable under § 2053 and § 2054. Notice also that the expenses deducted in computing the *adjusted gross estate* for purposes of determining the *pre*-E.R.T.A. marital deduction were only $70,000, because an additional $30,000 was attributable to the husband's half of community property, not eligible for the marital deduction. However that same reduction from $100,000 to $70,000 does *not* take place when computing the *taxable estate*, since the deductible costs, expenses, etc. that are attributable to the husband's half of community property should be allowed in determining his *taxable estate*, since his half of the community property is included in the gross estate.) So far, the deductions amount to $100,000.

Computing The Taxable Estate For Pre-E.R.T.A. Decedents—The Limited Marital Deduction. In addition to the foregoing deduction, the marital deduction itself is allowed under § 2056. By prior calculations, the pre-E.R.T.A. marital deduction amounted to $315,000. All together, the pre-E.R.T.A. deductions total $415,000. As a result of these deductions, the husband's *gross estate* of $1,000,000 is reduced to a *taxable estate* of $585,000. The *estate tax* on his taxable estate of $585,000, determined under the rate schedule of I.R.C. § 2001, is $187,-250, assuming the decedent had made no prior taxable gifts. Any unified credit remaining to the decedent will be credited to him via the computation of § 2001, which will also bump his rate bracket up if he has in fact made prior taxable transfers. In addition, if any *credit* (see Ch. XIV, *infra*) is available for the payment of state or foreign death taxes or for gift taxes during life, such credit would be allowed, pursuant to I.R.C. §§ 2011–2016, in determining the actual tax liability. Under I.R.C. § 2002, the executor is liable for the payment of the actual tax owing to the government.

Computing The Taxable Estate For Post-E.R.T.A. Decedents. If, on the other hand, the husband died after 1982, the marital deduction would equal the entire $900,000 which passes to the wife. Then total deductions are $1,000,000, which reduce his taxable estate to zero, so that no tax is payable.

In the foregoing example, the wife will continue to enjoy $300,000 of community property in which she had a fully vested interest before her husband's death. Although this was part of the family's net worth, it is not included in the husband's gross estate. It did not pass from him to her by reason of his death. (If the couple had lived in a common-law, separate-property state, the husband's gross estate would have been larger and he would have enjoyed a larger pre-E.R.T.A. marital deduction by virtue of passing all of the land and house and surrounding ranch or vineyard to his wife.) In the example, the separate property owned by the pre-

E.R.T.A. decedent-husband at death passed to his wife under his will and he received a deduction equal to half the value of that separate property, less the allowable, deductible expenses that are attributable to the separate property he gave her. (As a result, he is treated just as he would be if all the property owned by him and his wife had consisted of community property, in which case half would not be in his gross estate because not owned by him at death.)

For purposes of comparison, consider the tax consequences if the same husband and wife had owned the same family wealth of $1,300,000 but all in the form of community property. To determine the *taxable estate* of the pre-E.R.T.A. decedent-husband, one must begin with the gross estate, which would consist of one-half the family wealth since the wife's half of community property will not be included in his gross estate. Nothing will be eligible for the marital deduction because of the rule of former I.R.C. § 2056(c)(2)(B)(i) which states that in computing the adjusted gross estate there must be subtracted from the gross estate the sum of the value of property which is at the time of the death of the decedent held as community property. The adjusted gross estate will thus be zero in the example at hand. Since the $250,000 minimum deduction must also be reduced to take account of the community property in the gross estate, the minimum marital deduction will also be zero. Therefore, to calculate this decedent's taxable estate, the gross estate of $650,000 is reduced by $65,000 (deductible under §§ 2053 and 2054, and consisting of one-half the total expenses, and losses experienced by this estate). The other one-half of actual expenses and losses is allocable to the wife's half of community property which is not in the husband's gross estate. The net result is that the taxable estate consists of $650,000 minus $65,000 or a total of $585,000, the tax on which will be $187,250. In other words, this example shows that these community property spouses end up with the same tax bill as the spouses having some community property and some separate property eligible for the marital deduction.

By way of further comparison, one may consider the tax situation if the same family with the same wealth had lived in a separate-property state or had owned only separate property, all of which was owned by the husband at his pre-1982 death and was willed to his wife. In that event, the family net worth would still be $1,300,000. To compute the adjusted gross estate one would subtract the total expenses, debts, taxes, etc. allowable under §§ 2053–2054. This would total $130,000 since all the expenses and losses would be attributable to property in the husband's gross estate. The adjusted gross estate would then consist of $1,170,000, half of which would be $585,000, the ceiling on the available marital deduction. To determine this taxpayer's taxable estate, the net wealth of $1,300,000, which would also be the taxpayer's gross estate, can be reduced by deducting $130,000 in expenses and $585,000 for the marital deduction. The net result is a taxable estate of $585,000 which will produce an estate tax exactly the same as in the prior two examples.

The arithmetic of these examples is not as important as the conceptualization of what has taken place. In all three instances, the tax bill is the same because all the property of the family has been left to the surviving spouse and all the family wealth was thus enjoyed by her, either in the form of community property in which she held a vested interest before her death, or in the form of property she received from her husband, half of which she could receive tax free if, and only if, it was his own separate property. Of course all *post*-E.R.T.A. estates in which all property passes to the surviving spouse will have the same estate tax liability, namely none.

These pre-E.R.T.A. examples may give a misleading impression, because the tax liability did turn out to be exactly the same amount in each instance. If the facts were varied somewhat, for example, if the decedent's spouse did not leave everything within his power of disposition to the surviving spouse or if both spouses had contributed equally to the family wealth, however uniformly for all three examples, the tax would sometimes differ. The most that can safely be said is that the pre-E.R.T.A. marital deduction approximately and usually, but not perfectly and always, equalized the tax position of families who were of equal wealth and who made the same dispositions of community property and of separate property.

It may be noteworthy that the amount of the pre-E.R.T.A. marital deduction, when it was available at all, was keyed (except for smaller estates, when the fixed dollar amount controlled), to the size of the decedent's adjusted gross estate which in turn was determined with reference to the size of his gross estate. Therefore, generally, the larger the gross estate, the higher the *ceiling* on the marital deduction. The marital deduction in any event was limited by the property actually passing to the surviving spouse from the decedent.

Sometimes the marital deduction plays a role in what is called post-mortem estate planning. For example, in one case a decedent wife willed all her property at her death to her son. Her surviving husband, who evidently had enough wealth to live on (and evidently was not disinherited by his wife out of spite), elected under state law to take against the will. He thus became entitled to a substantial portion of the decedent wife's wealth. He soon gave to the couple's grandchildren the property he received from his wife's estate. The motive behind this conduct probably consisted of a desire to employ the marital deduction in the wife's estate by arranging for a disposition to him as a surviving spouse and then for the surviving husband to use his own gift tax lifetime exemption (no longer extant; replaced by unified credit) and annual exclusions to make tax-free gifts to the couple's grandchildren. In the process the surviving spouse skipped the son's generation for purposes of a transfer tax at the son's death. See Isaac Harter,

Jr., 39 T.C. 511 (1962) (Acq., 1963 C.B. 4). That the transfer to the husband after his election to take against the will would qualify for a marital deduction is borne out by the Regulations. See Regs. § 20.2056(e)–2(c). See also Rev.Rul. 66–139, 1966–1 C.B. 225 (settlement payment made by the executor with the decedent's widow in compromise of a good faith claim for dower under state law qualifies for the marital deduction). See also Rev. Rul. 68–271, 1968–1 C.B. 409, ruling that a payment made by the executors of the decedent's estate to the surviving spouse pursuant to her claim under an ante-nuptial agreement is considered, under the circumstances, as having passed from the decedent to his surviving spouse for the purpose of the marital deduction. Qualified disclaimers are to be taken into account when calculating the marital deduction, so that if, for example, some third party disclaims an interest under a will and that property then passes to the surviving spouse, the marital deduction, if otherwise available for that interest, will be allowed. The converse is also true.

In 1988, Congress added § 2056(d), which disallows the marital deduction for noncitizen spouses, unless the property passes to the surviving spouse in a qualified domestic trust (QDT). A QDT must have at least one trustee who is a U.S. citizen or a domestic corporation, either of which must have a right to withhold taxes from any distribution. See § 2056A, which governs QDT's. Section 2056(d) does not apply if a noncitizen spouse becomes a U.S. citizen before the estate-tax return is filed, so long as the spouse was a resident of the U.S. at all times after the decedent's date of death and before becoming a U.S. citizen. § 2056(d)(4). The purpose of § 2056(d) is to prevent the decedent's estate from escaping taxation completely, which otherwise could happen if a U.S. citizen husband died, left his estate to his foreign wife, and claimed the marital deduction, and his foreign wife then died in her home country. Section 2056(d) ensures that the property will be taxed either upon the husband's death or at the time of distribution from a QDT.

§ 64. The   Terminable   Interest   Rule— § 2056(b)

Following the general marital deduction rule set forth in § 2056(a), limitations are imposed by succeeding sub-sections, the most important of which is the *terminable interest rule* of I.R.C. 2056(b). The terminable interest rule arises from the basic premise of the marital deduction that property which qualifies for the deduction in the estate of the first spouse to die will eventually be taxed in the estate of the surviving spouse (if not disposed of before death). This premise follows from the attempt to correlate the treatment of property transferred tax-free under the marital deduction with treatment of property enjoyed by the surviving spouse tax-free under community property law. Accordingly, no marital deduction should be allowed when an interest in property given to the surviving spouse will, after the termination of that spouse's interest, pass to someone else without taxability in the surviving

spouse's gross estate. A terminable interest, such
as a life estate in the surviving spouse, with remainder to children or other beneficiaries, will avoid
taxation in the estate of such surviving spouse
because I.R.C. § 2033 does not reach interests in
property terminating at death. See § 17, *supra*.
Therefore, property disposed of in this manner
should not be allowed to avoid taxation in the estate
of the first spouse to die by qualifying for the
marital deduction, if that involves any "cost." See
Regs. § 20.2056(b)–1(g) ex. 1. In other words, the
value of the terminable interest should not escape
tax both at the time it is created and at the time it
terminates.

Specifically, I.R.C. § 2056(b)(1) states that an interest in property will not qualify for the marital
deduction if the interest passing to the surviving
spouse will fail or terminate upon the lapse of time
or on the occurrence or non-occurrence of an event,
if an interest in that property passes or has passed
for less than adequate consideration from the decedent to a third person and if such third person may
upon termination or failure of the spouse's interest
possess or enjoy any part of the property. Also, the
deduction is not allowed for a terminable interest
which is to be acquired for the surviving spouse,
pursuant to directions of the decedent, by his executor or by the trustee of the trust. Notice that the
mere termination of the surviving spouse's interest
alone or the passing of an interest to a third person
alone will not make the bequest ineligible for the
marital deduction. Rather, the terminable interest

rule is designed to reach situations where the wife is given an interest (such as a life estate) that will expire at her death, after which someone else (such as a remainderman) will possess the property. Its purpose is to insure that no transfer to a surviving spouse will qualify for the marital deduction if the interest transferred could not be taxed in the recipient's estate at death.

The statute now makes five exceptions to the terminable interest rule. One, under I.R.C. § 2056(b)(3), is applicable when the only way in which the surviving spouse's interest can terminate is upon her death in a common disaster or within six months of the death of the decedent and when her death does not in fact so occur. The purpose of this rule is simply to permit a will or trust to use a common disaster or early death clause without running afoul of the terminable interest rule. See Regs. § 20.2056(b)–3. The second exception, under I.R.C. § 2056(b)(5), applies if the surviving spouse has a life interest in income from property and a general power of appointment with respect to that property. See Regs. § 20.2056(b)–5. Since the ownership of the general power of appointment will entail taxability of the property subject to the power in the gross estate of the surviving spouse when she dies, under I.R.C. § 2041, nothing is lost by permitting the transfer to qualify for the marital deduction even though the wife has a terminable interest. The wife's rights will be regarded as the equivalent of outright ownership of the property at her death for purposes of inclusion in her estate, since she could have appointed the entire interest in favor of herself. See generally Regs. § 20.2056(b)–5. A third exception is provided by I.R.C. § 2056(b)(6) for life insurance, endowment or annuity contracts payable in installments where the surviving spouse has rights in the contract similar to those which she could receive and qualify for the deduction under the preceding section, § 2056(b)(5). See Regs. § 20.2056(b)–6.

The fourth (and exceedingly important) exception to the terminable-interest rule was enacted by E.R.T.A., and is therefore available only to the estates of post-'81 decedents. See new I.R.C. § 2056(b)(7). Under this exception, a life estate in "qualified terminable-interest property" will *not* be treated as a terminable interest, provided that the decedent's executor so elects. The entire property subject to such an interest is treated as passing to the surviving spouse, and its entire value thus qualifies for the marital deduction. "Qualified terminable-interest property" ("Q.T.I.P.") is defined as property with respect to which a proper election is made and which passes from a decedent to a spouse who is entitled to all income from the property (or a portion thereof) for life, payable at least annually. No person, including the spouse, may have the power to appoint any portion of the property subject to the interest to any person other than the spouse during the spouse's life. Creation or retention of any powers over the corpus are permitted, so long as they are exercisable only on or after the death of the spouse. Income interests for a term of years, or

a life interest subject to termination upon the occurrence of a condition, *e.g.*, remarriage, do not
qualify.

The fact that this exception necessarily involves
an election provides an interesting opportunity for
"post-mortem estate planning", depending on conditions obtaining after the decedent's death.

This important exception allows a decedent to
qualify property for the marital deduction while at
the same time keeping complete control over the
ultimate disposition of the property. Under the
older exceptions to the terminable interest rule, the
transferee spouse must be given control over the
ultimate disposition.

Eligible property for which an election is made
will qualify in its entirety for the estate tax marital
deduction, and thus will not be taxed in the decedent's estate. Since the property *need* not be subject to a testamentary power of appointment in the
surviving spouse, although it *may* be so subject,
special rules govern when the property will be
taxed. In the absence of these special rules, the
property could pass to the next generation without
being taxed in the spouse's estate, since the spouse
owns only an income interest, which expires upon
her death. Therefore such property will be subject
to the transfer tax at the earlier of (1) the date on
which the spouse disposes of all or part of the
qualifying income interest (by gift, sale or otherwise), in which case the entire value of the property, reduced by any consideration received for the

transfer, constitutes a taxable gift (see I.R.C. § 2519), or (2) the date of the spouse's death, when the value of the entire property on the date of death (or alternate valuation date) will be included in the wife's estate (see I.R.C. § 2044). The spouse may recover from the recipient of the property any gift tax paid with respect to the remainder interest transferred, including any penalties or interest. Likewise, her estate may recover any estate tax paid as a result of the inclusion of the property in her gross estate. See I.R.C. § 2207A.

Note that E.R.T.A. introduced still another exception to the terminable-interest rule, whereunder a life estate granted to a surviving spouse qualifies for the marital deduction if the remainder is to pass to a qualified charity upon the spouse's death. See I.R.C. § 2056(b)(8).

Whenever the marital deduction is placed in issue, the question must be asked whether the survivor has received a *non*-deductible terminable interest. Some examples may help illustrate the scope of the terminable interest rule. Suppose, for example, that the husband is the first to die and his will creates a trust providing that the income shall be paid to his wife for life with the remainder at her death payable to her estate. This is *not* a non-deductible terminable interest. Under I.R.C. § 2056(b)(1)(A) a marital deduction would be allowed, because there will be inclusion in the wife's estate under § 2033 and no interest is passing from the decedent to any person other than the spouse or her estate. Suppose instead that the husband has purchased a joint and survivor annuity which will pay an annual amount to the husband and wife during their joint lives and will pay to the survivor of them for his or her life a somewhat lesser amount, at the end of which there will be no refund and no payment to other recipients. When the husband dies, the wife will become entitled to receive the lesser annual payment for her life. This is *not* a non-deductible terminable interest, since no one else will receive the interest at the wife's death; it will simply expire. See the Regulations § 20.-2056(b)–1(g) Example 3. In other words, there is a requirement, as part of the definition of a non-deductible terminable interest, that someone else receive something from the husband when the wife's interest terminates. The reason for this rule is that if the wife were to get the entire interest (whatever its value), it is solely a gift to her and should be deductible in order to equalize the common law and community property situations. If the wife receives everything, there is no gift over to a non-spouse from the husband.

Some of the *exceptions* to the terminable interest rule may be illustrated by examples also. Suppose the husband's will provides that all his property shall go to his wife if she survives him by five months, and if not, the property is to be distributed to his children. (A clause to that effect would probably be inserted to avoid double probate and double estate tax costs in the event of a common disaster or simultaneous or near simultaneous deaths of the two spouses.) Also suppose that the wife does survive the husband for more than the required five-month period. The wife's interest appears to be a non-deductible terminable interest because her interest will fail on a contingency. However, the exception in § 2056(b)(3) makes this interest deductible since the survivorship requirement did not exceed the 6-month limitation of that rule. If the clause had said that the wife had to survive until "my estate has been administered" in order to take, her interest would not be deductible because it would be a terminable interest and the estate administration might require more than six months, thus exceeding the statutory exception. See U.S. v. L.A. Mappes, 318 F.2d 508 (10th Cir. 1963).

Similarly, a bequest in trust for the benefit of a decedent's surviving spouse will not qualify for the marital deduction under § 2056(a) if the bequest is contingent on whether the spouse survives until the trust is funded, and, due to the requirements of local probate law, the possibility exists at the time of the decedent's death that the funding of the trust may occur more than six months after the decedent's death. See Rev.Rul. 88–90.

The terminable interest rule can apply in rather unexpected situations. For example, the Supreme Court of the United States held, in Jackson v. U. S., 376 U.S. 503 (1964), that no marital deduction could be taken with respect to the allowance paid for the support of a surviving widow during the settlement of her husband's estate under state law. Her interest was deemed to be a terminable interest and hence not to qualify for the marital deduction. It should be added that the result will differ if the widow is the sole beneficiary of the husband's estate. Then the allowance constitutes a deductible interest, for what she does not receive during her life will pass through her estate and thus be taxed in the widow's gross estate. See Regs. § 20.-2056(b)–1(g) Example 8. In a more complex case, the percentage of the widow's allowance equal to her percentage of the residuary estate will qualify for the marital deduction. See Estate of Cunha v. Comm., 279 F.2d 292 (9th Cir. 1960), cert. den. 364 U.S. 942 (1961).

The many dimensions and intricacies of the terminable interest rule require that the statute and regulations and judicial and administrative authorities be consulted in detail and with great care before a specific plan of disposition is approved. Although the philosophy of the statute has been used from time to time to explain the general thrust of a statutory rule, it is risky to reason from the general logic of the statute to a particular prediction about the outcome of a disputed or undecided point.

§ 65. The Estate Tax Marital Deduction in Review

The marital deduction provides a way of postponing part of the federal estate tax that otherwise would have to be paid on a married person's estate, as well as actually reducing the aggregate tax that ultimately will have to be paid. The marital deduction does this by making it possible for the spouse who dies first to leave some or all of his or her estate in a manner that makes it deductible for federal estate tax purposes. Of course, any property that qualifies for the marital deduction in the estate of one spouse will, theoretically, be taxed in the survivor's estate to the extent that it is retained until the survivor's death.

In addition to postponing the payment of tax on some or all of the family wealth, the marital deduction also will probably result in payment of a much lower tax because the wealth can be split between two estates and thus will not rise so high in the graduated rate structure. The larger the separate estate of the first to die, the larger will be the interim saving of estate tax.

The ultimate saving is more difficult to calculate, because it will depend on the intervention of unpredictable facts. In particular, the property qualifying for the marital deduction in the estate of the first spouse to die, when taxed in the survivor's estate to the extent it has been retained, will be valued at the time of the survivor's death rather than at the death of the first spouse. It is even possible that if the surviving spouse owns separate property and the deceased spouse takes too great advantage of the marital deduction, the combined taxes may be *increased*, even though there is an interim saving. This possibility was made much more likely by the passage of the unlimited marital deduction. So it frequently will be advisable not to use the marital deduction in full. However, the additional taxes may often be a small price to pay for the financial and psychological advantages of having the use of the interim saving (postponement) of taxes for the survivor's lifetime.

In general, the task is to balance the advantages of having the use of interim savings for the remainder of the survivor's lifetime against the additional taxes that will be incurred when the survivor dies.

In planning for the marital deduction, the tax counselor should keep three factors particularly in mind. The first is that except in small estates, where the surviving spouse will need unfettered access to all the family wealth for her future needs, the unlimited deduction probably should be foregone, at least to the extent of the decedent's exemption-equivalent, currently $600,000. Not doing so is unwise, because it pyramids property in the survivor's estate and unnecessarily increases the combined federal estate taxes. Even better estate economy often can be achieved by limiting the spousal transfer in large estates to the excess of the total net estate over $3,000,000 and leaving the rest of the property in a trust that will not be taxed in the survivor's estate at all. This plan takes full advantage of the unified credit for both spouses and also provides two trips up the graduated rate schedule.

Secondly, the use of growth assets, assets that are likely to appreciate in value, for the transfer eligible for the marital deduction, is likely to prove disadvantageous. Since property qualifying for the marital deduction will be taxed in the survivor's estate at its value at the survivor's death, the use of growth assets will minimize the tax benefit by increasing the tax on the survivor's estate. Therefore, lawyers sometimes provide in a property owner's will that certain assets, ones that are likely to increase in value such as a piece of real estate or common stock in a closely held corporation, shall not be used for marital deduction purposes.

Thirdly, it is often desirable to take advantage of the marital deduction by the use of a trust for the surviving spouse's benefit. The trust may have substantial non-tax advantages, in terms of management and conservation of the property. The trustee can be given broad power over the property for the benefit of the surviving spouse. In fact, since the principal of the trust qualifying for the marital deduction will be taxed in the surviving wife's estate, she can be given an unrestricted power to withdraw principal from the trust without thereby creating any additional estate tax liability. Often, two trusts are used, one that qualifies for the marital deduction and one that will not be taxed in the survivor's estate. The so-called marital-deduction trust must be drafted with one eye on the Internal Revenue Code in order to make sure that all the requirements for the marital deduction are satisfied. For example, all the income must be paid to the wife each year. If necessary for her support and maintenance, the income from the residuary trust can also be paid to the wife. If not needed for this purpose, the income from a residuary trust can be paid to the children or accumulated for their benefit. If principal may have to be invaded for the benefit of the wife, estate tax can be saved in the wife's estate by using principal from the marital trust rather than from the residuary trust. In point of fact, every dollar of principal that is consumed from the marital trust will escape taxation in both the husband's and the wife's estate. Therefore, plans are sometimes laid for systematic use of principal from the marital trust rather than to have any income from the residuary trust paid to the wife. There is an income tax reason for this planning as well; dollars coming from principal can be spent entirely for the benefit of the wife, whereas only the after-tax dollars from income can be spent for that purpose.

In conclusion, the marital deduction is a very important tool in estate planning. It can provide substantial interim savings which will give the surviving spouse additional income and greater financial protection. In some instances, it will also produce an ultimate saving with the result that more capital is left for the children or other beneficiaries. The marital deduction also relieves problems of illiquidity by making it possible to pay the combined tax in two installments, part at the death of the first spouse to die and the balance at the death of the survivor. Since the marital deduction thus shifts some estate tax burden from the first estate to the estate of the survivor, the need for liquidity in the survivor's estate must be remembered. Also, since the order of death is never certain, an estate should always be planned against the eventuality that the expected order of deaths will be reversed.

396 MARITAL DEDUCTIONS Ch. 13

In general, the purpose of the *pre-1976* marital deduction may be seen in its historical role as an attempt to adjust the tax treatment for family property for couples residing in separate property states, or residing in community property states but holding separate property, in order to equalize that treatment with the "automatic splitting" of the family property for couples residing in community property states. The rules of the statute and other authorities in general attempted to provide equalization between separate property and community property situations by contriving permissive division of non-community property estates, so as to tax the decedent's estate in two halves if he were willing to leave at least half of his property to his surviving spouse. The exceedingly complex rules of the statute ended up providing tax equality in only a general and loose fashion. At times, it appeared that the overall objective of the marital deduction had been lost in the details of the statutory and administrative provisions. Under the post–1981 law, the purpose of the marital deduction is to make possible the tax-free transfer of wealth between spouses, while assuring that such wealth will be taxed upon its transfer to others. This additionally assures equality between separate and community property owners, as well as considerably simplifying transfer tax planning.

§ 66. The Gift Tax Marital Deduction— § 2523

Just as community property provided automatic estate splitting for estate tax purposes, it provided automatic inter-spousal gifts (and gift-splitting) for gift tax purposes. Therefore, the introduction of a marital deduction into the estate tax in 1948 was accompanied by introduction of a marital deduction in the gift tax.

Prior to 1977 I.R.C. § 2523 allowed a gift tax marital deduction for an amount equal to one-half the value of a transfer of an interest in non-community property to a donee who was at the time of the gift the donor's spouse.

From 1977 through 1981 a gift tax marital deduction was allowed for the greater of (a) $100,000 cumulatively, or (b) ½ the value of the gift. The Tax Reform Act of 1976 amended § 2523(a) to provide (very circuitously) for a deduction of all of the first $100,000 of inter-spousal gifts of separate property, of none of the second $100,000 of such gifts, and for a deduction equal to 50% of all inter-spousal taxable gifts over $200,000. The advantages of this upping of the limit, however, were greater in small estates, since as cumulative inter-spousal gifts increased from $100,000 to $200,000, the percentage deduction dwindled from 100% to 50%. Also, any deductions that in fact exceeded 50% were recaptured at the donor's death, in the form of a reduction in the then available estate tax marital deduction. See former § 2056(c)(1)(B). In any event, this alternative deduction limitation represented at least a deferral opportunity for those situations where the initial quarter's gifts were under $200,000. Under E.R.T.A., there is now an *unlimited* deduction for all qualifying post-1981 interspousal *gifts*.

The gift tax marital deduction closely resembles the estate tax marital deduction, even to the extent of including its own terminable interest rule and other rules for interests in unidentified assets, joint interests, a life estate with a power of appointment in the donee's spouse and qualifying terminable interest property. The following paragraphs will deal mainly with the differences between the gift tax marital deduction and the marital deduction in the estate tax.

Prior to 1982, and disregarding the fixed dollar alternative amounts of both taxes, the gift-tax marital deduction was allowed for one half of the amount of the property transferred, whereas the estate tax marital deduction could equal the entire value of the property transferred but was limited to one-half of the decedent's adjusted gross estate. (Under E.R.T.A., of course, there is *no* limit on the amount of either deduction.) The terminable interest rule in the gift marital deduction is broader than that in the estate tax, because a greater variety of terms is possible when a transfer is made inter-vivos. In particular, I.R.C. § 2523(b)(1) disallows any marital deduction for a transfer under which the donor has retained an interest that may ripen into possession or enjoyment at the termination of the donee-spouse's interest (except when the interest retained by the donor consists of his right of survivorship in a joint tenancy and if the two spouses are the only tenants). Similarly, the deduction is disallowed if the donor retains a power to create another interest in such a way as to change the donee-spouse's interest into a terminable interest. § 2523(b)(2).

The gift tax marital deduction statute does not contain a provision exactly like that in the estate tax [§ 2056(b)(6)] explicitly to permit the deduction with respect to proceeds of life insurance or annuity policies held by an insurance company; the same result follows, however, from I.R.C. § 2523(e).

The marital deduction available under § 2523 is allowed only to the extent that the gifts there specified are included in the amount of gifts against which such deduction is applied. In other words, the marital deduction in the gift tax may not exceed the aggregate of the donor's includable gifts to his or her spouse for the period.

In connection with the gift tax marital deduction of § 2523, attention should be turned again to I.R.C. § 2516 which exempts some property settlements in the marital context from gift tax and to the rule that a transfer of property in satisfaction of certain marital rights will sometimes be regarded as transfer for adequate and full consideration in money or money's worth and hence not taxable under the gift tax. Also, recall the rule for the deductibility of claims against an estate when the claim is based on a contract or agreement without full and adequate consideration in money or money's worth, often the situation in the case of antenuptial or other marital agreements.

In 1988, Congress added § 2523(i), which prohibits a marital deduction for gifts to noncitizen spouses. However, the law also raised the annual exclusion under § 2503(b) from $10,000 to $100,000 for gifts to noncitizen spouses. § 2523(i)(2).

The Regulations under I.R.C. § 2523 provide substantial additional guidance to the application of that section. See Regs. § 25.2523.

§ 67. Split Gifts and the Gift Tax

I.R.C. § 2513 contains a split-gift provision designed to give spouses in a separate property setting much the same gift tax treatment as that afforded by community property laws to a gift made by spouses to a third person. Under community property law, if the wife is deemed to have a vested half interest in property saved by the married couple during marriage, a gift of community property by a husband and wife to their child, for example, would be treated as a gift of half the property by each spouse. Hence, two annual exclusions and two unified credit allowances would be available to offset the gift. In the absence of I.R.C. § 2513, spouses making a gift of separate property held in the name of the husband would have available only one annual exclusion and one unified credit allowance.

To allow similar tax treatment with respect to non-community property, I.R.C. § 2513 provides that a gift by either a husband or a wife to a third person will be considered to be a gift of one-half the property by the husband and one-half by the wife if they both consent to such treatment of all gifts made during the calendar quarter by either spouse while married to the other.

Section 2513 does not amount to a joint gift tax return filed by the spouses and it does not enable them to share each other's unified credit under I.R.C. § 2505. See Rev.Rul. 54–30, 1954–1 C.B. 207 for the same issue under the specific exemption of old § 2521.

If one spouse pays the gift tax owed by the other, where a § 2513 consent has been given, the payment will not be treated as a gift by the spouse paying the tax since the liability for tax is joint and several. See Regs. § 25.2502–2 & § 25.2513–4.

It would seem that the post-1982 availability of an unlimited gift-tax marital deduction has robbed the split-gift doctrine of some of its vitality. One spouse, H, can simply give some property to the other, W, preparatory to giving the property to a third party, A. A possible barrier to this type of transaction, however, is the theory of the "indirect transfer", which would collapse the two gifts, and treat the gift from W to A as an indirect transfer from H to A, with W acting as a "mere conduit". See, *e.g.*, Regs. § 25.2511–1(h)(2). This theory could apply if the gift to W were conditioned on her making the gift over. Perhaps § 2513, which now allows gift splitting only in a rigid 50–50 ratio, should be amended to permit splitting in any ratio. Then it would allow the flexibility inherent in the above plan, without the uncertainty of success caused by the "indirect-transfer" theory.

Section 2513 has gained importance now that section 2562(a)(2) allows § 2513 gift-splitting to be used to relieve gifts under the annual exclusion from the generation-skipping tax (as well as from the gift tax).

§ 68. The Former Estate Tax Orphans' Deduction—§ 2057

The Reform Act of 1976 introduced a new (and short-lived) estate tax deduction for property passing to a minor child when a decedent dying after December 31, 1976 left no surviving spouse and the minor had no known surviving parent. The purpose of the deduction was to mitigate the estate tax burden so as to provide greater support for the decedent's family in cases where the marital deduction was not available to serve that function because there was no surviving spouse. (See H.Rep. at p. 59).

The deduction was limited to $5,000 per minor child, times the difference between 21 and the minor's age at the date of decedent's death. See former § 2057(b). The deduction also contained limitations similar to those applying to the marital and charitable estate tax deductions.

This deduction was repealed by E.R.T.A., and is not available for the estates of decedents dying after 1981. It was repealed because its value was not commensurate with the additional complications it occasioned, and because its repeal was more than compensated for by E.R.T.A.'s increased unified-credit amounts. See the General Explanation of E.R.T.A. (P.L. 97–34), prepared by the Joint Committee on Taxation, 12/29/81.

CHAPTER XIV

CREDITS AGAINST THE ESTATE AND GIFT TAXES: LIABILITY AND PAYMENT OF THE TAXES

§ 69. Unified Credit—Estate and Gift Tax— § 2010, § 2505

Prior Law. In computing taxable gifts, each citizen or resident taxpayer was, prior to 1977, allowed an *exemption* of $30,000 over his or her lifetime. This lifetime exemption, which operated as a deduction in computing the amount of taxable gifts, could be spread over any number of taxable periods. (See former § 2521.) The difference between an exemption and a deduction largely consists of the fact that the exemption is a flat amount fixed by the law for every taxpayer, whereas deductions vary from person to person or estate to estate, according to the facts in each instance.

Similarly, the *exemption* available in the estate tax was that provided by old I.R.C. § 2052 which stated that the value of the taxable estate should be determined by deducting an exemption of $60,000 from the value of the gross estate. This $60,000 exemption, available to every estate, had the exceedingly important result of freeing from tax any estate computed to have a gross estate that did not exceed $60,000. (Recall that the "gross estate" as determined under I.R.C. § 2031 may well exceed the amount of property owned by the decedent at death, since the gross estate can consist of property transferred during life but included in the gross estate under I.R.C. §§ 2035–2038, annuities, life insurance, and property subject to a power of appointment.) Even though the function and purpose of the $60,000 exemption was to free small estates from estate tax, the exemption was available in every estate, no matter how large. It thus reduced the progressivity of the estate tax rates, since those rates began to apply only to the excess of the gross estate over the $60,000 exemption.

This means that these pre-'76 T.R.A. exemptions were worth more to high-bracket donors than to those in lower brackets. For example, using the 1976 estate tax rate table, the $60,000 estate tax personal exemption represented a savings of $9,500 for a taxable estate of $60,000, but saved $46,200 for taxable estates of over $10,000,000. In other words, the exemptions, acting as deductions, came "off the top," and thus eliminated tax on $30,000 (gift tax) and $60,000 (estate tax) of taxable transfers at the donor's *highest* marginal rates.

Another possible vertical inequity in prior law was that the entirely separate gift tax exemption could be exploited by only the relatively rich, since those with more modest fortunes cannot afford to make large lifetime gifts, needing the capital for other lifetime purposes. This disparity was compounded by the fact that lower rates applied to *inter vivos* transfers, ¾ of the estate tax rates.

New Law. In order to remedy these inequities, the Tax Reform Act of 1976 abolished the separate gift tax rate table of old § 2502 and replacing it with a reference in new § 2052(a) to the new estate tax rate schedule of § 2001(c), now referred to as the *unified rate schedule*. It also abolished the gift and estate tax exemption sections 2521 and 2052, and added new sections 2505 and 2010, the unified credit sections for the gift and estate taxes, respectively.

I.R.C. § 2505 provides a credit for each calendar year against the gift tax of § 2501 of $192,800 less the sum of such credits allowable for all preceding calendar periods. The amount of the credit was gradually, but not evenly, phased in [see § 2505(b)], and reached the final level of $192,800 in 1987. The unified credit amounts for this purpose are the same as the estate tax unified credit under § 2010, except for a special limit of $6,000 on gift tax credits for gifts made prior to July 1, 1977. By its terms, the credit is, in general, not reduced for any amounts previously exempted from pre-1977 gifts by virtue of the old § 2521 specific exemption. The sole exception is for gifts made after September 8, 1976, the date of passage of the Reform Act, and before January 1, 1977, the effective date of the new provisions. The unified credit is to be reduced by 20% of any amount allowed as a specific exemption for gifts made between the above dates (§ 2505(c)). This exception was of course intended to prevent intentional exploitation of the fact that generally the unified credit allowable is unaffected by prior allowable exemptions. The reduction was set at 20% of the value of the exemption, since the unified credit is, in general, roughly equivalent to a gift tax deduction (at the lowest marginal rates) of five times the credit amount. Thus, under the new rate table of § 2001, a gift of $30,000 (for example) made in November, 1977, by a donor with no prior taxable gifts, would incur $6,000 in taxes, which is also the amount of his unified credit, leaving no net gift tax liability.

No part of a donor's unified credit of, ultimately, $192,800 may be used against tax on a gift to the extent the gift is attributable to his or her spouse when the spouses consent, under § 2513, to have gifts made during a calendar year considered as having been made one-half by each. So, one spouse cannot claim any of his or her spouse's unified credit either by a joint gift tax return or by attribution. But it would appear that a gift to a spouse, tax-free under the new unlimited marital deduction, followed by a gift from the donee spouse to the third party, would allow the use of the unified credits of both spouses, unless the steps were telescoped into a single gift. (See § 67, supra).

The unified credit (unlike the former $30,000 exemption) not only is cumulative over the lifetime of the donor, but any amount left unused at his or her death is available as a credit against estate taxes.

The mechanics of the unified credit in the estate tax situation are somewhat complicated, due to the cumulation of lifetime gifts into the estate tax base. I.R.C. § 2010 allows the *full* unified credit, reduced only by 20% of post-September 8, 1976 specific exemptions allowed, to be applied against estate tax liability, seemingly regardless of whether any or all of the available credit has already been taken in the gift context. This, in spite of appearances, however, does not amount to a double allowance of the credit, since the § 2001 estate tax is determined by computing a tentative tax on the sum of the taxable estate *plus* any taxable gifts made after December 31, 1976 (§ 2001(b)(1)) *minus* the "tax payable under Chapter 12" on such gifts (§ 2001(b)(2)). The unified credit is then applied against this amount. To the extent that the unified credit was taken on inter-vivos gifts, the "tax payable under Chapter 12" has been reduced (§ 2001(b)(2)) and the amount subtracted from the tentative tax under § 2001(a)(1) is less. (The net result is the application of any remaining unified credit against the estate tax, regardless of how much was used during life.)

Note that the maximum rates themselves were lowered by E.R.T.A. If a *post*-E.R.T.A. decedent were credited under § 2001(b)(2) with the amount of gift taxes payable for *post*-'76, *pre*-E.R.T.A. years, the computation mechanics would, in effect, give retroactive effect to these rate reductions. Therefore, post-1981 estates are credited under amended § 2001(b)(2) with only the amount of gift taxes that *would have been payable* under the *new* rate schedule.

Not only does the unified credit free small estates of tax, it also frees them of the necessity of filing an estate tax return. Under I.R.C. § 6018(a)(1), an estate tax return must be filed for a citizen or resident decedent only if the gross estate exceeds $600,000.

This $600,000 represents the "exemption-equivalent" of the ultimate 1987 unified credit of $192,-800. In other words, $192,800 is approximately the tax liability on a taxable estate of $600,000, and that tax is completely offset by the credit. This amount of $600,000 is also to be gradually phased in between 1977 and 1987 to correspond with the phase-in of the unified credit amount. Further, just as the unified credit is in effect reduced in § 2001, the exemption-equivalent amount is to be reduced by the sum of all "adjusted taxable gifts" (*i.e.*, all post-1976 taxable gifts not included in the gross estate) plus all specific exemptions allowed for gifts during the period between September 8, 1976 and January 31, 1977.

In many instances, no tax will be payable even though an estate tax return must be filed; although the *gross* estate exceeds $600,000, the *taxable* estate may well be reduced to zero by virtue of various deductions. (Moreover, any tax computed on the taxable estate may be offset in part or as a whole by other credits against the estate tax. See § 70, *infra*.)

§ 70. Other Credits Against the Estate Tax— I.R.C. §§ 2011–2014

Credits against the estate tax liability determined under I.R.C. § 2001 are allowed for gift tax paid by the decedent on property that is also included in his gross estate, for death tax paid to a state or a foreign country, and for estate tax previously paid on prior transfers of the same property.

For gifts made before 1977, the estate tax credit for *gift tax* previously paid is determined under I.R.C. § 2012. In general, the credit is designed to prevent a double tax when property that is transferred during life in a fashion that is complete for gift tax purposes also becomes taxable in the gross estate of the decedent because the transfer was not complete for estate tax purposes. The law limits the credit to an amount that bears the same ratio to total gift tax liability for the year of the gift as the amount of the gift bears to total taxable gifts in that year. I.R.C. § 2012(d). It also is limited to an amount that bears the same ratio to the federal estate tax as the value of the gift bears to the decedent's gross estate. I.R.C. § 2012(a).

For post 1976 gifts, there is an automatic "credit" for the tax payable on those total transfers under the general estate tax calculation method of § 2001. See § 2001(b)(2). This "credit" is computed at the rates in effect at the time of decedent's death, and is not limited by any of the percentage formulae of § 2012, which is inapplicable to gifts made after 1976.

The credit for *state death taxes* actually paid is established by I.R.C. § 2011. Under that section, the credit will not exceed a percentage of the tax imposed by I.R.C. § 2001. The creditable portion is determined under the graduated schedule in § 2011(b). The credit amounts to 80% of what was called the basic estate tax in the 1939 Code, when the estate tax consisted of a "basic tax" and an "additional tax." The credit for state death tax acts as an incentive for the states to levy death taxes up to the creditable amount, sometimes called "pick-up" taxes, since to do so does not increase the overall tax burden on their decedents. Note that increased unified credit amounts have the ancillary effect of reducing state pick-up tax revenues, due to the fact that this death tax credit comes after the unified credit is applied. See I.R.C. § 2011(f).

Under I.R.C. § 2014, a credit is allowed for a *foreign estate tax* paid with respect to any property situated within a foreign country and included in the gross estate. Were it not for this credit, a double tax could arise because (i) the United States imposes a tax on all of the property in the estate, even if that property is located outside the territory of the United States, and (ii) many foreign countries impose an estate tax on part or all of the same property to the extent it is situated within their territorial jurisdictions. The credit is restricted to the amount of the foreign death tax which is attributable to the value of the property situated in the foreign country and included in the decedent's gross estate. It is also limited to the portion of the U.S.

estate tax that is attributable to the foreign property included in the gross estate. A foreign tax credit is also granted for resident aliens if the foreign country in which the decedent was a citizen will allow a similar foreign tax credit in the case of United States citizens who are residents of that country. See § 2014(h). In some instances, a double tax treaty or convention has been entered into by the United States and the foreign country in question. In that event, the estate will receive the credit provided by § 2014 or the credit allowed by the treaty, whichever is more advantageous. See Regs. § 20.2014–4. In a few, limited circumstances, a death tax credit may be taken under § 2014 and a treaty. *Ibid.*

Under I.R.C. § 2013, a credit is allowed for all or a part of estate tax paid on *previously taxed transfers to* the decedent. The purpose of this credit is to ameliorate the impact of transfer taxes imposed on successive deaths within a relatively short period of time. An estate is entitled to a credit for estate taxes paid on prior transfers of property to the decedent if the property was transferred to him or her by someone who died within ten years before, or within two years after, the death of the decedent. There is no requirement that the property be traced or identified in the estate of the decedent or even that the same property be in existence at the time of the decedent's death. See Regs. § 20.2013–1(a). The amount of the credit depends on the amount of the estate tax paid by the other person and also by the length of time between the death of the transferor and the decedent. The larger the estate tax and the shorter the interval of time, the larger the credit. Further, limitations and qualifications are imposed by the remaining subsections of I.R.C. § 2013.

No parallel credit is allowed either in the gift tax or in the Chapter 13 tax on generation-skipping transfers.

§ 71. Liability and Payment of the Estate Tax

The amount of estate tax liability is determined under I.R.C. § 2001 by applying the tax rates there provided against the sum of the taxable estate, defined in § 2051, and all prior taxable gifts, with a credit back for gift taxes paid.

Payment of the estate tax shall be made by the executor, § 2002 specifies. The term "executor" is defined by I.R.C. § 2203 to apply to the executor or administrator of the decedent or, if no person is appointed, qualified and acting as such, then any person in actual or constructive possession of any property of the decedent. I.R.C. § 2205 declares that if the tax or any part of it is paid by or collected out of any of the estate passing to somebody other than the executor in his capacity as executor, such person shall be entitled to reimbursement out of the undistributed estate, or by equitable contribution from those whose interests in the estate came unreduced by payment of the tax. I.R.C. § 2206 provides for the liability of life insurance beneficiaries and I.R.C. § 2207 deals with

the liability of a recipient of property over which
the decedent had a power of appointment. Section
2207A(a) provides for the recovery by the executor
of any estate taxes attributable to "qualified terminable interest" property. This recovery is at the
highest marginal rate incurred by the estate, in
contrast to the §§ 2206 and 2207 recoveries, which
are pro-rata. The period of limitations on assessment and collection of the tax is established under
I.R.C. § 6501(a) to be a period lasting three years
from the time a return was filed except in instances
of willful attempts to evade tax, where no return
was filed, where a false return was filed or when an
extension has been given. I.R.C. § 7403 sets forth
the rules governing an action to enforce a lien or to
subject property to the payment of tax.

Under I.R.C. § 6324(a)(2), if the estate tax is not
paid when due, any person who, on the date of the
decedent's death, receives or holds property included in the gross estate under I.R.C. §§ 2035–2042 is
personally liable to the extent of the value of such
property at the time of the decedent's death.

State law often requires payment of the estate tax
to be made out of the general residuary estate
unless the will otherwise directs. However, in
many states statutes have been enacted to appor-
tion estate taxes in the absence of any provision of
the will to the contrary.

Payment of the Estate Tax and "Flower Bonds".
Until 1971, the U.S. government issued some Treasury Bonds that could be used at *par value* to pay

estate tax on the owner of the bonds. Some such bonds are still outstanding. Carrying relatively low interest rates, they can be purchased at big discounts from par or face value. Since they can be "redeemed" at par by using them to pay the tax, they recommend themselves to a person nearing his or her deathbed, since they will "flower into maturity" upon the death of the investor. Though the taxable estate is enlarged, no *income* tax is payable upon the increase in value, because of the fresh-start basis rule of I.R.C. § 1014. See Treasury Dept. Circular 1052; and see CCH, Federal Estate and Gift Tax Reporter at ¶9764.45 for a list of qualified bonds.

§ 72. Liability and Payment of the Gift Tax

The gift tax is computed under I.R.C. § 2502 by applying the rates provided in § 2001 against the taxable gifts of the taxpayer. As spelled out in § 2502, the rates are applied on a lifetime, cumulative basis.

All in all, the primary liability for the gift tax imposed by § 2501 falls on the donor. See I.R.C. § 2502(d). (But note new § 2207A(b), whereunder any gift tax paid by the donor with respect to "qualified terminable interest property" may be recovered from the person receiving the property.) But if the donor does not pay the tax when it is due, the donee becomes personally liable to the extent of the value of the gift—even if there has been no particular effort to collect the tax from the donor and even if he or she is perfectly able to pay it. See

I.R.C. § 6324(b), whose lien provisions aid in the collection of this tax. The period of limitations under I.R.C. § 6501 is three years, except with respect to the donee for whom the period is four years, since he or she is a transferee within I.R.C. § 6901. See § 6901(c). The time and place for paying the gift tax are governed by I.R.C. § 6151 and extensions of time for paying the tax are governed by I.R.C. § 6161.

The Regulations under the various Code sections cited in this Chapter provide helpful elaboration and explanation of the statutory rules.

§ 73. Liability and Payment of the Tax on Certain Generation–Skipping Transfers

Liability for, and payment of, the new Generation-Skipping Transfer Tax is outlined in Chapter II, § 15, of this text.

Reporting the New G.S.T. Temporary Regulations on the new Generation–Skipping Transfer Tax were issued on March 31, 1988 for guidance on reporting and filing returns. See Regs. § 26.2662–1 and see I.R.S. Ann. 88–71, 1988–16 I.R.B. 37.

CHAPTER XV

A FEW FUNDAMENTALS OF ESTATE PLANNING

§ 74. Introduction

Estate planning is a specialty involving complicated techniques and sound legal judgment; it cannot be mastered merely with the comprehension of a few basic principles. Nevertheless, some general introduction to the maxims and attitudes of estate planning can serve to review the basic structure of the federal estate and gift and generation-skipping taxes and also convey something about the nature of estate planning possibilities given the impact of these transfer taxes. (Income tax factors also form an important component of estate planning, but they will be subordinated here.)

In general, taxpayers contemplating transfers of substantial wealth probably should make at least some *inter vivos* gifts, and thus utilize the annual gift tax exclusions, the split gift provision and the marital deduction wherever possible. The annual exclusions are lost year by year if they are not used.

Similarly, the unified credit is lost for gift tax purposes to the extent not claimed in the year "allowable". Of course any unified credit amounts allowed against the gift tax will decrease the amount later available to the estate, but the deferral value of the credit alone makes it advantageous to utilize it during life, whenever feasible.

By the use of the marital deduction and split gift provisions it is possible to make gifts indirectly, or in sequence, at a lower tax cost. However, tax considerations alone should not lead a taxpayer to make a transfer that is undesirable from a non-tax point of view.

§ 75. The Marital Deduction

For purposes of the estate tax, the marital deduction should carefully be considered whenever it makes sense for non-tax purposes. In employing the marital deduction, the taxpayer and the tax advisor must be knowledgeable and wary to avoid some of the traps that lie in its complicated provisions.

Because of the $600,000 exemption-equivalent of the unified credit, a person or a married couple can make substantial gifts of a testamentary nature without imposition of a transfer tax. In general, assuming no post-1976 taxable gifts were made during life, a husband can transfer an unlimited amount to his surviving wife (or vice-versa) tax free, by using the new, unlimited marital deduction. If the wife (or husband) who survives consumes part of what her husband left her and holds only about $600,000 at her death, she will be able to transmit that property outright without a tax in her estate because a unified credit will be available to her also.

Tax planners often seek to equalize the taxable estates of a married couple or of other persons in the same generation, thus subjecting as much of the property as possible to each spouse's "ride" up the graduated rate schedule. A numerical example will demonstrate this point. The tax on an estate of $3,000,000 is $1,290,800. The tax on an estate of $1,500,000 is $555,800. Thus, the total tax on two separate estates of $1,500,000 each is $1,111,600, or $179,200 less than the tax on a single, combined $3,000,000 estate. A significant tax savings thus results from equalizing the two estates. Conversely, if each spouse has separate property approximately equal in value and if the husband dies first, there may be no tax saving if he uses the marital deduction to transfer property to his wife, since his bequest to her will eliminate tax on the exemption-equivalent amount in his estate but produce a tax on it in hers. Moreover, if the husband's estate is much lower in value than the property that the wife holds or will hold at her later death, it can even be that the use of the marital deduction by the husband (the first to die) will create a greater (though later) tax bill in the wife's estate than the tax saving accomplished by using the marital deduction for postponement and for reducing the tax in the husband's estate. Indeed, in this situation, it often will be desirable for the wife to use her *gift-tax* marital deduction to make sure that the husband, upon his death, will obtain full use of the unified credit, a separate "ride" up the graduated estate tax rates, and the new $1,000,000 generation-skipping exemption.

In general, however, the marital deduction is attractive and should be considered when a transfer to the surviving spouse is desired. The marital deduction postpones taxes on the portion eligible for the deduction until that property is taxed in the estate of the surviving spouse. If the surviving spouse consumes or dissipates the property during her life and does not hold it at her death, it will escape transfer tax altogether. In any event, she will have the use of the taxes saved in the first estate.

State transfer taxes often complicate the tax planning that is made under the federal transfer taxes. For example, a bequest to a surviving spouse may turn out to be taxable in the husband's estate and then later in the estate of the wife, if she is the surviving spouse, under state tax law. In that event, it might prove better for the husband to transmit his property directly to their children or to use a trust for his wife with remainder to the children, if she can get along without outright ownership of the property after his death.

In connection with the marital deduction, careful use should be made of the exceptions to the terminable interest rule, especially the new "qualified terminable interest" device, or "Q.T.I.P." as it has come to be known, so as to preserve the marital deduction and maximize the family planning goals. These exceptions include survivorship or common disaster provisions, life insurance proceeds payable to the wife in installments, a carefully drafted marital deduction trust and an estate trust providing the income to be paid to the wife for her life, with remainder to her estate, if she is the surviving spouse.

Occasionally *post-mortem* estate planning can serve to reduce taxes and to better tailor the disposition of property to the family situation. For example, a wife might take action after her husband's death, with the additional facts then known to her, to disclaim an outright gift made to her by her husband's will if doing so will cause the property to go to a child or someone else she would like to receive the property. She may choose to do this if she does not need the property and if keeping it out of her hands will reduce transfer taxes because she has separate property that will make her estate larger than her husband's (as reduced by the marital deduction) and because she cannot make a great many *inter vivos* gifts without a heavy tax bill. She may do this even if the property renounced thereby passes to a trust in which she has a life income interest. See § 2518(b)(4). A "qualified terminable interest" trust ("Q.T.I.P.") makes this kind of post-mortem planning even easier.

A common form of estate planning structure in a family with substantial wealth is the creation of two trusts at the time of the death of the first spouse, usually the husband (on an actuarial basis). One trust, perhaps determined by a formula designed to maximize the tax benefits obtained by utilizing the unified credit and a separate trip up the rate schedule in both estates, is called the credit shelter trust (or "A" trust) and is designed in such a way as *not* to give the surviving spouse a taxable interest and thus to avoid tax in her estate—which arrangement will entail a transfer tax in the estate of H, the first spouse to die. A second trust, sometimes called a marital deduction trust (or "B" trust), can then be created to give the wife an interest that will be taxable in her estate but deductible in the husband's estate. The surviving spouse can be given the income from both trusts. If she is also entitled to receive corpus from either, it is better that she consume the corpus of the marital trust, since the B trust corpus remaining at her death will be taxable in her estate. In contrast, the corpus of the credit shelter or A trust will not be taxed in her estate since she has only a terminating life interest in that property.

One big problem with all the pre-E.R.T.A. exceptions to the terminable interest rule was that the surviving spouse had to be given the ultimate right of disposition over the qualifying property. One spouse's choice of beneficiaries would often differ, or be feared to differ, from that of the surviving spouse. The post-E.R.T.A. "Q.T.I.P." trust permits the decedent to exercise more control over the property without foregoing the marital deduction to that extent.

§ 76. Transfer Tax Advantages of Lifetime Gifts

For transfer tax purposes, it is usually desirable— for propertied taxpayers who can afford it—to make *inter vivos* gifts of part of their wealth—even if those gifts will be taxable when made. (And substantial amounts of property may be given away even before giving does become taxable. The $10,-000 per-year per-donee exclusion is not an insignificant allowance. A person with plans eventually to cause her estate to be distributed to, for example, five other persons, can in the space of 20 years give away $1,000,000, with no transfer tax consequences whatever, merely via the annual $10,000 per-donee exclusion).

Until 1977, the clearest and most often cited reason for lifetime gifts was to split the property eventually to be transferred during life or at death between the two transfer taxes, the gift tax and the estate tax. Taxable gifts should have been split between the two taxes because each had its own graduated rates and thus a progressive effect, so that the tax imposed on a million dollars of taxable transfer under one tax would exceed the tax imposed on a transfer of $500,000 under each. In addition, of course, the pre-1976 T.R.A. lower rates of the gift tax tables made it advantageous to give gifts; the separate gift tax lifetime exemption of $30,000 further intensified the advantage.

As explained in previous sections, none of the above advantages survived the 1976 Tax Reform Act. There always existed, however, two other advantages of lifetime gifts, which were not taken away by the reforms. Against both these factors, however, must be balanced the postponement in tax until death that can be accomplished by holding property until death, rather than paying tax on *inter vivos* gifts when made.

First, the property valuation dates are different under the two taxes. Thus a gift is valued at the time it is made, while property passing through a decedent's estate is valued at either the date of his death or six months later, at the election of the executor. A completed gift therefore insulates any future appreciation in the gifted property from exposure to the transfer taxes. This creates an opportunity for what is called "estate freezing," a technique whereby a donor makes gifts of those items of his property which are expected to appreciate in value greatly before the date of his death, while retaining only those relatively non-volatile assets with a fairly stable value. The usefulness of this technique, however, like that of all inter-vivos giving, must be weighed against the *income* tax advantages of a stepped-up basis available for property taxed in a decedent's estate. (See § 77, *infra*.) See Cooper, A Voluntary Tax? New Perspectives on Sophisticated Estate Tax Avoidance, 77 Colum. L.Rev. 161 (1977), also General Series Reprint 329, The Brookings Institution (1977).

The second general tax advantage of making gifts is that the estate tax base includes the amount of estate tax payable, while the gift tax base includes only the value of the gift. Thus the amount of gift tax paid, since it will not itself be part of the decedent's estate either (having been either already paid out to the I.R.S., or else, if still owing, will be a claim against the estate and thus deductible under § 2053), will never be subject to either tax (except when the gross-up requirement of § 2035 applies). In small estates this difference may well be inconsequential; however in very large estates it can be almost staggering. For example, a 1977 taxable gift of $10,000,000 would have incurred a tax of $6,050,800. Thus a donor with $16,050,800 could have made an effective after-tax gift of $10,000,000, paying a tax of 38% of the gross amount that he parted with. In contrast, if the same donor died in 1981 with an estate of $16,050,800 the tax bill would have been $10,286,360, 64% of his total assets, while the sum received by the donee would be only $5,764,440, somewhat over one-half of the net lifetime gift.

It is mainly these two factors, the differing valuation dates and the fact that there is no "gross-up" for the amount of gift taxes paid, (except under § 2035) which provide the remaining reasons for the complex rules of I.R.C. 2035–2038, whereunder some lifetime gifts are nonetheless included in a decedent's estate, lest otherwise significant taxes be avoided. Note that while E.R.T.A. made § 2035 inapplicable in all but a few situations, the § 2035(c) "gross-up" for gift tax continues to apply to all gifts made within 3 years of death.

§ 77. Federal Income Tax Consequences of Certain Property Dispositions *

When planning transfers to effect the wishes of a donor and to minimize the transfer tax consequences, it should never be forgotten that various dispositions may have markedly different income tax consequences as well. To take a simple example, a completed gift (if there is no § 2035 problem) of corporate stock will not only take that stock out of the donor's estate, but will also cause any future dividends from it to be taxable to the donee for income tax purposes, and not to the donor. The interrelations between the gift, estate and income taxes are many and complicated, and in this chapter discussion will be confined principally to the effects of gifts or bequests on the sale or other disposition by the donee of the gift property, *i.e.*, to the question of the donee's *basis* in the donated property.

First, it must be remembered that neither the receipt of a gift nor a bequest is treated as income to the donee. I.R.C. § 102 excludes the gift or bequest property from income at the time of its receipt. The donee may, nevertheless, have occasion to report income as a result of a gift or bequest that is later sold by the donee. For as a price of tax-free receipt, the donee of a gift must take the donor's own basis as his basis in the gift property

---

* For a more extensive introduction to U.S. Federal Income tax principles see McNulty, Federal Income Taxation of Individuals (In a Nutshell), 4th Ed., West Pub. Co. (1988), and for materials on income taxation of income in respect of a decedent and income of trusts and their beneficiaries and settlors, see Id. at §§ 76–82.

for purposes of determining gain on sale by the donee. See I.R.C. § 1015(a); Taft v. Bowers, 278 U.S. 470 (1929). Consequently, if A owns Blackacre for which he paid $10,000 (his cost basis) and gives it to B when Blackacre is worth $15,000, and if B later sells Blackacre for $17,000, B will have taxable gain of $7,000. If Blackacre had been worth just $8,000 when A gave it to B, B would still have $7,000 gain when he sold it for $17,000 later. This is an entirely lawful and proper way to shift taxation of the gain in appreciated property to a donee.

Deductible loss, however, cannot be shifted in this way. For purposes of determining loss on subsequent sale, the donee must take as his basis the lesser of (i) the donor's own basis or (ii) fair market value (FMV) of the property at the time of the gift. Consequently, if A's basis had been $10,000 and FMV $8,000 at date of gift and B later sold the gift property for $7,000, B would have a realized loss of $1,000; A's loss of $2,000 will never be recognized by A or B. If, perchance, B had sold Blackacre for $9,000 (an amount in between A's basis—$10,000— and FMV—$8,000—at the time of gift), B would realize neither gain nor loss, a strange result that follows from selling the property in the "gray" area between the two bases and basis rules of I.R.C. § 1015(a). (The rule for determining loss is irrelevant because if it applied, donor would be seen to have gained; if the rule for computing gain is used, the result shows a loss.)

The potential loss deduction will have disappeared; no deduction will be available to anyone.

Perhaps the policy justification for allowing gain and tax burden to be shifted is that the donee will be in a more liquid position than the donor when the gain is realized by sale; similar policy does not support shifting losses between taxpayers.

Very different rules apply to bequests (or lifetime transfers included in the estate of the decedent, because made in contemplation of death, for example). The legatee's basis is the fair market value of the property at date of death (or the alternative valuation date elected for estate tax purposes). I.R.C. § 1014(a). Thus if A bequeathed Blackacre, which cost him $10,000, to B, and if Blackacre was worth $12,000 at the date of death, or alternate valuation date, B's basis in Blackacre is $12,000. If the FMV at death had been $9,000, B's basis would be $9,000. Thus, in the *gift* situation, the donor's gain is later taxed to the donee, if the donee sells the property and realizes a price in excess of the donor's basis, but in the bequest situation the donor's gain (or loss) goes untaxed (or undeducted) and the legatee begins with a new basis equal to valuation of the property for federal estate tax purposes.

In the bequest situation, gain accrued before death often goes untaxed. Pre-death loss in property can not be shifted, just as in the *inter vivos* gift rule, because an heir takes FMV at death as his or her basis for purposes of computing gain or loss when he/she sells or disposes of it. Again, the reason for not taxing gain at death may be a concern over lack of liquidity. And the decedent's old basis is not carried over after death because of the heavy administrative burdens involved in tracing the decedent's basis. So potentially taxable gain escapes tax altogether, and potentially deductible loss disappears without a deduction.

Under these rules for death transfers, strong income-tax motivated incentives are created for an elderly taxpayer to sell property that has decreased in value below his basis, in order to realize and deduct the loss, and to retain property that has risen in value in order to avoid realizing the gain, and to give his heirs an elevated basis—equal to fair market value—at death. Gift property with gain inhering in it can often be donated to a low-bracket (or tax-exempt) person and the gain transferred to that person; loss property is better sold, if the loss is deductible by the high-bracket original owner.

The Tax Reform Act of 1976 attempted drastically to change the basis rules for property transferred at death. For bequests and devises or includable lifetime transfers by decedents who died after December 31, 1979, rules somewhat similar to the gift rules were to apply. In general, recipient's basis was to be the transferor's adjusted basis of the property immediately before the death of the transferor, adjusted for transfer taxes paid.

The former elevation of basis at death or *"fresh-start basis"* principle was (apparently) reversed in 1976 largely for reasons of equity and economics. Formerly the income tax did not reach pre-death appreciation in the hands of the decedent or the heir, an escape from tax thought to be unacceptable as a matter of tax equity. And the resulting incentive to retain appreciated property until death but to sell loss property in order to realize the tax deduction before death was believed to create a skewing of investment incentives and, at least in terms of price level increase, a serious lock-in effect. To be sure, the estate tax law would include property held at death at its fair market value, but that did not justify failure to tax the unrealized income since the estate tax also would apply to the proceeds of sale, or property in which those proceeds were invested, in the case of a taxpayer who sold before death. The main advantage of the old rule was that fair market value at death was easier to ascertain than the decedent's basis, and particularly easy if it had been established for estate tax purposes.

The old elevation of basis at death rule could have been maintained while closing the escape route for unrealized appreciation if death had been deemed a (constructive) realization of gain. *Constructive realization*, however, was thought by many to involve undue liquidity problems; assets often would have to be sold to pay income tax at a time when there had not been a voluntary disposition, such as a sale or exchange, so as to make invocation of a tax bill suitable. Especially, small businesses, farms and estates consisting mainly of a family residence or other illiquid assets, would be hard hit by constructive realization at death. Instead, Congress opted for the carryover-of-basis rule to enable the income tax to get at the pre-death appreciation.

See (former) § 1023. In doing so, however, very serious administrative and compliance responsibilities were created. How is the decedent's basis to be determined after his or her death, on an asset acquired years earlier, perhaps affected for tax purposes by depreciation or capital adjustment? And how is an executor or administrator fairly to distribute assets when they have bases different from their respective fair market values, and when various recipients stand in different tax brackets and tax positions from each other? A piece of property worth $100,000 and carrying a basis of $90,000 would be worth more than another asset having an equal fair market value but a lower basis. And the basis differential would matter more to a high bracket taxpayer than to a lower one, or to someone needing or planning to sell the asset soon, or to use it in a trade or business when depreciation deductions would be a factor, than to someone planning to retain the asset in a non-depreciable capacity.

Following passage of the 1976 Reform Act, the new carryover basis rules became the focus of much comment and criticism, both because of basic policy questions and the greatly increased burdens on estate administrators. Originally intended to be applicable to property passing through the estates of decedents dying after December 31, 1976, these rules were, in 1978, postponed, and their effective date delayed until January 1, 1980. Efforts to repeal, or to postpone, the carryover basis rules of I.R.C. § 1023 continued, and were finally successful in 1980, when the Windfall Profit Tax Act eliminated the new provisions, and restored the pre-'76 Act fresh-start basis rules. Thus, except for those estates whose executors elected carryover treatment under the election available for decedents dying after 1976 but before 11/7/78, the carry-over basis rules have been repealed without ever having come into effect.

Consider the following plan in the light of the stepped-up (fresh-start) basis rules of I.R.C. § 1014(a)–(e). S owns appreciated property, which he cannot sell without realizing substantial capital gains. S's father, F, is terminally ill, and S is his sole beneficiary. Can S give the property to F, and get it back with a stepped-up basis after it passes through F's estate? This plan probably would have worked prior to E.R.T.A., although the device was never well publicized, and probably only infrequently used. Note also that in many cases the plan would not work at all, since the additional estate tax attributable to the property would often exceed the capital gains tax saved, especially at the then 20% maximum capital gains rate. Another factor to be weighed is the possible gift tax liability attaching to the original gift.

In any event, E.R.T.A. added new § 1014(e) to the Code, whereunder the step-up rule will not apply to property given to a decedent within one year of his death (and after August 13, 1981, the date of enactment of E.R.T.A.), and *reacquired* by the donor or his spouse from the decedent. Rather, the donor, S above, will take as his basis the basis of the property in the decedent's hands immediately before his death, *i.e.*, S's original basis plus any additions to basis made by the decedent, F. A similar rule will cover the case where the property is sold by the estate and the donor, S, or his spouse has the right to the proceeds. Note the possibility that this rule may easily be avoided, merely by having F bequeath the property not to S or his spouse, but to anyone else, perhaps S's son, etc.

§ 78. Planning and the Generation-Skipping Tax

The tail shouldn't wag the dog. Sage tax planners believe that individuals should decide how they will dispose of their wealth during their lifetimes and upon their deaths without first concern for the estate, gift, or generation-skipping taxes. This is a fundamental principle of family estate planning. Preferably the tax advisor's role is to analyze the tax consequences of the individual's plan, advise of tax savings that could be achieved with major or minor alterations to the plan, and then let the client decide whether the tax savings are worth the non-tax-related costs of deviations from the initial plan. Of course, in practice, many clients do not know what they want and will seek the estate planner's advice for both the tax and non-tax aspects (e.g., how much wealth is it prudent for an 18-year-old to control?) of lifetime and testamentary estate and personal financial planning.

Tax–Free Transmission of Wealth to Remote Generations. If a client wishes to transfer wealth to individuals who are removed from the client by two or more generations, it will be important to consider all the ways that such transfers can be accomplished without paying any generation-skipping tax.

The most obvious planning tool is the $1 million GST exemption provided by section 2631. As was discussed in the outline at Ch. II, § 15, this exemption can shelter either $1 million of direct-skip transfers from immediate taxation, or trust assets worth $1,000,000 at the outset from the tax effects of distributions and terminations, (or a $1 million combination of direct skips and transfers into generation-skipping trusts). Spouses planning significant generation-skipping transfers will want to be sure that the GST exemptions of both spouses are used to the fullest effect. Spouses may therefore wish to ensure that both of them have sufficient assets to make full use of their GST exemptions. Also, because the GST exemption cannot be freely traded between spouses, couples who do not wish to pay estate tax on the death of the first to die may wish to take advantage of the section 2652(a)(3) election. This allows the spouse who establishes a marital deduction Q.T.I.P. trust to allocate GST exemption amounts to it; the election enables that spouse to be treated as transferor of the Q.T.I.P. remainder for GST purposes even though the corpus is includable in the transferee spouse's estate for estate tax purposes.

Also important is the exclusion under Ch. 13 for gifts that are excluded from Ch. 12 by the annual exclusion, and § 2652(a)(2) allows the spouses to use § 2513 gift splitting for this purpose.

Another potentially important provision is the unlimited exemption for direct-skip transfers by a grandparent (or his/her spouse) to a grandchild whose relevant parent predeceased the transferor grandparent. See I.R.C. § 2612(c). Finally, recall that an election by spouses as to lifetime gifts can often double the $1 million § 2631 G.S.T. individual exemption and the annual $10,000 exclusion. See I.R.C. § 2652(a)(2).

Minimizing the Generation-Skipping Tax That Must Be Paid. Even with the array of complete generation-skipping tax avoidance devices available, some clients will want to make taxable transfers to individuals removed from themselves by 2 or more generations.

It will be important that they plan very carefully. First, they should try to avoid transferring GST-exempt assets to non-skip persons. As a practical matter, this means that trusts should be designed with inclusion ratios of 0 (totally exempt) or 1 (totally non-exempt) with no exempt assets distributed (including distributions on termination) to non-skip persons. Second, they should consider the benefits of direct-skip transfers as opposed to taxable terminations and distributions. Not only are direct-skips tax-*exclusive*, but they can also be readily used to skip *more than one* generation with no additional generation-skipping tax liability.

Perhaps taxable terminations should be avoided wherever possible. Not only are they tax-*inclusive*, they will also quickly decimate the trust corpus. It should be possible to forestall taxable terminations by appropriately designing interests in non-skip persons [while keeping a watchful eye on the nominal interest rule of I.R.C. § 2652(c)(2)]. See Kalik & Schneider, *Generation-Skipping Transfer Taxes Under the Tax Reform Act of 1986*, 21 U. Miami Inst. of Est. Plan. ¶¶900, 909.3 (1987) [reprinted at 39 Major Tax Planning ¶¶1600, 1609.3 (1987)]. However, technical corrections may be enacted so as further to close this door.

Estate and Gift Tax as an Alternative to the Generation-Skipping Tax. Generation-skipping trusts were originally designed to transmit wealth to remote generations without incurring *any* transfer tax. With the advent of a generation-skipping transfer tax, the question in many cases has become not *whether* there will be a transfer tax but *which* tax will apply. In many cases, estate or gift taxation will be preferable to generation-skipping taxation, and in them otherwise generation-skipping trusts should be deliberately subjected to estate or gift taxation, given these comparisons: The estate and gift taxes give each taxpayer a unified credit that provides an exemption-equivalent of $600,000. The generation-skipping tax has no such credit. If a transferor has more than $600,000, she (or her estate) can take advantage of graduated tax rates that do not reach their maximum until *inter vivos* and death transfers (after allowing for deductions) total $3,000,000. The generation-skipping tax has no graduated rates. It taxes all non-exempt transfers at a flat rate equal to the highest estate or gift tax rate, except for the surcharge that applies to transfers over $10,000,000 up to $21,040,000. The estate tax includes a credit for tax paid on prior transfers. I.R.C. § 2013. The generation-skipping tax does not.

At one time, generation-skipping transfers were the perfect end-run around the federal transfer tax scheme. Now many taxpayers will seek estate or gift taxation, for at least part of their estates, as a safe harbor from the potential ravages of the generation-skipping transfer tax. Unfortunately for the complexity of the estate planning profession, there also will be times (difficult to foresee) when this will prove disadvantageous.

Often the optimal estate plan will involve judicious acceptance of tax costs from both the estate (or gift) tax and the generation-skipping tax.

The following example shows how the use of powers of appointment can facilitate the desirable mixed use of both estate taxation and generation-skipping taxation as wealth, and beneficial interests in that wealth, are transmitted through a number of generations.

Example: Grandfather bequeaths $500,000 to fund a non-exempt trust for the benefit of his grandchildren. This is a direct skip to a trust and is subject to the generation-skipping transfer tax. Immediately after the transfer, the trust property will be treated as if its transferor (grandfather) were only one generation above the grandchildren beneficiaries. See I.R.C. § 2653. Subsequent distributions to the grandchildren will not be taxable as generation-skipping transfers because the grandchildren are no longer skip persons relative to the trust. If the trust called for distribution outright to the *great-grandchildren* upon the death of the last surviving grandchild, there would be a taxable termination since the great-grandchildren would be skip persons relative to the trust. (Note that two generation-skipping transfer taxes must be paid in order to get property to the great-grandchildren. Had grandfather made part of the transfer a direct skip to a special great-grandchildren's trust there would have been only one round of taxation on that property.)

Alternatively, grandfather could have given a general power of appointment to the last surviving grandchild. The trust property would then be included in this grandchild's estate (and possibly sheltered by grandchild's $600,000 exemption equivalent and/or the estate tax graduated rates) and in the grandchild's spouse's estate via a Q.T.I.P. This grandchild would then be the new transferor [see § 2652(a)(1)] so that the great-grandchildren would not be considered skip persons. The last surviving grandchild could even make provision for a substantial new trust to make distribution to *great-great grandchildren* (and beyond) by allocating his GST exemption to shelter the trust property. Had grandchild not been given a general power of appointment over the trust property, he would not be the "transferor" and this would not have been possible.

CHAPTER XVI

REFORM PROPOSALS AND FUNDAMENTAL ALTERNATIVES TO PRESENT TRANSFER TAX SYSTEMS

§ 79. Introduction; Reform Proposals

In order constructively to discuss possible transfer tax reform, it must first be decided what general qualities such a tax must have. Many analysts would agree with most of the following *desiderata*. First, the tax should produce a reasonable amount of revenue, without necessitating large administrative costs, which also means that it must be easy to understand and therefore comply with. Second, the tax must impose significant restrictions on the passage of large amounts of capital to succeeding generations, without at the same time drastically reducing the incentives to accumulate such capital. Third, the tax should be perceived as fair, which entails treating similarly situated taxpayers alike, and not providing disparate treatment for transactions which are the same in substance and only formally different. Thus it should not interfere with a taxpayer's dispositive plans by intruding technical rules, favoring certain forms, such as trusts, over other more or less equivalent dispositions. Finally, a tax on wealth transmission should be consistent with, and mutually reinforcing of the income tax, at least as long as the two are kept separate.

The 1976, 1981 and 1986 reforms wrought large changes in the transfer tax system.

The emphasis in general seems to have been upon reducing or eliminating those provisions which operate mainly for the benefit of wealthy people and are of little utility for people of more modest wealth, to attempt in general to increase the revenue from these taxes and to simplify, unify or coordinate them whenever possible. Although the changes have been characterized as a sweeping reform, they hardly rise to the level of a radical change in our transfer taxes. One must not be too chagrined by that fact, however, since changes in the taxes are likely to take place gradually and by incremental steps; it would probably be somewhat unrealistic to expect a prompt and wholesale repeal of our present taxes and substitution of something very drastically different. Nevertheless, important reforms are still to be desired. In addition to those changes explicitly or implicitly suggested in previous chapters, the following specific reforms are among those discussed by commentators.

Some have suggested, even before E.R.T.A., that the rates and exemptions be changed to produce greater revenue. In 1987, Congress did enact I.R.C. § 2001(c)(3) which phased out the benefits of both the unified credit and the graduated rates by applying a special 5% surcharge tax bracket to large taxable estates (in 1993, those exceeding $10,000,-000). In order to keep small estates out of the transfer tax but to pick up some revenue from estates more modest than those presently covered, the basic exemption-equivalent might be reduced, for example, to $75,000. See Bittker, Federal Estate Tax Reform: Exemptions And Rates, 57 ABA Jour. 236 (1971). But note that the trend of the law, as evidenced by E.R.T.A.'s increased credit amounts, has been in precisely the opposite direction. Inflation, of course, may explain or justify higher nominal exemption levels.

It has also been suggested that transfer tax rates be assimilated to the levels of the income tax. Greater progression, in somewhat broader brackets, with a steeper increase and a higher beginning point, perhaps a beginning rate of approximately 25%, have been advocated. (Note that because of the unified credit, the lowest transfer tax rate can in fact be said to be 37% in 1993.) Note also that E.R.T.A. and the 1986 T.R.A. took divergent approaches, by compressing the rates applicable to the largest estates, while foregoing maximum rate parity by lowering the highest *income* tax rate to 28% (or 33%) (on income of any kind). See Bittker, op. cit., *supra*. Since then, the highest estate and gift tax rate was set in 1993 at 55% of the amount of a taxable estate over $3,000,000, and the top income tax rate was raised to 39.6%, or more through the effects of certain phase-outs of benefits with higher income. As discussed below, if gifts and bequests were treated as income under the income tax, an assimilation of rates would happen automatically.

It has been argued that the transfer taxes are psychologically and financially "good" taxes in the sense of getting at ability to pay and having a minimal effect on risk taking, resource allocation and entrepreneurial drive. The taxes are fairly efficient from a fiscal point of view, as well as from an economic point of view. At the same time, Professor Westfall has argued, in his article entitled Revitalizing the Federal Estate and Gift Taxes, 83 Harv.L.Rev. 986 (1970), that the taxes should better take into account the support responsibilities of a decedent or other transferor. As a consequence, a deduction should perhaps be allowed for transfers to minor children to a larger extent than was provided by the 1976 "orphans' deduction." To increase revenues and reduce the leakage in the base of the transfer taxes further, the annual exclusion might be reduced to an amount that would still exempt Christmas gifts and other incidental giving but would require a transfer tax on more substantial gifts; and the credit for state death taxes might be repealed as a rather crude and obsolete form of revenue sharing. (Note once again the opposite approach taken by E.R.T.A., which abolished the "orphan's deduction" completely, while increasing the annual gift tax exclusion from $3,000 to $10,-000, and leaving the state death tax credit intact.)

A post-1976 Tax Reform Act examination of concrete trouble spots in the transfer tax has suggested, among other possibilities, that the special rules qualifying minors' trusts for the gift tax exclusion should be replaced by a rule allowing one exclusion for a gift to a minor and his estate without regard to time of distribution. This would take away the present tax incentive to distribute the corpus of minors' trusts at a time when such a "forced" distribution may run counter to important societal or familial goals. Another desirable reform in the area of trusts might be to eliminate the complicated terminable interest rule of the marital deduction. A simple solution, assuming that all marital property will be taxed in one of the spouse's estates, would be to provide a simple election by the surviving spouse to have "her" half (or some other portion) of the property taxed in her own estate, upon her death, and not in the estate of her spouse. Another suggestion is that retained managerial powers over property should entail that property's inclusion in the estate of the person who has given away all of a piece of property except that which he or she values most, the powers to buy, sell, reinvest, mortgage, etc., the property; in short, the power to control it.

Another felt shortcoming in present law is the exceptionally lenient treatment given to much insurance. Not only is life insurance not taxed in the decedent's estate (at least if certain easy-to-comply-with restrictions are met), but in addition it will cause no income tax consequences for the beneficiary. It could be said in support of present law, that no other property completely irrevocably transferred during life is included in the donor's estate. And yet no other type of property so magically increases in value by virtue of death nor so closely resembles a testamentary transfer.

Most importantly, perhaps thought should still be given to a *complete* unification of the gift and estate tax system, as the Treasury Department recommended in 1969. In spite of the 1976 reforms, significant differences remain between the tax consequences of a completed *inter-vivos* gift and a gift passing through a decedent's estate. A separation of the gift tax from the estate tax induces complexity and controversy, in particular because complicated rules have been devised to apply when a donor transfers property during his life but retains some interest in it or some opportunity to recover it. Slight differences in these transfers lead to differences in the amounts of transfer tax that will have to be paid.

This fact makes it difficult to simplify, or perhaps even abandon, the complicated rules as to when the heavier estate tax consequences attach, without at the same time both losing revenue and allowing some taxpayers to avoid a measure of tax liability. Thus, for example, if the gift and estate tax burdens were completely equalized by dropping the $10,000 annual gift exclusion (administratively unwise, however) and grossing-up the gift tax base by the amount of gift tax payable, then the special provisions of §§ 2035–2038 relating to transfers within 3 years of death and grantor retention of certain powers perhaps could be completely eliminated from the Code. The result would be immediate taxation on the present value of the gift property.

Revenue would be lost in comparison with present
law with respect only to the element of appreciation
in the gift for the period between the gift date and
the donor's estate valuation date. This would be
compensated by immediate donor liability at the
time of the gift, and thus the enormous simplification that would result could even be coupled with
an "easy to complete" approach to lifetime gifts,
without much revenue loss.

§ 80. Fundamental Alternatives *

Lawyers tend to think "inside" the law, rather
than to stand back and view it from a distance.
This kind of thinking also characterizes some attempts by lawyers to propose revisions, or alternatives to existing laws, including tax laws. Perhaps
the lawyer does what he is best fitted to do, by
training or by inclination or native ability, but it is
worth noting that more sweeping proposals than
those mentioned above have been made for a
change in the federal transfer taxes.

The basic structure, characteristics and problems
of estate and gift taxes have been explored in the
preceding chapters. The preceding section then
discussed some possibilities of further discrete
changes to existing law. The main general concerns, however, about the transfer tax system as it
now exists are its formidable complexity, which is,

* The following passages are based upon and expanded from
McNulty, Fundamental Alternatives to Present Transfer Tax
Systems, Ch. 6, p. 85, in Halbach (ed.), Death, Taxes and Family
Property (Essays and American Assembly Report) (West 1977),
excerpts reprinted with permission.

of course, only exacerbated by attempts at piece-meal reform, and its non-neutrality. For example, the now-aborted carry-over basis provisions would have created enormous planning problems, and greatly increased the compliance burdens of the executor. Tied to this complexity is the need to create ever more sophisticated schemes of disposition in order to take advantage of the many perfectly legal means of tax minimization. This in turn very often forces schemes of disposition which are other than would have been adopted had no unfavorable tax consequences inhered in a donor's natural and preferred plans. The transfer taxes as they stand thus may be overly intrusive into private affairs and yet unsuccessful in redistributing wealth, or distributing the tax burden, as fairly as could be.

This section, therefore, turns to fundamental and perhaps drastic alternatives to, rather than mere reforms of, the present transfer tax systems. More dramatic, ambitious (and perhaps politically difficult) possibilities include: systems that attempt to measure and tax the "bequeathing-power" exercised by the donor (such as the "Vickrey proposal"); proposals to tax more heavily or to confiscate inherited property over a period of several generations (such as the "Rignano proposal"); a so-called "accessions tax"; and finally a suggestion that separate transfer taxes be repealed and that gifts and bequests be taxed as income to the recipient. Also mentioned are a wealth or net worth tax and the possibility of and arguments for not taxing donative transfers at all.

Preliminary Note on Our Estate and Inheritance Taxes. Some salient features of the existing U.S. Federal estate and gift taxes are: the transferor or his representative are treated as the taxpayer; rates are applied to the transferor and geared to the value of the property transferred; taxation (or exemption) and valuation occur at the time of each transfer (rather than receipt); the same tax rate structure applies to all property transferred without regard to its origin (earned, saved or inherited); rates do not take account of age differentials between transferors and transferees; and taxation is at positive and graduated rates that do not reach 100 per cent, or confiscation. Some of these characteristics have been viewed as deficiencies, for the correction of which other forms of transfer tax should be designed.

Inheritance Taxation. Although the federal death tax takes the form of an estate tax, the inheritance tax form is widely used by the states. Under an inheritance tax, the amount of tax paid would vary with the amount of a bequest or devise to a specific recipient, and perhaps would also vary according to the recipient's relationship to the transferor. Thus, rates would be progressive, or in any event different for a gift to a single recipient of a small amount and a gift of a large amount, possibly also differing according to degrees of closeness of the relationship, with a higher rate of tax applicable to the larger gift and to the gift to a more distant relative or an unrelated recipient.

The principal arguments for general reliance on the inheritance tax format rather than the estate tax are: (1) If the tax burden is viewed as falling on the successors, the inheritance tax form seems more fair in that it takes account of the number of recipients of a decedent's wealth and makes the tax depend on the size of their shares, rather than simply on the size of the donor's estate; (2) The inheritance tax structure facilitates preferential treatment of close relatives or other classifications of beneficiaries via varying exemptions and rate schedules. The main objections to the inheritance tax have been: (1) as contrasted with an estate tax, technical difficulties often result from the need to identify beneficiaries and value their interests, especially in the instances of discretionary trusts and those involving contingent future interests; and (2) each inheritance is taxed separately, without regard to other gifts to, or inheritances by, the same taxpayer either contemporaneously or over a lifetime—a deficiency rather naturally handled by the accessions or income-tax models to be discussed later.

Taxing the Exercise of "Bequeathing-Power". Estate and inheritance taxes apply on the death of each transferor. Consequently, they create differential results, and some would say inequities, depending on whether a transferor uses "generation-skipping" transfers and depending in any event on how closely the death of each transferor is followed by that of a recipient. (Notice also that many generation-skipping transfers incur no tax under Chapter 13 because of its many exclusions and exceptions. Even if the impact of successive taxation is ameliorated by credits of limited amount or duration, as under the present federal estate and gift taxes, estates that are taxed at several transmission points end up being diminished more by greater taxes than are estates taxed fewer times during the same period.

To counteract these inequities and generation-skipping incentives, a succession tax structure could be set up to impose essentially the same tax burden on transmission of wealth from one individual to another without regard either to the number of steps or the time lapse involved. Notable among such proposals is the "bequeathing-power succession tax" advocated by William Vickrey in his Agenda for Progressive Taxation (1947). The purpose of the "bequeathing-power" concept is to equalize the death taxes paid in two families in which the timing and sequence of deaths would otherwise produce heavier taxation in one than in the other.

Vickrey's mechanism would be complex in operation, but the goal and basic conception can be simply stated. "Bequeathing-power" expresses a property owner's ability to place value in the hands of various transferees of varying degrees of remoteness. The tax on a transfer would be based on the "bequeathing-power units" used, reflecting differences in age (*i.e.*, based on date of birth rather than generation) between the transferor and the recipient; the greater the differential, the greater the tax incurred by the donor or testator. As a result of this system, the bequeathing-power value of an estate (*i.e.*, the power to benefit) with regard to any particular potential recipient remains constant as the wealth is passed from person to person, although the actual after-tax value of the estate declines with each transfer.

Unfortunately, like other transferor-oriented schemes that seek to equalize tax burdens regardless of the number of transmission points along the way, this proposal raises a host of administrative and technical problems that tend to recede in the transferee-oriented systems discussed below. In addition, like so many transfer taxes, it does not distinguish—as the next proposal does—between wealth the transferee had inherited and that which he or she had earned and saved.

Earned and Inherited Wealth Distinguished: The Rignano Proposal. In the view of some, it is inequitable or socially undesirable to tax the transfer of earned wealth as heavily as the transfer of wealth that was itself earlier inherited. This is the idea underlying proposals such as one made by an Italian count named Rignano.* Under his scheme, transmission by gift or at death of inherited wealth would be taxed more heavily than would transfer of wealth that has been currently saved by the transferor. Thus, the rate of tax applied to property earned and saved by the decedent might be 5%, while that applied to property the decedent inherit-

* The Rignano proposal has been described in greater detail in Tait, The Taxation of Personal Wealth, Ch. 10 (1967).

ed from his or her parents and then transmitted to another generation might be 20%, and a still higher rate, say 50%, would apply to property the decedent had received from grandparents, and so on.

Such a proposal can be designed gradually, over several generations, to confiscate inherited wealth but yet to encourage work and saving. The rates in Rignano's own plan reached 100% on the further transmission of wealth that had been inherited from grandparents. Alternatively, the scheme can be diluted by more limited rate increases or by spreading them over a greater time span.

Serious administrative and practical problems inhere in distinguishing between inherited and earned wealth. Tracing and taxing the Count's family estate and vineyard as it passed through several generations might have seemed feasible; it would be quite another matter to trace the proceeds of its sale through securities, cash, reinvestments and secured transactions over two or three generations in the contemporary world. Also, if based on any but the most sophisticated and complex tracing principles, the system would induce persons to consume their inherited wealth and to transfer only earned property.

A distinction between saved and inherited wealth could be introduced into other forms of transfer tax. Such a proposal can be viewed as a palatable alternative to immediate confiscation of property that an owner attempts to transfer during life or at death. Analogous proposals have suggested allowing the first successor no more than an income or annuity interest in the property, or adding a "re-inheritance" duty to existing death taxes.

Heavier taxation of re-inherited wealth rests on the intuitively appealing proposition that human beings care more about leaving assets to their immediate heirs than to their remote heirs. Also, when final taxation is removed by two or more generations, the effect on work/savings or consumption incentives would seem to be minimized. The more favored position given to currently saved wealth (defined as including earnings on one's inherited investments as well as from one's labors) should serve as an incentive for property holders to invest for maximum return and thus most efficiently from the viewpoint of the economy at large.

Nevertheless, any attempt to impose heavier taxes on the transfer of inherited wealth tends to be swamped by the awesome problems of identifying, tracing and valuing the inherited property, and of distinguishing it from the earned and saved, or more recently inherited, assets.

An Accessions Tax—Built-in Unification, Simplification and Equity? The preceding chapters have pointed up the problems of our traditional dual system of separate estate and gift taxes and the objectives of having a single, unified transfer tax. Unification may take any of several forms. One of these is the so-called "accessions tax", which has been concisely described as "a progressive, cumulative tax on the total lifetime acquisitions of an individual through inheritances and gifts." * The key feature of this tax is that it is not one upon transferors but is instead levied upon, collected from, and calculated with reference to the transferees or recipients. In this respect it may seem to resemble an inheritance tax, but it differs in several important and fundamental particulars. The principal difference is the fact that it would be geared to the cumulative accessions of a particular recipient from all sources during his or her lifetime and would be graduated accordingly. Also, at least in the form in which it is now most often proposed, it would come to bear at the time when property reaches the recipient, rather than when the recipient's interest is created; troublesome problems of valuing contingent future rights of uncertain beneficiaries are thereby eliminated. Thus, the timing of the tax will often differ from the usual estate, inheritance and gift taxes, which focus on the transferor's parting with the property; and the amount of the tax would not vary with the size of the estate of the transferor (as it does under an estate tax),

* For early elaborations of the accessions tax model of transfer tax, see Rudick, A Proposal for an Accessions Tax, 1 Tax L.Rev. 25 (1945); Rudick, What Alternative to the Estate and Gift Taxes, 38 Calif.L.Rev. 150 (1950). See also Sandford, Willis and Ironside, An Accessions Tax, Institute for Fiscal Studies Publication No. 7, London (1973).

And see the "accessions tax" proposal developed by Professor William Andrews as part of the American Law Institute's Estate and Gift Tax Project (1969), outlined below under "*A recent model*". For a more recent legislative model, see Halbach, *An Accessions Tax*, 23 A.B.A. Real Property, Probate and Trust Journal 211, (Fall 1988).

nor would it vary so much with the amount of the particular receipt (the inheritance tax method) as it would according to the recipient's lifetime history of receiving gratuitous transfers from all sources.

The accessions tax for the current year would be computed by subtracting all accessions taxes paid in prior years from the total tax on all lifetime accessions through the current year. A lifetime exemption and small annual exclusions would apply. Although rates and exemptions could be varied on the basis of the donee's relationship to the donor, such differentiation is not necessarily a part of an accessions tax. Also, it need not but effectively and simply could be designed to deal with the generation-skipping problems posed by the varied array of trusts and related arrangements that have proved so troublesome under present systems. By its very nature, it is a unified transfer tax, thus eliminating the dual system of separate exemptions and rate schedules.

One Accessions Tax Model. A fully elaborated model of an accessions tax was developed by William Andrews as part of the American Law Institute's Estate and Gift Tax Project (1969). By his definition, an accession occurs only upon receipt of a gift or inheritance—that is, for example, not upon the creation of a trust but rather when the trustee makes a distribution, whether of income or corpus. Professor Andrews' proposal included an annual per donor exclusion for gifts up to $1,500, a lifetime exemption of $24,000, and a complete exclusion of interspousal accessions and of accessions for cur-

rent consumption. It also efficiently, though blunt-
ly, dealt with the problem of generation skipping by
providing a deduction equal to 40 per cent of the
amount of any accession from a parent, parent-in-
law, parent of a deceased parent, sibling or child
(calling them "immediate relations"), thus making
the effective rate of tax lower than on accessions
from other sources ("remote accessions"). A later
version of an accessions tax, with excellent and
different solutions to some of its problems, is developed, described and analyzed in Halbach, *An Accessions Tax*, 23 A.B.A. Real Property, Probate and
Trust Journal 211 (Fall, 1988).

*Consequences of Taxing Recipients Instead of
Transferors.* One of the most powerful arguments
for an accessions tax approach is that of enhanced
equity. That is to say, if the burden of a tax on
transfers at death primarily falls on the decedent's
successors, the burden is appropriately correlated
with each recipient's ability to bear the tax, or at
least with his or her total overall benefits from
donative acquisitions. The accessions tax is not
concerned with the size of the transferor's estate
(the estate tax approach) or merely with the size of
the particular accession apart from all others (the
inheritance tax approach). In this respect, it appeals to many of the same notions of equity that are
sought in the income tax: horizontal equity requires that people in an equal position (*i.e.*, similarly situated) pay an equal amount of tax; vertical
equity requires that those in a better position pay a
larger tax (either proportionately or progressively).

One consequence of the present estate and gift taxes' focus on transferors is that the tax on a specified amount received often is greater in the case of a recipient who takes from one transferor than for a person who receives the same amount from several transferors. Also, the amount of the tax depends on the size of the estate or the transferor's donative history, rather than upon the lifetime receipts of the transferee—that is, under a transferor-oriented tax, one who inherits a given amount as one of several heirs bears a heavier burden than one who receives the same amount as a sole heir. In contrast, an accessions tax is neutral with regard to the number of other successors, the number of transferors, and the size of the estate or the donative history of the transferor. It is concerned with the overall, lifetime accessions position of the one who bears the tax, the transferee.

More Advantages and Disadvantages. As noted earlier, the accessions tax by its very nature unifies the transfer taxes and avoids the problems of our traditional dual structure. It thereby avoids the problem of how to tax gifts arguably made in contemplation of death. It lends itself to dealing effectively with generation skipping, and it naturally shoulders aside many of the technical problems that have plagued other systems. In many respects it copes effectively with the tax problems presented by trusts, particularly discretionary trusts, but it does offer possibilities of tax deferral—even though at a high cost that may make them neither worthwhile to the taxpayer nor harmful to revenue in the long run. The tax offers greater neutrality and therefore greater equity with regard to estate and gift splitting between married individuals. Also, an accessions tax would offer a desirable background for reform of probate laws.

Some Questions. Probably most controversial and difficult to assess are arguments concerning revenue production and about the extent and desirability of redistribution of wealth under an accessions tax. The questions are significantly interrelated.

It is often said that an accessions tax probably would not raise as much revenue as the present estate and gift taxes do, unless rates were raised and exemptions lowered. It is not as clear as initial impressions might suggest, however, that this argument is entirely valid, even if taxpayers engaged in "planned dispersion" among numerous recipients in several generations, for the effect could largely— although not entirely—be counteracted by a combination of cumulation over a lifetime of receipts from the increased number of donors dispersion would produce and differential rates to handle the generation-skipping element involved. As the number of descendants multiplies when generations are jumped (*e.g.*, in addition to two children, each pair of husband-wife transferors is likely to have four grandchildren) so does the number of ancestors from whom accessions are received and cumulated over a lifetime (*e.g.*, each such grandchild has four grandparents as well as two parents). In addition, an associated element of what might be called "accession-splitting" between a natural donee and his or her spouse can be handled in accessions tax legislation, though not without injecting an element of complexity into the system. With regard to the problem of tax deferral resulting from taxing trust distributions rather than trust creation, it is important to note that such a tax does not involve the "interest-free loan" element that is present in the income tax but rather is compensated for by the enlarged tax base that is reached by an accessions tax that has been postponed, only to be levied on distributed or accumulated income as well as on the original trust corpus.

Supporters of the accessions tax argue that it would produce greater, earlier and more desirable redistribution of wealth, as well as greater equity. Because property tends to be kept within the immediate family anyway, however, the extent to which this is true and the results and benefits of such redistribution are highly speculative, as is the distribution of transfer tax burdens.

Some Further Questions. One of the accessions tax's strongest appeals is its apparently close coordination between the amount of the tax and the ability to pay of those who are viewed as bearing the burden. However, the question of who bears the burden may be more complicated than appears on the surface. Are the bearers necessarily the beneficiaries who receive some property (but perhaps less than they would have but for the tax), or might the burden be borne by unnamed beneficiaries who would have received transfers had the donor not recognized that his or her distributive wealth would be diminished by transfer taxes? This we cannot presently determine, nor can we know how much the anticipation and presence of the tax affected a decedent's inclination to work and save as compared with a disposition to forego earnings and to consume existing savings. Consequently, a comparison of the equity of various transfer tax regimes, including—but not limited to—the accessions tax, must now proceed without regard to relevant information concerning who bears the tax.[†]

In addition, the argument that the burden of an accessions tax corresponds to ability to pay is true only in the limited sense that the tax relates to the recipient's life-long history of benefits from *donative* transfers. The income or other wealth of the recipient is not taken into account. Whether the progression of rates based solely on donative transfers under this and other forms of wealth-transfer taxes is desirable deserves further analysis. If one wishes to take into account overall taxpaying ability, including income, one naturally looks for other

[†] For further discussion of the incidence and economic effects of death taxes generally see Jantscher, The Aims of Death Taxation (at p. 40) and Boskin, An Economist's Perspective on Estate Taxation (at p. 56) in Halbach (ed.), Death, Taxes and Family Property, West Pub. Co. (1977). See also Shoup, Federal Estate and Gift Taxes, Washington, D.C., The Brookings Institution (1966). For a comparative study see Wheatcroft, Estate And Gift Taxation: A Comparative Study, Sweet and Maxwell (1965). See also Rolph and Break, Public Finance, Chapter 12 (1961). And see Pechman, Federal Tax Policy, Chapter 8 "Estate and Gift Taxes," Washington, D.C.: The Brookings Institution (3d ed., 1977).

tax structures. These might include a periodic, comprehensive wealth tax or an income tax that includes donative receipts in its base.

Wealth Taxes (vs. Transfer Taxes). An alternative, or possibly even a supplement, to a transfer tax could be a wealth or net worth tax, levied periodically on a comprehensive base of the taxpayer's net worth (wealth minus liabilities). The timing and frequency of the levy would depend on the rate of the tax and its revenue or redistribution goals.*

Since such a tax is imposed without regard to a transfer, it would pose problems of periodic liquidity, probably require increased holdings of assets in liquid form, and would involve wealth being significantly consumed by taxes while property remains in the hands of the same (increasingly unhappy) owner. For a sense of some other issues and questions about the effect of such a tax on risk-taking and investment and other aspects of economic behavior, consider alternatively: (a) an *ad valorem* tax of 3% per annum (*i.e.*, a fraction of likely overall return on property); (b) an annual tax of 8% or 10%; and (c) a tax of 20% yearly. One might consider also whether some effort should be made to value and tax human capital, for omitting such "wealth" from the tax base may make a wealth tax inequitable and

* For thoughtful recent treatments of the periodic wealth tax proposal, see Isaacs, Do We Want a Wealth Tax in America?, 32 U.Miami L.Rev. 23 (1977); Sandford, Willis and Ironside, An Annual Wealth Tax, Institute for Fiscal Studies, London (1975); Cooper, Taking Wealth Taxation Seriously, 1978 Mortimer Hess Memorial Lecture, May 22, 1978 ("The Record").

allocatively biased, although some may think that this form of "investment" should be encouraged by leaving it exempt.

Simple Repeal of the Federal Transfer Taxes. Much could be said in favor of repealing transfer taxes altogether and enacting nothing to replace them. The revenue they raise is small, as may be their redistributive effect. The executive, judicial and legislative costs of administering, interpreting, and reforming these taxes are fairly large. The capital accumulation and other economic effects of such taxes may be substantial and in important respects negative. Also, huge costs of compliance or legitimate avoidance are borne by taxpayers, and tax-motivated planning involves more than transaction costs—it also produces intrusions, distortions, and apparent inefficiencies in the allocation of economic resources, not to mention inequities among taxpayers depending on whether they can avail themselves of expert advice. All this for a small revenue and the supposed addition of some slight progressivity to the overall tax structure.

To repeal all taxes on transfer of wealth may seem politically impossible and philosophically retrogressive, but it is quite arguable that the present tax structure, or any of the more politically realistic reforms, simply is not worth the price paid in complexity, transaction costs, allocative inefficiency, incentives to earn and save, and in our employment level, which depends on the nation's capital base. Evidence that these taxes have served to redistribute or equalize wealth or to break up concentrations of economic power during recent decades is missing, or melts away in a critical economist's hands. The last word is not in, and perhaps inequalities of wealth and tax burdens would have been greater if these taxes had not been in effect, but one cannot merely assume that their net effect is significant in any particular direction, or even that it is favorable.

Still, wholesale repeal may not be the best effort Congress can make. Repeal of these taxes as a separate revenue source would provide an excellent occasion to merge them with another form of taxation that would read more understandably, yield more revenue, bear more fairly on taxpayers, administer and generally operate more simply, impose lower transaction and compliance costs, redistribute more effectively and produce a more neutral or otherwise more desirable influence on the allocation of resources. An alternative that some believe may offer most of this imposing list of advantages is considered in the next paragraphs.

Taxation of Gifts and Bequests as Income. An elegantly simple and economically attractive alternative to the present mode of taxing bequests and gifts would be to stop applying special transfer taxes to either transferors or transferees and merely tax the latter as having received income. Technically, at the federal level, this proposal consists of repealing Internal Revenue Code § 102, which excludes property acquired by gift, bequest, devise, or inheritance from the income tax law's definition of income and also repealing the Federal Estate and Gift Tax laws.*

One goal of such a change would be simplification of the law. In its basic form, the proposal would add nothing to existing law on the books; in fact, it would repeal many sections of the Internal Revenue Code. Some amendment in the income tax law probably would be necessary, however, to deal with particular problems to which reference will be made subsequently. (Moreover, some theorists would even insist on a new deduction for the donor if the donee is to be taxed on a gift as income; others would vehemently disagree.)

Why tax gifts and bequests as income? A gift or inheritance enlarges the recipient's power to consume or invest, just as does other income, which economists have long defined as any accretion in

* See Statement of John K. McNulty before the Committee on Ways and Means of the U.S. House of Representatives, hearings on Estate and Gift Taxes, March 15–17, 1976, pp. 485–491; McNulty, A Transfer Tax Alternative: Inclusion Under the Income Tax, Vol. IV, Tax Notes, 24–28 (June 28, 1976); Dodge, Beyond Estate and Gift Tax Reform: Including Gifts and Bequests in Income, 91 Harv.L.Rev. 1177 (1978).

A more recent discussion of this viewpoint, and of treating the making of a gift or bequest as an event of realization by the donor, for income tax purposes, is Galvin, C., To Bury The Estate Tax, Not To Praise It, 52 Tax Notes 1413 (Sept. 16, 1991). In response, one commentator raises the problem of valuation uncertainties and disputes, and recommends imposing a carry-over-basis income-tax rule instead. See Smith, R., Burying the Estate Tax Without Resurrecting Its Problems, 55 Tax Notes 1799 (June 29, 1992). Galvin responded. See Galvin, C., Burying The Estate Tax: Keeping Ghouls Out Of The Cemetery: A Reply to Professor Smith, 56 Tax Notes 951 (Aug. 17, 1992).

wealth or any net receipt. In Haig-Simons' definition, income is the sum of the value of rights exercised in consumption plus the change in the value of the store of property rights between the beginning and the end of a period. Probably for this reason, responsible tax reform proposals (such as Canada's Carter Commission Report, 1966) have recommended that the income tax include gifts and bequests.

Gifts and inheritances have been expressly excluded from the income tax, evidently because of early Supreme Court definitions of income, as the term was used in the Sixteenth Amendment, as "gain, derived from capital, labor, or both combined." Since then, except for cases of specific exclusions, the judicial definition has gradually expanded to include any "undeniable accessions to wealth, clearly realized, and over which the taxpayers have complete dominion." The present statutory exclusion of gifts and bequests may also have been designed to "keep the Tax Commissioner out from under the Christmas tree." And, of course, inertia has probably been a major factor in continuing the income tax exclusion after enactment of the estate and gift taxes.

Some Advantages of Taxing Gifts and Bequests as Income—Fairness. To tax gifts and bequests as income would be to expand the base of the income tax and to comprehend within its single set of graduated rates, its annual computation, and its other structural characteristics these important items of accretion to one's ability to pay tax as well as to consume or to invest. The result has the advantage of fairness, at least to those who view the federal income tax in its basic provisions as the fairest tax in the federal system, especially because the proposed inclusions would enable it even better to "get at" overall ability to pay. The proposal would also do away with the different tax rates and exemptions applicable to gifts and bequests—as we have seen, disparities that give rise to much tax planning, controversy and ultimately inequity. Finally, although it is premature to advance a definite conclusion about redistributive effects, a likely surmise is that taxing gifts and bequests as income would lessen concentrations of wealth both by better gearing the tax to ability to pay and by inviting wider lifetime and testamentary distributions of property to lower income taxpayers, as the present transfer taxes do not.

Preventing Tax Avoidance—Another Aspect of Fairness. The Federal Estate and Gift Taxes are well known as taxes that can be avoided or at least greatly reduced, legitimately, if competent tax advice is available, and the Gift Tax is one that often goes unpaid even when due. Consequently these taxes both produce little revenue and quite unevenly burden similarly situated taxpayers. The costs of administering and enforcing the present transfer taxes, and those of complying with or minimizing them, as noted earlier in this chapter, are very substantial. Private dispositions of wealth are deterred or accelerated or otherwise distorted by the transfer taxes. While a system of taxing gifts and inheritances as income would not be fully free from these costs, it is likely that the costs would be much lower.

Some Concerns and Possible Solutions. One concern in taxing gifts and bequests as income is that a taxpayer might in one year receive a large inheritance all of which would be taxable at once and at graduated income tax rates. The unfairness to such a person is obvious in comparison to another who receives a like amount over a number of years. One answer for this "bunching" lies in existing provisions that allow "income averaging" over a period of five years. If this period is not regarded as sufficient, more extended averaging might well be afforded to gifts and bequests, or the general averaging period might be extended.

Another concern is the necessity for reporting birthday gifts and many other small exchanges that would heavily burden taxpayers or may go unreported. The answer to this problem is to include in the income tax law an annual or lifetime exclusion of a certain amount, or both, as in the present transfer taxes.

Another major problem would arise from the need to value many more taxable gifts, if income tax exemptions were set lower than present transfer-tax levels.

It is likely that some additional statutory enactments would be necessary in order to cope with the multifarious and complicated devices that taxpayers have learned, or tried, to use to minimize or avoid

the present transfer taxes. These include powers of
appointment, revocable and amendable transfers,
gifts disguised as loans, annuities, life insurance
and many other matters now dealt with by the
estate and gift tax law. Some other types of questions that will undoubtedly arise can also be handled without undue complexity;   these include
whether a special exclusion should be afforded to
surviving spouses and children, whether the family
(including dependent children, a la The Canadian
Royal Commission on Taxation, under Ch. Carter,
1967) or the individual should be the taxable unit,
and whether the donor should realize gain or loss
on disposing of property by gift. Unduly heavy
taxation of estates that are subject to multiple
transfers in quick succession could be handled by a
graduated credit, exemption, or other allowance.
Generation-skipping transfers and discretionary
trusts, however, would present more serious problems, the solution to which might return some
significant complexity to the law, since the income
tax approach, unlike the accessions tax, does not
inherently tend to correct for them. Other current
issues will be less of a problem. For example, the
question of what is a "gift" or "bequest" under the
present system's § 102 exclusion would be of less
significance. Taxing gifts and bequests as income
also bypasses the problems of integrating an *inter-
vivos* transfer tax with a death transfer tax.

Broader policy questions are also involved. An
income tax approach would tend to invite distribution of gifts to low-bracket recipients—the very

young, the very old, or those having low income
years to average with the year of receipt. These
incentives and the inequity of results among taxpayers would differ somewhat from those created by
an accessions tax, where gifts to low-accession recipients make later gifts to those same recipients, by
the same donor or others, taxable in higher brackets. No lifetime cumulation of that kind would be
likely to find its way into the income tax model—
although it could.

The allocational economic effect of an income tax
approach, in the private sector, must not be ig-
nored. If incentives are created for different distributions of wealth, effects on capital accumulation
and spending can be expected to follow from differences in the marginal propensities of the wealth
holders to consume or save. Both the altered tax
base and the alteration of distribution and wealth
holding patterns may in turn affect the progressivi-
ty/regressivity of taxes on the transferred property
and on its future income.

Revenue Losses or Gains? Reliable estimates of
the revenue impact of the proposal to tax gifts and
inheritances as income are not readily available.
Such admittedly rough estimates as have been made
by responsible sources, however, offer some general
impression of the order of magnitude of revenue
gains that might result. Based on certain reasonable assumptions about the tax circumstances of
recipients and assuming (for want of a reliable basis
for any particular contrary assumption) no change
in behavior as a result of a different tax law, one

study estimated that the inclusion of inheritances in income would have produced about $13 billion added revenue from the federal income tax in 1966. Obviously, the inclusion of gifts in these estimates would have added somewhat to this revenue figure. By contrast, revenue from federal estate and gift taxes amounted only to $4.68 billion as recently as 1975.

Economic and Social Effects. The redistributive effect of taxing gifts and bequests as income, instead of the manner in which the present system taxes them, probably would be positive, but the available data and analysis are insufficient to demonstrate or quantify this point.

Both the income and accessions tax models shift the focus from the transferor as taxpayer to the transferee, and, more importantly, the income tax model would no longer differentiate donative acquisitions from earnings and the like. These changes will alter society's property and reward structure, especially viewed from the donor's perspective. They may also involve an actual shift of tax burden, in the sense of incidence and "who pays the tax?" Important effects may follow from simply removing amounts of funds from different pockets or from creating different incentives to which both potential donors and donees respond differently—in working, saving, or consuming—than they would to a separate transfer tax. The results could be expected to appear in allocation of national resources, distribution of wealth, consumption patterns, formation of capital, employment levels and productivity. Beyond the economic issues lurk significant social and moral questions about what roles the transfer tax plays that may differ from the roles best served by an income tax model.

Taxation as Income—Conclusion. The structural reform that would result from taxing gifts and bequests as income to the recipients and repealing the transfer taxes on decedents' estates and lifetime donors would produce a simpler federal tax law, a law less costly for the government to administer and for taxpayers to comply with. It would produce a fairer tax, because it would coordinate the tax bill with ability to pay—as measured by all income, not just donative receipts. Although income may not be a perfect measure of a person's ability to pay tax, it seems to be the best measure the U.S. tax system has yet given us and would be made more comprehensive by including in it gifts and bequests. Consequently, this structural reform would produce a fairer taxation both of gifts and bequests and of other items of income.

Conclusion. To propose drastic alternatives to the existing Federal Estate and Gift Taxes is to seem to invite trouble, in part because of the many unknown effects and costs attached to employing taxes with which we have little or no experience. To stay with the familiar forms, and to attempt little adjustments to perfect them, seems more agreeable.

Nevertheless, so little is known about the real economic and social effects of our present transfer taxes, and even today there is so much litigation and dissatisfaction, that a shift to some new structure may not be as disadvantageous as it would at first seem. If major gains in simplicity, equity or allocative efficiency were likely, a change could well be worth the risk and costs. Among the main alternative forms explored, the accessions tax and the taxation of gifts and bequests as income have the most to recommend them in principle and the fewest political and legal obstacles as a practical matter. Each merits further study and serious consideration instead of the endless tinkering and complexifying tax "reform" efforts that have so preoccupied Congress in recent years.

*

INDEX

References are to Sections of this Book

473

†